Outside *the*
GATES

"And so Jesus also suffered outside the city gate to make the people holy through his own blood. Let us, then, go to him outside the camp, bearing the disgrace he bore. For here we do not have an enduring city, but we are looking for the city that is to come."

— Hebrews 13:12-14 (NIV)

Outside *the*
GATES

REVISED *and* EXPANDED EDITION

Chaplain Robert D. Crick, D.Min., Supervisor, ACPE

Co-Authored by Brandelan S. Miller, MACE, MABS

The Need for, Theology, History and Practice

of Chaplaincy Ministry

Outside the Gates –Theology, History, and Practice of Chaplaincy Ministry
by Chaplain Robert D. Crick and Brandelan S. Miller

Published by HigherLife Development Services, Inc.
400 Fontana Circle
Building 1 – Suite 105
Oviedo, Florida 32765
(407) 563-4806
www.ahigherlife.com

ISBN 13: 978-1-935245-57-5
ISBN 10: 1-935245-57-0

Second Edition

10 11 12 13 — 9 8 7 6 5 4 3 2 1

Printed in the United States of America.

In appreciation for...

Jeanette, my life and ministry companion, who has ministered with me for more than 50 years in chaplaincy and other ministry assignments. She has loved me unconditionally, but with a critical and discerning spirit of my need for both freedom and boundaries.

Our children and their families: our son David, his wife Robyn, their daughter Samantha, and twins Dylan and Mackenzie; Jonne Lynn, our daughter; and our son Robert Dale, his wife Carmen, and their twins, Rachel and Jonah. My family is my pride and joy.

Our thousands of chaplains, serving around the world, who have helped teach the church that "care leads and evangelism follows." They have turned the church toward this vast opportunity for ministry "outside the gates."

Brandelan Miller, for her scholarship, chaplaincy research, and love of God, her family, and now, chaplains and chaplaincy ministries. She has been a fast learner in discovering that chaplaincy is at the core of God's call for a church of compassion and care.

— Chaplain Robert D. Crick

It has been an honor to work with Dr. Robert Crick on this writing project. As an educator and minister, it has been my desire to develop a practical theology of care. Through this project I was given the opportunity to express my core convictions. Along the way, under the leadership of Dr. Crick, I was given the additional opportunity to grow in my understanding of how those convictions are played out in critical life situations. Dr. Crick helped me to move from a philosophy of ministry to a theology of practiced care. For that, I am eternally grateful.

I'd also like to thank my grandfather, Lester Thomas, who nurtured my spiritual growth with unwavering steadfastness. It is because of his compassion and love that I came to more fully understand the love and compassion of Christ. He was my biggest fan, and, likewise, I am forever his.

To my children, Eliana, Alexia, and Hunter, and my husband, Gregory Miller: thank you for allowing me to work on this project and supporting our efforts to create a document in which we could be fully satisfied.

— Brandelan S. Miller

In Remembrance

REVEREND THOMAS J. OFFUTT, JR

Thomas J. Offutt, Jr, (1938-2010) was a relentless supporter of chaplaincy training and development.

During and following a most successful business career, Tom and his wife, Elaine, had a life-changing spiritual encounter which included a deep call to care for others. This special call led them with deep convictions into a ministry of care for those devastated by poverty, disaster, addiction, and both physical and mental illness. Having personally experienced divine deliverance in various areas of their own lives, they passionately dedicated themselves and their resources to their calling to be "wounded healers."

It was through chaplaincy training and ministry that Tom and Elaine's call was firmly developed and focused with miraculous results. Giving unconditionally of their time, funds, energy, and creativity, this dynamic couple made possible the distribution of this text, *Outside the Gates*, and other chaplaincy and care materials. Additionally, they gave to the development of chaplaincy and care facilities, disaster response ministries, and chaplaincy training programs around the world.

Prior to Tom's untimely death, he, Elaine, and others had established Outside the Gates Ministries, Inc. as a means to carry out care and chaplaincy endeavors into the next several generations. It is our greatest desire to honor Tom's ministry by continuing in this ministry through his example of dedication and compassion for individuals in need of care.

Table of Contents

Preface xiii

UNIT ONE: A Practical Theological Approach to Chaplaincy Ministry

Introduction 3

Chapter One: Why Chaplains Do What They Do 5

Chapter Two: Working for a Global God 13

Chapter Three: The comPassion of Christ:
A Model for Chaplaincy Ministry 25

Chapter Four: "I Am What I Am": Understanding
Your Pastoral Identity and Pastoral Authority 35

Chapter Five: Prepare Ye the Way: A Theology of
Spiritual, Professional, and Personal Formation for Chaplains 49

UNIT TWO: A Survey of the History of Pastoral Care and Chaplaincy

Introduction 65

Chapter Six: Pastoral Practices from the Days of
the Ancient Israelites through the 17th Century. 67

Chapter Seven: Pastoral Practices from the
18th through the 20th Centuries. 87

Chapter Eight: The Contemporary Context
of Pastoral Care and Chaplaincy 107

UNIT THREE: Understanding the Practice of Chaplaincy

Introduction 117

Chapter Nine: Military Chaplaincy. 125

Chapter Ten: Clinical Chaplaincy 139

Excursus: Mental Health Chaplains. 149

Chapter Eleven: Correctional Chaplaincy 153

Chapter Twelve: Marketplace Chaplaincy. 169

Excursus: Campus Chaplaincy 176

Chapter Thirteen: Volunteer Chaplaincy 181

Chapter Fourteen: Ethics, Morality, and the Law in Chaplaincy . . . 205

CONCLUSION

Chaplaincy: A Commitment to the Marketplace and the Temple. . . 219

Appendix A 225

Bibliography 227

Foreword

by Steven J. Land, PhD

I cannot commend this groundbreaking work from a seasoned practitioner without commending to you the man. As you read this text, you may find yourself asking, "Who is this guy?" That's how I felt when I became acquainted with this decorated Vietnam veteran with a strong presence and a good heart. He had returned from his tours in Vietnam and was processing those traumas, his own tumultuous upbringing, and life and death situations that would forever mark and deepen his ministry, while at the same time representing wounds which he kept clean but open. This is a man with whom to reckon.

We were, and are, two different people with obvious differences but a deep affinity. We both strive to be good Pentecostal ministers, teachers, caregivers, husbands, fathers, practical theologians, churchmen (Church of God), and friends. I have known and loved this man and his family for almost 40 years now. As you read this account of chaplaincy (theology, history and practice) you will come to know the author "between the lines." So, who is he?

He is a Pentecostal mystic whose wife, Jeanette, led him early on to a Pentecostal Christian commitment. He "saw" her in a night vision with a kind of Holy Spirit hologram on an old flint rock. So before you think he's too clinical and scientifically skeptical, remember, he is a mystic.

He is a son who grew up, like many of us have, in a difficult family. But rather than becoming bitter, he took the good things and the hard things and came out with a compassionate understanding of those who don't have the advantage of a strong, dependable, idyllic family upbringing. He has remained true to his family.

Bob is a devoted husband who definitely "married up" to his beloved Jeanette. She is the love of his life and represents the voice of God to him so often. Caring for him, their kids and their grandkids, she has been with him in churches, military posts, schools, and many other settings. But she has remained constant in her devotion to him and the family, because she is constant in her love and obedience to God.

Dr. Crick can be putty in his grandkids' hands. He is a caring father to his two sons and daughter—fierce in his devotion to their well-being and prayerful about their future. They enjoy being together.

Bob and Jeanette are devoted to their church in their covenant of attendance, finance, prayer, witness, and service.

The exponential global expansion of the chaplains' ministry and its new relevance to the local church has required sustained teaching and gifted administration. Robert Crick is a tireless, gifted administrator with a strong work ethic. He expects and inspires everyone around him to be fully engaged.

Bob is a gifted counselor, without parallel in his clinical abilities to comfort, support, and be present in difficult situations—especially in cases of grief and loss. He has seen people at their violent worst in war but has witnessed care, courage, and compassion under duress. He is not easily overwhelmed. This in itself is a gift to those who are.

This man, the author of this unique book you are about to read, is more than the sum of the parts I have briefly noted above. We can argue with some of his insights, conclusions, emphases, or omissions (and he would want that). But we can't argue with the devotion, passion, and diligence with which he has worked in the confines of numerous institutions and in a variety of life situations.

We have been teachers and dialogue partners together in the PTS for several decades. I have been the better for it. Welcome to the conversation.

Steven Jack Land
President, Professor
Pentecostal Theological Seminary

Preface

The title for this project evolved out of a concept I coined "Outside the Gates" in my early years of chaplaincy ministry. After nearly fifty years of personal and professional reflection, this concept has taken form in what I believe to be a developed theology for and approach to chaplaincy ministry. This practical, theological approach speaks primarily to that great need for us to minister outside the gates of our Christian community. However, a prerequisite to this is a personal and revealing inventory that assesses our availability for such a calling. It speaks to all the barriers that prevent us from effectively ministering to those neighbors before us who are in great crisis. It speaks to our fears, our cynicism, our biases, our religious, political, and cultural indifferences, and yes, even racism. For so many, Christianity has become a "gated community" with access limited only to those who will rise to our created standards in ideology and practice. And, from behind our gates, we offer prayers of supplication, and even financial support, for those outside our gate—not for their immediate or eternal benefits, but for ours. While there is immediate relief in communities from these efforts, if the motive is not from a shared love of God's beloved sons and daughters, it is merely a sounding gong before our Lord. Ministry isn't just measured by what we do; it is also measured by why we do it and how much we are willing to suffer with (have compassion for) another human being in the midst of their crisis. Chaplaincy is unique in this approach. It is more than spiritualizing personal, real-world events; it is making room for those real-world events to be experienced, processed, and "owned" under the careful guidance of the chaplain, who invites the still and quiet presence of a merciful God into the circumstance.

While chaplaincy has been present since the foundations of the Judaic faith (as evidenced in Old Testament Scriptures) this specialized field of pastoral ministry has only recently become a recognized and distinct ministry of the church; this, in part, is because for much of history pastors, priests, and nuns have played a dual role of ministering to troops, prisoners, and the sick while maintaining their specialized role in the local pastorate. Chaplains had already been well recognized among the military for hundreds of years yet their dedicated work among the poor and needy in vulnerable positions had largely been unrecognized as a specific field outside of the traditional role of the local pastor. The nineteenth and twentieth centuries began to reshape those roles with the entrance of psychology and psychotherapy into the church. The recognition of the need for pastoral care specialists was undeniable.

So, who are these pastoral care specialists known as chaplains? They are those called to the office of pastor and teacher, but they are called, set apart, and sent out to a specific context outside the borders of the local church. Chaplaincy may not fit perfectly into a precise category as identified by the five-fold ministry; it does, however, possess the possibility of operating out of any one of the five on any given day. Chaplains preach when appropriate; they teach as opportunities arise, both formally and informally, on daily life and spiritual matters; they are witnesses for Christ in the secular community; and they work to build up the church. This does not take away from chaplains their pastoral authority, for they are still sent and commissioned as a pastoral presence in non-traditional settings.

The distinction between the two specialized fields of the local church and the secular community is greater than their foreseen contexts, yet that context helps to define the very nature and approach that undergirds those fields. Traditional pastors are trained and equipped to lead, edify, and equip a body of believers at various stages in their Christian walk. Along the way they counsel, teach, encourage, advocate, and guide congregants toward a spiritual life that is more and more fully realized in the natural. Chaplains are trained and equipped to do many of the same things, but in a context that is pluralistic, non-religious, and even oppositional to religious figures. They minister to individuals who are generally not privy to the language and jargon of the church community. They minister to individuals who are entrenched daily in the trials and crises of life. Their training is practiced theology in the muck of dysfunction, woundedness, and despair. And they are trained as practitioners who are counselors, advocates of justice, and available presences in times of need. While they operate out of a pastor's heart, their congregation is not bound to the walls of a believing, religious institution. They are, like the apostles, sent out among the people to be with them as a willing presence of hope and compassion.

The goal of this work is that the seasoned or student chaplains who read it will internalize a theology that values all of human life (no exceptions) and will be compelled to reach and love a wounded world through thoughtful and compassionate chaplaincy care. Please note: this book is not a novice collection of lofty chaplaincy ideals; rather, it is the evaluation of the principles, history, and practice of a care ministry approach—now recognized officially as chaplaincy—that has been present since the foundations of the Judaic faith (as evidenced in the Old Testament). While this text is written from a distinctly Pentecostal perspective, it is not limited to those who subscribe to this specific Christian ideology. Within this text is a common theme in Christian practice and belief that permeates each page while maintaining an authentic faith-based identity.

— Chaplain Robert D. Crick

Copyright Notes

UNIT ONE

A Practical, Theological Approach to Chaplaincy Ministry

When we honestly ask ourselves which person in our lives mean the most to us, we often find that it is those who instead of giving advice, solutions, or cures, have chosen rather to share our pain and touch our wounds with a warm and tender hand.

— Henri Nouwen

Introduction

An Examination of Core Theological Principles for Chaplaincy

Since Chaplaincy is a unique ministry that operates primarily "outside the gates" of the church community, it is important to understand why chaplains do what they do. First, chaplains are motivated by the core belief that God is Creator of all things; therefore all things must belong to Him—even the secular. Since all things belong to God, all of His creation possesses worth and dignity equally. Second is the belief that God is a global God. Chaplains understand and believe in God's global vision for the redemption of individuals, families, subgroups/cultures, nations, and systems. In order to do this, they must be sent by the local ecclesiastical body into a given context fully equipped personally, intellectually, and spiritually. In preparation for that specialized context, chaplains must be compelled by the love and example of Christ to bring ministry to the hurt and needy of all races, classes, and faiths. Jesus took ministry outside the temple gates; so must the church. Thus, chaplains, as moral authorities, must be pastors and counselors, as well as advocates before God and the agencies or institutions they serve. Third, chaplains must do all of this and still maintain their authentic Christian identity as Presbyterian, Pentecostal, Lutheran, Southern Baptist, etc, in an arena of ministry where the ideology is diverse and multifaceted. In doing so, they give families permission to embrace the tenets of their faith and their source of strength. Finally, this unique ministry demands its ministers to be intellectually, spiritually, and emotionally mature in character and in person.

In this first volume, these key theological principles for chaplaincy ministries will be explored within the context of this unique and specialized field. The attempt here is not to put forth a comprehensive theological argument, but to introduce and develop these theological topics which will undergird an *ethos*—the particular character of a chaplain as it is lived out in one's attitudes, habits, and beliefs—necessary for chaplaincy ministry.

Chapter 1

Why Chaplains Do What They Do

Do you not know? Have you not heard? The LORD is the everlasting God,
the Creator of the ends of the earth. — Isaiah 40:28

The pastoral heart is the heart which grasps the Kingship of God that is still present in every context of existence and beyond. It is the heart that is *incapable of dichotomizing* our present existence between Divine ownership and demonic ownership or anything else considered outside of God's dominion[1]. An unfortunate mistake that is often made by believers and some ministers is the separation of "us" and "them"; "our" domain and "theirs". "They" are those outside of God's protective Kingdom; "we" are those hidden within its protective gates. This approach separates and divides; it does not heal or restore God's original creative purposes. In our privileged position, we peer out of our walled fortresses to see the unknowing masses of the "other" and offer up an apathetic prayer of help alongside our passionate prayers of condemnation. Unfortunately, those who miss the Kingship of the Creator God lose sight of His original purpose in the creation texts. Thus, what is not seen is our wounded and broken brothers and sisters—created in the image of God—who have been granted the same privilege of existence in a world still governed by the King of Kings. When this is missed, we have chosen to see with eyes of flesh rather than through the eyes of the Spirit; for the Spirit recognizes that all things and all people still belong to God and seeks to redeem them for their intended purposes.

The first chapter of the book of Genesis opens with the acknowledgement of God as the Originator of creation. It was God who, in three days, created the atmospheres. It was God who, in three days, filled those atmospheres. And it was God who designed a place for humanity, fashioned in His own image, to dwell. What makes this concept/truth so remarkable is that God is more than just a potter working on His great opus; He is also the life source that dwells within all life. This mystery gave rise to an understanding by God's people that all life is sacred. When animals, for example, were killed for food or cultic practices, the priests

---

1   Scripture never indicates that God relinquished His position as Sovereign. While Satan may have been given a position of influence on Earth (John 12:31, 2 Corinthians 4:4, Ephesians 2:2, 2 Timothy 2:26, and 1 John 5:19), he is not, nor will he ever be, the Sovereign Creator and Lord over God's creation. For, *the Lord is the everlasting God and Creator of the ends of the world.*

had to follow strict guidelines in the taking of these lives as a way of reverencing the sacred life within them. Similarly, the ancient Hebrews' notion of humanity was far distinct from its surrounding neighbors. Life was sacred because all humans possessed the breath or Spirit of God. Paul affirmed this notion in Acts 17:25 (NIV), stating that God has given life and breath and everything else to all people. From this essential theological starting point two points can be made that are relevant to the work of the chaplain: (1) because all things belong to their Creator God, nothing and no one is outside of His reach; (2) all people—regardless of race, class, and religious affiliation—have inherent value and deserve to be treated with the greatest dignity and the respect due their Creator.

Does God Really Own Everything?

Although the whole earth is mine, you will be for me a kingdom of priests

and a holy nation. — Exodus 19:5b-6 NIV

Since *all* life originated from God, all things still belong to God. That means anyone or any thing that exists belongs to God. Nothing came to be without God. Plants, animals, solar systems, etc., belong to God. The wicked, the inconsiderate, and the inhumane belong to God. Their lives are even sacred simply because they possess the breath of God. What else is meant by "all"? Scripture says that interpretations (Gen. 40:8) belong to God; the secret things (Deut. 29:29) belong to God; power (Ps. 62:11) belongs to God; vengeance (Ps. 94:1) belongs to God; shields (kings and the political bodies) (Ps.47:9) belong to God; mercy and forgiveness (Dan. 9:9), death and salvation (Ps 68:20), and all nations (Ps. 82:8, 89:11) belong to God.

Jesus and Paul are both worthy examples of men who understood this principle. Because of their understanding that the world outside the walls of their religious community still belonged to its Creator, they included that world in their ministerial efforts. Jesus ministered to Jew and Gentile alike. He touched the untouchable leper and—as the holy, transcendent God—made a way for a prostitute to touch the Untouchable, Holy Christ. Above all, He was present in the lives of people in crisis. For the adulterous woman He was an advocate of mercy (John 8:1-11); for the socially rejected tax collector He was a friend and receptive guest (Luke 19: 1-9); for the woman at the well He was the revelation of eternal, committed love (John 4:1-42); and for the grieving Centurion, while healer and intercessor, He was available—even in His busyness (Matt. 8:5-13; Luke 7:1-10). He even traveled to a foreign land to cast a legion of demons out of a man living in a cave outside his city walls (Matt. 5). While their social, economic, and ethnic differences were recognized, even identified, they were decidedly Jesus's beloved neighbors: worthy of love, attention, and care.

The book of Acts 1:8 explains that Christ's message of care and salvation was to be taken to the ends of the earth. Compelled by the gospel message, Paul took this model of ministry to the masses. He ministered to Jew and Gentile alike, through prayer, counsel, and instruction. He raised money for the poor, discipled a former slave, and worked among the people as a tent maker. Likewise, chaplains work among people within various industrial (corporations and businesses), institutional (hospitals, campuses, prisons, etc.), and governmental (such as the military) settings (at home or abroad) as they are assigned. Their motto is always to care first and to let evangelism follow.

Chaplains, like Christ, have committed themselves to being present with those in the worst circumstances. The sick receive holistic care[2]; the poor are given sustenance; the vulnerable are given a voice; the grieving a place to weep; and the wealthy business executive is given a moral compass to navigate through the muck of corruption and greed. Just as Christ was drawn to some of the neediest places and people in and outside of His community, so chaplaincy has been defined by a great compassion for individuals and families in the midst of suffering.

God's Love for His Beloved Creation

All of Scripture points to the endless love of God for His creation. In John 13:34, readers are instructed to love one another in this same manner. Chaplains who believe this communicate it through an intentional attentiveness to the care and the needs of individuals while simultaneously recognizing needs that are universal. A specific need of a family may be grief related, while a universal need may be rest, shelter, or food. An attentive chaplain must be aware of both.

In Genesis chapter two, God recognizes a need that is both specific and universal: it is not good for man to be alone. In fact, God is concerned enough about Adam's aloneness—his need for human affection and connectedness—that He creates Eve. The Creator God's activity identifies an innate need within all of creation to belong with or to someone or something. God, in his infinite wisdom, recognized that while the divine-human relationship is necessary, humans need a counterpart, a friend, a beloved dressed in the human essence and marked by the divine Creator.

2 Holistic care: "taking into account all of somebody's physical, mental, and social conditions in the treatment of illness." North American Dictionary.

Mother Teresa once stated that the greatest disease and the greatest poverty to overcome is loneliness. God loved Adam enough to recognize that it was not good for him to be alone. Similarly, chaplains will be confronted with people and families whose circumstances have isolated them from their known world. Chaplains may, in many instances, be that individual or family's only connection to the world. By simply being present, they have validated a forgotten or neglected life.

Amazingly, God created this world in such a way that He communicates our worth and dignity in every aspect of His creative activity. We learn from these passages that the Creator God is a fatherly God who earnestly attends to His beloved sons and daughters. Hence, the role of the Father is not limited to a select group of people; it is an unlimited love to an unlimited number of individuals without limits in presence, in compassion, or in purpose. Likewise, we must be committed to love as He loves.

Of course, wisdom suggests that there are moments when care recipients are in greater need of being alone with their pain, their thoughts, and their God. Sometimes they need to be given permission to retreat, to be alone, and to recuperate from tending to those around them—as so many people are prone to do. Some care recipients are just not able to be still and process their pain in the presence of others; they want to take care of things or play host to the chaplain and/or visitors. It is acceptable and necessary for the chaplain to be aware of an individual's need. How? Ask. Ask recipients if they need some time alone. Ask if they would like a pastoral care presence, such as the chaplain. Allow them to decide what their need is and communicate that to the chaplain. The most effective chaplains are those who simply make themselves available to serve, allowing care recipients to identify what they need from the chaplains.

Somewhere we know that without silence words lose their meaning, that

without listening speaking no longer heals, that without distance closeness

cannot cure. — Henri Nouwen

Chaplaincy is about both giving and receiving. And sometimes we find it difficult to receive what our parishioners want to give us. In hospital settings, with a dying patient, most often it is the "gift" of their fears and pain. For a soldier, it may be anger at being in a most difficult and dangerous place. For an inmate, the gift could well be a confession of hopelessness. In other words, we have to receive with grace whatever it is that our parishioners give us at that critical moment and in that special encounter.

This is an area that must be walked very cautiously for ethical reasons. However, there is a benefit when care recipients are able to give back in some way. Please note: we are not referring to monetary gifts. We are referring to those gifts that allow care recipients to be an equal participant in the relationship. Consider, for example, the woman who washed Jesus feet. It was just as important for her to give something back to Christ as it was for Him to receive it from her: not for His sake, but for hers. In ministry, it may be the gift of their time, their story, or something that is a reminder of their life and experience. This small and seemingly insignificant gift may be central to removing the stigma of "needy" or the feeling of inferiority from the care recipient; or it may simply be a symbol of their willing participation in the ministry relationship.

The following story describes one such example of gift giving. It describes one man's need to reclaim his dignity. He would not receive the disaster response team's offer of food and other support following a hurricane until he gave the gift of some of his experiences. Only after he shared with the group could he receive their support.

> Following Hurricane Ike's devastation in 2008, the Church of God Chaplains Commission sent a group of care responders to Houston, Texas. The storm swept through communities with rage and water levels that were unbelievable. At times, the winds reached well over 125 mph. In visiting the small community of San Leon, I had the privilege of walking down the street with our Disaster Response Chaplains, visiting homes and talking to families whose entire belongings were in their yards, water-soaked, beyond salvaging.

> One rather rugged truck driver at first refused the meal we prepared for him and his family. But, after taking it, he asked, "Would you like to see what this storm did to my home?" In other words, all he could give in return for our gifts were the emotions he had felt when faced with a deadly situation. With a note of personal pride, he showed me the watermarks, the damage to a recently purchased large television, and the hole in the roof that he made in order to pull his wife from the raging waters. That was all he had to give; and, hopefully, we received his "gift" in a manner that affirmed his worth as he dealt with the crisis. Regardless of the gift, a story, a smile, or even the deepest pain, we help restore human dignity so broken lives are reassembled and hope restored.[3]

This story is a reminder that though recipients of care may be sick or in need, they are not powerless. Their shared gift may be nothing more than their story or some other common reality, but it puts them on equal ground with the chaplain. It returns to them a gift misplaced in the crisis: their dignity.

---

3   Robert D. Crick, *Weekly Update* (Cleveland, TN, Church of God Chaplain's Commission, 2005).

I Know I Have to Love Them, but Do I Have to Like Them?

Being unwanted, unloved, uncared for, forgotten by everybody, I think that

is a much greater poverty than the person who has nothing to eat.

— Mother Teresa

Not every ministry experience is easy. Sometimes the Lord brings people into the lives of chaplains that may be more difficult to receive than others. Yet, at the heart of this ministry—as modeled by Christ—is the belief that all people are worthy of love, even the most vile and inhumane. In John 13:34-35, Jesus instructs the disciples to love one another as He loves them. In Matthew 5:43-48, Jesus exhorts the people to love their neighbor *and* their enemy and to pray for them. Later, in chapter 22, Jesus further instructs the believers to love their neighbor as themselves. In Luke 6:26-28, love of enemies is defined in the following way: "Do good to those who hate you, bless those who curse you, pray for those who mistreat you." (NIV) The root term in these examples and others used by Jesus is *agape*, which refers to an altruistic love of others. According to Stephen Post, altruistic love is:

> "...an intentional affirmation of the other, grounded in biologically given emotional capacities that are elevated by worldview... and imitation into the sphere of consistency and abiding loyalty... Altruistic love is closely linked to care, which is love in response to the other in need. It is closely linked to compassion, which is love in response to the other in suffering; to sympathy, which is love in response to the other who suffers unfairly; to beneficence, which is love acting for the well-being of the other; to companionship, which is love attentively present with the other in ordinary moments."[4]

When Christ instructs his hearers to love their neighbors, to love one another, and to love their enemies, He is demanding they love altruistically. John 13:34-35, "Love one another," is addressed to a community of believers. This has its challenges, but it can be accomplished. To love an unknown neighbor identified only by faith, ethnicity, or another marker, may also have its challenges, particularly if your belief is that love is a measure or determinant of intimacy. Not so if we love as Christ loves. Even a stranger becomes a beloved. But He doesn't stop there. He demands we love even our enemies, our persecutors. How is that possible?

---

4   Stephen G. Post, "The Tradition of Agape", 51.

Let's probe into a heart issue that has long plagued Christian practice: "I know I have to love them, but do I have to like them?" In all honesty, the question isn't about the worth of the other person; the question is about self. To what degree does God expect His church to deny itself for the love of others? Could it be with the same commitment that Christ sacrificially loved the world even unto death? How does this happen? According to Paul, "...more of you, God, and less of me." When this happens, that altruistic love previously mentioned becomes clearer to the caregiver. And then the opening questions can focus where they need to focus—the recipient.

God himself identifies human life as "very good." This does not mean that everything that people *do* is pleasing to God or anyone else—rather, the existence of the individual life itself is pleasing because God's essence is contained within the individual as a son or daughter. Thus, the life of a tormenting mass murderer is loved and valued because God's essence is still present in humanity. Chaplains cannot love him without liking him, and they certainly cannot offer her compassionate care if they don't genuinely like her. Why? Good care requires time, attention, and presence—all of which are recognizably uncomfortable when the chaplain does not like the recipient, and especially when a chaplain claims to not like, but "love," the care recipient.

Refer again to the quote by Post. He notes three essential prerequisites to love as Christ loves: intentional affirmation of other, elevated worldview, and imitation. First, in order to like the care recipient, the chaplain must be intentional about affirming the life before him/her. In other words, to like someone who is not compatible to the chaplain is a choice that evolves out of a worldview in which all people are inherently valuable to God, and therefore valuable to us. There are times when this demands denial of the chaplain's natural tendency to dislike the care recipient, and chaplains who desire a ministry modeled after Christ will do so intentionally. It is imperative, then, that chaplains affirm in their lives and communicate through word and deed that everybody deserves authentic and spirit-led care that is reflective of the Father's love for His children.

CHAPTER ONE
Questions for Further Reflection

1. What is the starting point for chaplaincy theology, and what two points can be made from that which leads us to ministry practice? Write a three- to five sentence response. (5 points)

2. Explain how human dignity can be maintained and what oversights can rob a person of their personal dignity. Why is it so important to communicate dignity and worth to those you help? Develop your answers through brief descriptions, illustrations, and/or examples in a well-developed paragraph. (5 points)

3. Explain why it is important for chaplains to truly care for those they minister to. What three things does good care require of chaplains? Write a three- to five-sentence response. (5 points)

4. In your own words, define both human dignity and holistic care. (5 points)

CASE STUDY: Case studies are provided for class discussion. The goal is to get you thinking about how you might approach ministry from the perspective of a chaplain. However, for this first study, you will work on developing a theological base that will undergird your ministerial practices. Reflect on the class materials and prepare/develop a response to the following discussion:

> Identify three (3) theological principles that you believe are core principles in your approach to ministry. Support each principle with Scripture and an explanation of their relevance in the ministry context. Write a two- to three-sentence description for each.

Chapter Two

Working for a Global God

For God so loved the world that He gave his one and only Son, that

whoever believes in him shall not perish but have eternal life. — John 3:16

S cripture clearly points to a global God. Isaiah 56:1-7 declares that
foreigners from all nations "who bind themselves to the LORD" will
share in the rich reward of covenant relationship with the Almighty.
He even declares in verse 7, "For my house will be called a house of prayer
for all nations." Echoing this declaration is Psalm 67, in which the psalmist
prays for God to grant salvation to all nations. W. David Buschart[1] points
out that though these passages call for a globalization of God's reign in the
lives of His creation, they do not call for the loss of diversity. Inherent in
these passages, written for a particular people, is the hope of salvation for
all people, individually. Both pagan nations and troubled individuals are
valued. God's love for humanity is not limited to our human value systems
or national borders. A person is not loved less because of a scandalous
past, and s/he is not loved more because of a social or ethnic background.
In fact, The Gospel of John teaches that God so loved *the world* that
He exchanged the life of His only son for the lives of His most valued
creation, human beings—the definitive image of redemption. Humanity is
universally loved by God as a particular, culturally-specific people with a
history and a story of its own.

In this section, we will examine how this principle helps us understand
why chaplains are called to work in a pluralistic society. We will examine
God's vision for global ministry; Jesus's role in revealing the global God;
the implications for chaplaincy ministry as a means to sanctify systems and
people outside the gates; and the equipping and sending of chaplains.

---

1   W. David Buschart, "Our Global God", Journey with Jesus website, (August 8,
    2005), http://www.journeywithjesus.net/Essays/20050808JJ.shtml.

A Divine Vision for Global Ministry

She gave this name to the LORD who spoke to her: 'You are the God who sees me,' — Genesis 16:13a

The Abrahamic Covenant is our first explicit indication of God's vision for a global ministry. In Genesis 12:3b, God promises Abraham that all people on the earth will be blessed through him. We then see glimpses of this lived out through stories such as Naaman's healing at the Jordan (2 Kings ch. 5), Rahab's rescue by the Israelite insurgent forces (Joshua ch. 2), Boaz's and Naomi's kindness to Ruth, and God's covenant with and provision for Hagar, the mother of Ishmael, Abram's first child (Gen. 16: 7-12).

Hagar's Story

Hagar was a woman, a slave, and a foreigner. She had no rights, no privileges, and no home. In fact, she was used to provide a child for a family in which she did not belong. In a moment of desperation, she made a run for the desert, and God appeared to her there. He comforted her, covenanted with her, and named her unborn child. The name given was "Ishmael" or "God hears," a revelation of Godself to Hagar. Yet, her response to God's attentiveness, "You are the God who sees me," seems to indicate something about how she saw herself—unseen. God alone saw this nobody, this rejected mother, and God alone heard her desperate cries in the desert. This story reveals a God who is absolutely attentive to ALL of His creation, especially, a wounded mother desperate for someone to be present, to be a witness to her pain, and ultimately to hear her cries. And so God heard, He saw, and He acknowledged this unseen, insignificant slave woman and her child. Later in the story (ch. 21:17-21), God again expressed His vast love for this foreigner and her son by extending a portion of Abraham's covenant (ch. 21:18b) to Ishmael. What evolved out of these passages is one of countless examples for pastoral practice.

God not only acknowledged Hagar's personhood and pain, but later acknowledged her need and made provision for her. This powerful model of chaplaincy ministry incites us (1) to listen and be attentive to the cry of those in need; (2) to see our care recipients as God's beloved creation; (3) to meet them where they are (outside and inside the city walls); (4) to acknowledge their wounds; and (5) to make provision for their needs (even if it is nothing more than some water and a place to lie down in the shade). Chaplaincy ministry demands attentiveness to another's unique and specific need given their unique and specific circumstance and, at times, in spite of our own social conventions.

14

While many of us may connect to Hagar's feelings of despair, rejection, and aloneness in the midst of a major life event, we may not readily connect with the magnitude of what was taking place in that desert experience. God *covenanted* with this foreign slave woman. This was unheard of in the ancient world. As a social convention, God (or gods or anyone else) did not make legal agreements with women or foreigners; those people had no legal rights. Yet, as "head of state" He elevated her to the status of a free man by making this contract with her. What an amazing statement about compassion and helps ministry. And, quite possibly, the assumption in this dialogue is that no elevation took place at all. As a person created in the image of her Maker, she was a worthy recipient of His promise, protection, and provision.

Certainly the church must follow this great example. We must minister to the many in need outside the walls of our churches and immediate contexts, approaching them on an equal plane as brothers and sisters worthy of our time and resources. This will most certainly bring little benefit to the ministering church, i.e., no monetary compensation. From a business perspective, it may cost more than the return; yet, from the belief and conviction that all life is sacred and worthy of dignity, we must respond to the needs of those wounded and in need outside of our proverbial gates. As with Christ, the cost is great, but the potential for even the smallest return is immeasurable.

This approach to chaplaincy ministry reveals to the care recipient the God who is near to the brokenhearted. It is out of this conviction that we can nurture the sick (physically, mentally, or spiritually) and care for the wounded or dying. Hagar was not only deeply wounded, but alone in the desert when the Lord ministered to her. Thankfully, the God she may have become acquainted with inside the security of Abraham's community loved her enough to have a vision for care that reached beyond the borders of that camp. God's vision was never limited to a small, select group of people. Like the often small Christian communities from which Christian chaplains derive, God chose this select group of people (Jews), sojourners, to be a conduit of His love, mercy, and care. This vision for care is what validates the global ministry of chaplaincy.

Christ As the Doorway to Globalization

Jesus spoke: "and you will be my witnesses in Jerusalem, and in all Judea and Samaria, and to the ends of the earth." — Acts 1:8b

While the Old Testament introduces the idea of a global God, it is Christ who legitimizes this mission. In the opening chapter of Acts, He lays out His vision for ministry which is essentially a vision to reach beyond racial, ethnic, and religious barriers. Isn't this the reason He gave His life? He died in order for salvation to be accessible to all people in all nations. He modeled this in His ministry to a Roman soldier, an adulterous Samaritan woman, a demon-possessed man from the region of the Gerasenes, and in our own lives. Never losing sight of His specific mission, Christ embraced a broken world in need of hope, redemption, and healing.

Three points can be made about this first-century mobilization of the Gospel. First, God's vision for humanity was never to differentiate between Jew and Gentile, as echoed by Paul in the book of Galatians. All of humanity has significance. Second, because of the fallen state of the world's population, Jesus sent his disciples, both men and women, outside the gates of the community to where the people were, to where the needs were (Matt. 20:28). Third, we discover in our effort to take the love, compassion, and comfort of Jesus to the "least of these" that Jesus is already there (Heb. 13:13).

> Post-veil: refers to the literal, physical divider between God and humanity which was torn as a result of Christ's work on the cross, thus giving humanity access to God. See also Matt. 27: 51, 2 Cor. 3.

The book of Matthew opens with Jesus's lengthy genealogy containing the names of several Gentile women. Among those listed were Ruth and Rahab, whose very appearance in this list indicates their significance. That is to say, from the very opening of the New Testament, the Spirit makes it clear that the family of God encompasses Jew and Gentile alike[2]. And, through the redemptive act of Christ, God reveals himself as the global God. Later in Matthew (ch. 8:11), Jesus prophesies: "I say to you that many will come from the east and the west, and will take their places at the feast with Abraham, Isaac, and Jacob

---

2 Please note that the references made to Jews and Gentiles are with the understanding that, in the modern world, this kind of separation still exists between followers of specific religions and non-followers. For many Christians, the world is divided into believers and non-believers.

in the kingdom of heaven." For, **post-veil**, God is no longer hidden from humanity (Heb. 10:1-22), and the redeemed are commissioned to take this revelation into all the earth (Matt. 20:28).

The earliest glimpse at the global mission of the early church came by way of Peter in Acts chapter 10. In verse 28, Peter explained to the people gathered at Cornelius' house that God had shown him that no man (or woman) should be called impure or unclean. While it was unclean and unacceptable for Jews to associate with Gentiles, God had a vision of unity for all His people. For God, what once distinguished clean from unclean; acceptable from unacceptable was unacceptable. He never let go of the secular; it has always belonged to Him. His vision is redemption, and His goal is the restoration of all of creation (*Hosea* 2:16-23). Thus, the work of Christ and His example of mercy to those outside the community made possible the salvation and healing of countless families and individuals throughout history.

> *… The one thing on which we can all agree, among all faiths and ideologies, is that God is with the vulnerable and the poor… God is in the slums, in the cardboard boxes where the poor play house… God is in the debris of wasted opportunity and lives, and God is with us if we are with them…*
>
> — Bono, *On the Move*

What is so remarkable about the work of Christ is that it reminds us that though we bear the presence of the Lord in our lives and desire to take that presence into a community of wounded people who may or may not know their Heavenly Father, He is already there! Hebrews 13:13 wonderfully challenges the church and chaplains in particular to go outside the church "gates" to find Christ. What a powerful revelation of our Lord. While 100% *with us and in us*, He beckons us to more fully seek Him as *He is with all people* in their sufferings and their celebrations.

It was no accident that Jesus suffered and was crucified in the manner recorded in the gospels (Hebrews 13). The message is clear. Going outside the gates is moving beyond the clean and ordered life of religiosity. It is moving beyond a failed system of external ritual and finite redemptive acts of sacrifice to identify with the lowly, rejected, eternal Christ—the essence of what is clean and ordered. He took on our sin, our refuse, our littered lives of chaos and disorder to make Himself available to those who would never—under the old system—have had access to the holy and cleansing nature of God. The irony of this as a starting place for a chaplaincy theology of ministry is that healing, salvation, love, transformation, redemption, comfort, provision, and hope were made available, not through a religious institution, but the local garbage dump. The challenge for chaplains is to not see their work as "taking Jesus to the unsuspecting masses." Rather, it is to foster an atmosphere where the already present Christ can emerge on a trash heap as the One who can identify with all of our rejection, loss, and woundedness, and offer life-giving hope in the midst of it for both caregiver and recipient.

This interpretation of Christ's role strikes at the very heart of why chaplains are the extension of the church's ministry to the "least of the least." Christ's role as described in Hebrews 13 is the reenacting of that process of dumping the used-up carcasses. When we think of His sacrifice on the cross, and especially in terms of ministry outside the gates, we see the significance of those who are the abused, used-up, and tossed aside. The unwanted carcasses, which tell us what the least of these really are, give us a more radical interpretation of His sacrifice for the church and the challenge that sacrifice now offers to the church of the Lord Jesus Christ.

Jesus Moves the Temple Outside the Gates; Now the Church Must Follow

Mark 12:30-31 is considered by many chaplains to be the definitive passage for their ministry. This passage reads: "[the greatest commandment is this:] 'love the Lord your God with all your heart and with all your soul and with all your mind and with all your strength.' The second is this: 'Love your neighbor as yourself.' There is no commandment greater than these." In this ministry, second to having a passionate and committed love for God is having an other-serving love for one's neighbor. Chaplains are called to a ministry of *other-serving*, to seek out those in crisis for the purpose of loving them as Christ loved, and loving them with the same level and commitment they give to themselves.

Jesus, in one of His greatest acts of mercy, moved ministry outside the gates of the Jewish community. He fully understood His commission from the Father who sent Him and empowered Him to act on the Father's behalf (John 8:12-30). As with many religious leaders, He could have come with a narrow scope, seeking only to bring the heaviness of the Law. But He did not. He brought love and mercy; and through Him profound possibility entered into the world.

An unknown author wrote, "Christian soldiers armed with virtue—hearts afire with blind obsession, cannot see the difference 'twixt compassion and oppression." Fortunately, Jesus could see the difference and chose a ministry of compassion rather than a work of oppression. His model of ministry reflected that of chaplaincy: care first, then evangelism. Consequently, their lives were transformed as they came to believe in Christ as their Lord and Savior. He gave them mercy through humility, instruction, and love. He proclaimed the Good News; He brought understanding concerning the cares of this world and God's response to them; and He provided counsel when necessary.

18

The diverse crowd that followed Jesus gave Him many opportunities to judge their sins, yet He did not. For example, Zacchaeus (Luke 19) was certainly deserving of a humiliating public rebuke for corrupt taxation of the Jews, but Jesus refrained, choosing instead to dine with him (Luke 19). The Samaritan woman with whom He conversed at the well (John 4:1-26) deserved correction for her many "marriages," yet He chose to give this lonely and rejected woman company (vv. 1-26), a voice (27-42), and living water (vv.13-26). And for the woman caught in adultery, He became her protector and advocate (John 8:3-11). Jesus's response to this ministry model is best described in Matthew 11:19: "The Son of Man, on the other hand, feasts and drinks, and you say, 'He's a glutton and a drunkard, and a friend of tax collectors and other sinners!' But wisdom is shown to be right by its results." The amazing results of Jesus's ministry are irrefutable.

The wisdom found in Jesus's ministry is the seeking of those outside the gate who are in need of what ministry has to offer: relationship, hope, and salvation. This happens in emergency rooms, prison yards, and even on battlefields.

> Between 1966-1967, while still in Vietnam, I realized that we had to acknowledge a church "beyond the gates." Therefore, when some of our Airborne troops gave their hearts to the Lord, we created what we called the *Sky Soldiers Christian Fellowship*. This was an in the field, "beyond the gates" church. When a young Airborne trooper was saved, he was baptized in water, given the right-hand of fellowship by fellow Airborne soldiers, and accepted into membership in the *Sky Soldiers Christian Fellowship*. This was truly a church "in the marketplace." As an induction into the *Sky Soldiers Christian Fellowship*, somewhat a substitute for membership in a church back home, the soldier first publicly confessed giving his heart to the Lord Jesus Christ, committed to daily Bible study, witnessed to fellow Sky Soldiers, and lived a life in accordance with the Word. Many of these soldiers were killed before they got back home to their churches. Parents would find this membership card in their wallet and inquire as to what it meant. For us it meant that by taking seriously the goal to move ministries beyond the gates, we could assure the parents and other family members that their loved one had made a commitment to serve God, and had a "church" in this unusual combat zone. This was deeply comforting to the parents.
>
> — Chaplain R. Crick, D.Min.

God was already present on that battlefield in Vietnam, but the chaplain provided a place for Him to be recognized and received. By going outside the gate, chaplains partner with a God who is already present in the needs of those housed in the secular world. We have, unfortunately and too often, operated under the elitist belief that we bring God to the world. Yet, experience shows us over and over again that He is already present in their brokenness, their hunger, and their loneliness. In going, chaplains bring awareness of the omnipresent God to the marginalized and impoverished of our world.

Reaching People by Redeeming Systems

All the ends of the earth will remember and turn to the Lord, and all the families of the nations will bow down before him, for dominion belongs to the Lord, and He rules over the nations. — Psalms 22:27

Unlike Jonah, an unwilling participant in the redemption of Nineveh, the heart of the chaplain must be for all people, even their enemy. Jonah's eventual obedience to be God's mouthpiece to the Ninevites led to the salvation and redemption of the people, their livestock, and their political system. Imagine an entire nation and its systems (family, social, and political) redeemed by God!

Esther is described as being chosen for "such a time as this" as she entered into a marital contract with Xerxes, the Persian king and captor of her people. As a result, her entire ethnic group was saved from destruction (Esther 10:3). Joseph, a mere slave and convict in Egypt, was willing to be a servant to both God and to Pharaoh in spite of many injustices. His willingness to seek God on behalf of Pharaoh led to the salvation of several nations (Gen. 41). The relevance of a moral presence in systems and with leaders is evident. Through faithfulness to both God and their "employers," Esther and Joseph found favor to advocate for the weak and disenfranchised. They impacted policies and changed the course of nations.

In Matthew 5-7, Jesus breaks into a lengthy discourse that challenged the status quo of His day. The *Sermon on the Mount* is not a call to discard the old system; rather, it is a call to a greater sense of righteousness and moral operations within the existing system. The system was not bad; God Himself initiated this system. However, the original purpose of sustaining a holy and separate people was lost. The best example of this is found in Jesus's discussion on giving (Matt. 6:1-4). Giving/caring for the poor had become a selfish act that brought attention to the giver instead of focusing on the needs of the recipient. Jesus's call to acts of higher righteousness and moral operations required givers to do so out of love for the poor, not love of accolades. Similarly, chaplains offer care recipients and employers a moral dimension to their present codes and operational standards. For example, a hospital may become so mechanical in patient management that they lose sight of patient care. A chaplain might offer a moral presence by reminding staff that, in spite of busy schedules and personal agendas, they are called to care for the needs of their patients by being attentive to the patient when present. The role of chaplains is to assist an institution in maintaining a humane system that values the lives they serve.

What is meant by systems?[3] Are they limited to kingdoms and nations? No. Systems are not limited to those functioning realities that govern a church body or even a nation. They can be as small as a family unit or a group of friends. What Scripture shows is the possibility and hope of reclaiming these systems for their created purposes: communities that give rise to spiritually, physically, and emotionally healthy and interdependent individuals. By helping a grieving family process through fears, hurts, and loss, individuals and families find wholeness and healing. Chaplains may simply bring understanding to issues of faith and mortality. Thus, systems provide a framework for chaplains to work within, presenting opportunities to bring a moral and spiritual dimension to everyday happenings.

God never gave away the **secular** (things considered outside the church community or to be non-religious). The secular is not outside God's reach; it still belongs to its Creator God. However, the reality is that "the universe as we know it does not fully conform to God's purpose for His creation"[4] As chaplains work to redeem world systems, they do so out of belief in the "already, not yet" kingdom theology: those realities of God's future kingdom that are already present but not experienced in their fullness yet. God's purpose for His creation (healing, peace, etc.) can be actualized in part with the expectancy of its fullness to be complete when Christ returns. Biblical authors, such as Isaiah and John, referred to this future redemption as the new creation (introduced in Isaiah 65:17 and developed in Revelation 21:1) in which all of creation, including its systems, will be redeemed.[5]

> Secular: those things considered outside the church community or non-religious.

---

3 *System*: the method by which a desired result is achieved; a governing body—large or small—made of collective parts. Example: a family is a system made up of individual contributors to the overall purpose of the group. This includes parent(s), children, and any extended family that may contribute to the home. Whether spoken or unspoken, all family members have a defined or assumed role within the family unit. The function as individuals and as a family may be healthy or unhealthy.

4 Grenz, *Theology for the Community of God*, 839.

5 Stanley J. Grenz, *Theology for the Community of God*, 840.

The great task before Christian workers, chaplains in particular, is to find a way to work within the systems of this world in order to redeem and sanctify those systems in the authority of our Lord Jesus Christ, who sends them. The balancing act occurs when one effectively operates in and under the authority of Christ while still functioning as an employee of an institution. For example, in most institutional settings, chaplains fill a traditional role of "moral conscience." That is why, dating back to ancient Israel, priests recognized as having moral authority were sought out for spiritual direction before, during, and after a combat situation. In keeping with that tradition, the chaplain is empowered by military or institutional leaders as the moral conscience.

The chaplain also serves as a key member on various committees that relate to ethics, civil rights, and other committees designed to protect the people that an institution employs or serves. For example:

> While working as a chaplain at a drug and alcohol facility, Fitzsimmons Army Hospital, I became aware that some of the more critical cases of addiction were not coming our way. One of the largest units on post had developed a very complicated system by which one would be released from duty in order to attend the addiction recovery classes. Additionally, the identity of the individual attending these classes was known to a number of persons, making it a rather suspicious process. In talking to the commander, we decided that this would be handled in a much more confidential and professional manner. To no one's surprise, those who most needed our help began to apply and become part of the addiction recovery program. In order to make this happen, though, a rigid, highly controlling senior officer had to be moved to another assignment. Sometimes the chaplain's redeeming role is most vital in first opening up the process for review and then fully participating in creating a new, more effective process.
>
> — Chaplain R. Crick, D.Min.

The vision and mission that Christ spelled out for the disciples in Matthew 28:20, Acts 1:8, and Acts 10 gave believers permission to expand their mission globally. Today, chaplaincy reaches around the world. Chaplains are present in some of the darkest, most impoverished, oppressed, and immoral places on this earth. Their mission is very clear: to be present with the brokenhearted and needy while working with and within the systems that affect the lives of those they seek to help.

CHAPTER TWO
Questions for Further Reflection

1. What does God promise to Abraham in Genesis 12:3? Select a biblical story which best illustrates this promise and explain how that promise is lived out through the story.

2. List the five components of the chaplaincy model identified in this chapter. (5 points)

3. In this chapter, three points are identified concerning how the first-century Christians mobilized the gospel message. List all three. (5 points)

4. Define what is meant by "systems," and explain what chaplains hope to gain from a ministry to "systems." Finally, what created purpose do these systems serve? (5 points)

Class Discussion: The following questions are provided for class discussion. The goal is to get you thinking about how you might approach ministry from the perspective of a chaplain. Carefully reflect on the class materials and prepare/develop a response:

> An important aspect of chaplaincy ministry is its focus on global ministry. Find a political article which addresses an issue that another country faces, such as literacy, extreme poverty, slavery, or violent oppression. Write a well-developed one paragraph response summarizing the author's points concerning the issue, and provide a Christian response. (10 points, worth two questions)

Chapter Three

The comPassion of Christ:
A Model for Chaplaincy Ministry

And if I give all my possessions to feed the poor, and if I surrender my
body to be burned, but do not have love, it profits me nothing.

— 1 Corinthians 13:3, NASB

Mother Teresa once wrote, "I have found the paradox that if I love until it hurts, then there is no hurt, but only more love." This is how Christ loved as He ministered in the cities, along the shores, in homes of strangers, and during His terrible public execution. While He certainly suffered a gruesome death for the love of humankind, one of the most beautiful aspects of His ministry is that He *suffered with* the people in their times of need. His ministry of compassionate care is summarized by the Old Testament prophet, Micah—hundreds of years before Christ presented Himself to us in human form. In Micah 6:8, the prophet declares that three things are required of God's people as caretakers in this world: to act justly, to love mercy, and to walk humbly. This is the essence of a compassionate Christ who advocated for the weak, cared for the sick, and became a servant to all He encountered.

In this section, the discussion will focus on Jesus as the model for chaplaincy ministry, particularly through **advocacy of justice**, **ministry of presence**, and **service to neighbor**.

Ministry of Advocacy: To Act Justly

Learn to do right; seek justice. Defend the oppressed. Take up the cause of
the fatherless; plead the case of the widow. — Isaiah 1:17

Chaplains not only behave justly, they are advocates for care recipients when injustice is present. They bring awareness to unethical policies and unfair treatment of clients, inmates, soldiers, employees, etc. They are a moral voice for the institution they serve, and they are the moral conscience amidst the daily routine of the work environment. This example of advocacy stems from Old Testament laws that sought to protect the dignity and rights of all people. For example, the Old Testament has much to say about ministry to the poor or needy. The socio-political system by which the ancient Hebrews functioned made intentional provisions for the poor, sojourners, the fatherless, and widows (Ex. 21:2, 23:10-11; Lev. 19:9-10, 25:3-6; Deut. 14:28-29, 15:9, 23:24-25 to name a few specific passages). While slaves existed, they were to be treated as human beings, not cattle (Ex 21:2). Paul even instructs in Ephesians (6:5-13) that they were equal before the impartial God. The problem was that people did not follow God's commands or example. Several Old Testament books (particularly the prophetic books) deal at length with the plight of the poor and the disenfranchised (Micah 3:1-4; Isa. 5:23, 10:1-2, 16:3-5, 61:1-4; Jer. 5:28; Prov. 31:8,9). These passages teach us that God does not hope that His people care for the lowliest of citizens; He demands it.

The prophets were advocates of justice for the casualties of injustice. They repeatedly and openly rebuked the Israelites for taking advantage of the vulnerable. They reminded people that their behavior was not the will of the Father. While chaplains are certainly not prophets, they do play a prophetic role in terms of pointing out present injustices and unethical practices. In a prison, a chaplain may be an advocate for a Muslim inmate whose religious rights have been denied. On the mission field, a chaplain may be influential in mobilizing aid for forgotten residents in ghettos or those impacted by natural disaster, such as those affected by Hurricane Katrina or the Haitian people left homeless, physically broken, and hungry following a devastating earthquake.

Passivity: Another Kind of Injustice:

To see an injustice and do nothing is the same as committing the injustice ourselves. We share in the guilt of oppressing the poor and the vulnerable when our elevated lifestyles are more important than submitting to the duty of caring for the poor, the orphan, the widow, the prisoner, the immigrant, and even the refugee.

While injustice and inhumane systems still exist in our present world and context, chaplains have the responsibility and privilege to pray for and work to change those systems. The wise chaplain recognizes that we not only struggle against the spiritual forces that oppose the work of Christ, but we struggle against the rulers, authorities, and powers of this world, too. The wise chaplain must learn to work with unjust authority figures and within inhumane systems to help them recover an ethic of humane operations. Psalm 72 records a psalmist's prayer for God to send a leader who would defend *and* a system that would protect the rights of the poor. He prayed for a government that would deliver the vulnerable from oppression and violence. And he prayed for a system that would remember the widow and the orphan. Chaplains must also be advocates before God and authorities for the casualties of systems that oppress and deny any human being of their right to dignity, freedom, and basic provisions. Proverbs 29:7 states, "The righteous know the rights of the poor; the wicked have no such understanding." Chaplains are given the opportunity to bring that understanding to communities and institutions.

Ministry of Presence: To Love Mercy

God is our refuge and strength, an ever-present help in trouble.

— Psalms 46:1

What is so merciful about presence? You don't do anything. You just stay and keep watch. And, honestly, having a front row seat to another's gaping wound is not an ideal image of ministry. Ministry is feeding the hungry, clothing the naked, and saving the lost, right? That is mercy in action. Or is it? This romanticized view of ministry often prevents us from a ministry of compassion through connectedness. Henri Nouwen referred to this as the "wounded healer." We are most effective as healers when we approach care with our eyes and hearts wide open: when we no longer fear connecting with another's pain through our own pain—without compromising the care given.

Think of Jesus in the Garden of Gethsemane (Matt. 26:38, 40). In His moment of overwhelming agony, His only request is for the disciples to stay and keep watch with Him. It is a plea for them to be present in His anguish; to dare to visit His pain with Him. And they failed. Hear the desperation when Jesus asks the three to stay with Him: "My soul is overwhelmed with sorrow to the point of death. Stay here and keep watch with me." Still overwhelmed and troubled by the impending events, He travails before the Lord: "Father, if it is possible, may this cup be taken from me." In Jesus's humanity, He didn't want to die, and He certainly didn't want to die and suffer the way He would. He needed a watchful presence, someone to be near to Him while He prayed through the fear and the anguish, but the disciples fell asleep. In chaplaincy, there are moments when care recipients

> Ministry of Presence—the intentional act of being fully attentive to the recipient of care in thought, emotion, body, and spirit; removes the focus from speaking and doing.

27

just want someone to be a watchful presence. There is a realization of one's vulnerability that occurs during crisis; care recipients are vulnerable to a multitude of emotions, thoughts, actions, etc. "Keeping watch" provides recipients of care with a necessary presence that reminds them that they are not alone as they process their fears, their grief, and their suffering.

In spite of the disciples' failed attempts to be a watchful presence for Christ, He was an amazing example of this kind of care. He did so through unending mercy and attentiveness toward the suffering. He went to where they were, and they sought Him wherever they could find Him. He was never put off by the smell of decaying flesh, the contaminants of sickness, or the lack of social standing. For Christ, they were all worthy recipients of compassionate, loving care.

A wonderful illustration of this kind of care comes from Luke 5:12-16, in which a man covered with leprosy came to Jesus, fell on his face, and begged him, "Lord, if you are willing, you can make me clean." As a chaplain, the art of listening will become a necessary discipline. Hear what the man asks Jesus: "If you are willing." The statement is not about the man's faith in Christ's ability or His power to heal. He is certain that Jesus can make him clean. What he is not so certain about is whether Jesus is *willing* to make him clean. Certainly, this diseased man has dealt with much rejection during his crisis. His leprosy would have greatly limited his life and his relationships. He was untouchable, unworthy. Perhaps he desired the fulfillment of a reciprocated love relationship, or to feel an embrace from a child, a handshake from a friend, or the love of a spouse—all those things that make us distinctively human.

The leper got more than he had bargained for when he approached Jesus. Note the order of events recorded in the passage. Scripture says that Jesus reached out His hand and touched the man; *then* He spoke healing into him. Have you ever considered why we lay hands on people to pray for healing or to impart something into the life of the recipient? Is it possible, here, that the model is care first? Touch is a powerful communicator of love and worth. We touch because we care; we touch because no matter how poisoned or diseased the life, love is much more profound and powerful. Jesus gave the leper dignity with that touch; then He gave him back his health. Mother Teresa, whose work among leper colonies made her famous, once stated, "One of the greatest diseases is to be nobody to anybody." Maybe the leper was "nobody to anybody," but that day, his Creator revealed Himself—through the work of Christ—as the God who saw him, who heard him, who touched him, and, consequently, who made him clean. The most important gift given to the man was validation that he was someone worthy of dignity and love. As chaplains, this is the message that is most vital to patients, prisoners, soldiers, students, etc. This is the ministry of presence. Jesus gave this man His time and His full attention. This does not discount or lessen the worth of or desire for recipients to find healing, deliverance, etc. It just reminds us that without love those things are as sounding gongs before God. Pit-stop prayers may produce healing, but they do not communicate compassion and validate the pain of those conflicted and wounded by life. Chaplains must be willing and attentive presences who are able to bring the compassionate Christ into the midst of the need.

Consider the military chaplain, for instance. Military chaplains often experience that sacred moment of *presence* in both tangible and intangible ways. It is tangible in that they physically represent the sacred; it is intangible in that God, the represented, is in their midst. Military chaplains wear a cross on their uniform identifying their sacred position; soldiers readily recognize this symbol. That tangible, sacred presence can be a source of great comfort for those preparing to parachute from an airplane into hostile enemy territory. That sacred presence captured in an ancient symbol worn on a helmet is a reminder that they are finite. Here, the infinite and intangible God is made tangible as soldiers are forced to consider their "life and death" realities.

> As an airborne chaplain with hundreds of jumps, I experienced first-hand what ministry presence means. During one flight, many soldiers who were expected to make an airborne jump were riding an airplane for the first time. They were scared out of their wits; but my presence as a chaplain, with a cross on my helmet, created a sacred presence that was repeated in similar crisis situations time and again. These crisis moments seemed to bind the chaplain to the soldier in a very special way, and these moments of presence were repeated on numerous occasions, particularly when a soldier would lose a close friend or colleague in battle. There are no words to explain the power of the chaplain's presence at critical moments such as these.
>
> — Chaplain R. Crick, D.Min.

The same optimal moments happen in hospitals and other institutions as the chaplain takes the hand of a patient, an inmate, or a grieving family member. Generally, there are no words spoken, just the holding of hands and experiencing what is often times labeled simply "presence." If a chaplain has not learned the value of this deeper, introspective relationship with the Lord and their care recipients, they will not understand their role in the "ministry of presence."

Ministry of Service: to Live Humbly

Do nothing out of selfish ambition or vain conceit. Rather, in humility value others above yourselves, not looking to your own interests but each of you to the interests of the others. In your relationships with one another, have the same mindset as Christ Jesus: who, being in very nature God, did not consider equality with God something to be used to His own advantage; rather, He made himself nothing by taking the very nature of a servant, being made in human likeness. And being found in appearance as a man, He humbled himself by becoming obedient to death—even death on a cross! — Phil. 2:3-8, NIV

Chaplaincy is a ministry of service to a diverse and pluralistic world. It is a ministry where preference, inequality, and self-glorification cannot exist. Christ is the penultimate example of this. As God, He made Himself as nothing (Phil: 2:6), becoming a servant of humanity. John Stott's book on Romans best illustrates the magnitude of Jesus's actions. He explains that if we truly understood the extent to which God hates sin, we would only begin to grasp the depth of His love for us in this one act of taking on human flesh. Yet, Christ was compelled to clothe himself in human flesh in order to preach good news to the poor, bind up the brokenhearted, proclaim freedom for the captives, and release prisoners from darkness (Is. 61:1).

He did not come to this earth to be received as a king, although He was worthy of that honor. He came to wash the feet of fishermen and tax collectors (John 13: 1-17); He came to touch lepers; and He came to befriend a population of common, everyday citizens. This amazing God-man set the bar high for ministry. His command was not to go and do your own thing; it was to go and do likewise. Chaplaincy is an opportunity to minister in like manner.

Chaplain Jones, a highly skilled physical specimen, is one example of this kind of humble ministry. He had taken first place on two occasions in a 25-mile endurance speed-walk. A real "man of men." Yet he felt somewhat detached from the soldiers who, for various reasons, fell out during the endurance speed-walk. Determined to identify with the fastest and the slowest, Chaplain Jones lead the pack for the first half of the speed-march and then gradually fell back to finish the race with those with damaged feet and other physical weaknesses. Not to his surprise, he identified with both: those that needed the chaplain to be the epitome of strength and power, and those that needed someone to understand their struggles and weaknesses. As humble servants, we approach the "least of these" on equal standing—as brothers and sisters—not "honoring one another above [ourselves]" or approaching them as beneath us. It is a response to God's command for us to "love one another. As [Christ has] loved you, so you must love one another." (John 13:34, NIV).

To live humbly is to live in submission and obedience, not regarding our comforts and pleasures as greater than His instruction and His agenda. It is living as the beloved creature of God and not as God Himself. There is no personal agenda; there is no hidden agenda there is only gratitude that we can express His profound love and share His hope with those in need of His divine intervention.

> Love fearlessly!
>
> In loving my neighbor, the wounded, and the poor, I offer up love to the Father; in letting them love me back, I open myself to more fully experience the greatness of his unlimited, unending, inseparable love.

"It is only through [this] humbling of ourselves that we will be allowed to walk with God. 'God resists the proud, but gives grace to the humble.' (1 Pet. 5:5) Paul points out that it is high-mindedness that leads to unbelief and lack of faith in the power of God (Rom. 11:20; 12:3). The humble attitude required by the Lord will make itself manifest in a life of prayer, contrition, and service."[1] In this way, humility is not only a professional ethic for chaplains, but also a personal ethic from which professional ministry manifests. "High-mindedness" or pride positions us to look down on or approach as *less than* those invaluable lives that we are called to serve.

In a sense, chaplaincy has evolved out of a response to those in need. It seeks to offer services and provisions for those who are in the worst of circumstances and distresses, including sickness, imprisonment, broken relationships, poverty, bereavement, etc. And it may simply be attentiveness to issues (great or small) that seem great to others. For example, Army Chaplain Megan Hodge was assigned to a year in Iraq; she also served as a vital link between the US Army Forces and the Iraqi people. On one occasion, she heard of an Iraqi youth soccer team that practiced every day without uniforms, sometimes even without the proper equipment. Their one desire was to compete with other Iraqi youth soccer teams and to have the privilege of traveling to another country to compete. Through an all-out effort with her local church and other church agencies,

---

1   Carey Dillinger, "What Does the Lord Require?".

she raised thousands of dollars for brand new uniforms, equipment, and eventually funds for them to compete abroad. Humility validates all circumstances and regards all individuals and groups, including these Muslim youths, as worthy of humble service.

In chapter six of the book of Micah, the prophet has brought his message to its climax as illustrated through a courtroom drama. He presents a series of rhetorical questions concerning what exactly God seeks from the people of Israel (6:6-7). Then, in verse 8, Micah answers by summarizing the totality of God's mission for His people: "He has showed you, O man, what is good. And what does the Lord require of you? To act justly and to love mercy and to walk humbly with your God." This passage summarizes the mission of chaplaincy as a ministry of compassion. Out of compassion, chaplains are advocates of justice for the voiceless and the vulnerable. Out of compassion, chaplains extend mercy to those who have not known mercy, such as prisoners or victims of abuse. Out of compassion, chaplains walk in humility, always approaching the "least of these" as brothers and sisters and seeing in them the great value and worth that is innately theirs.

CHAPTER THREE
Questions for Further Reflection

1. Actor Michael J. Fox once stated, "Pity is just one step away from abuse." In four to six brief sentences, explain what you think he meant. Why do you agree or disagree with this statement? (5 points)

2. Select a passage from the Pentateuch (first five books of the Old Testament) that requires us to care for a vulnerable or oppressed group of individuals. What does it ask, specifically? Who is asked to act, if anyone? How can this passage be made relevant for present chaplain ministries? (5 points)

3. Identify the three parts of Micah 6:8, and explain, in two to three sentences each, the application to chaplaincy ministries. (5 points)

DISCUSSION QUESTIONS: The following questions are provided for class discussion. The goal is to get you thinking about how you might approach ministry from the perspective of a chaplain. Carefully reflect on the class materials and prepare/develop a response to the following question:

> Call is an essential factor in the story of a chaplain; it is where it all begins. So, for this first study, you are the case to be evaluated. Reflect on your "call story." If you have one, write it out. Have you come to a certainty about your call? If so, how do you know you are called to this ministry? Finally, what core principle do you currently see as central to your ministry practice? In reflection, why is "calling" such an important aspect of one's chaplaincy ministry? Write at least a two to three-paragraph response.

Chapter Four

"I Am What I Am": Understanding Your Pastoral Identity and Pastoral Authority

He who sent me is trustworthy, and what I have heard from him I tell the world. — John 8:26b NIV

Who could forget the immortal words of Popeye the Sailorman: "I yam what I yam"?[1] His words declared he was not more or less than who he was, but exactly what he was supposed to be. He owned his identity and functioned effectively out of that identity. He knew his strengths; he knew the kind of person he was; and he never deviated from his personal identity in an attempt to be something or someone he was not. Wow! What a way to live.

Ministry in a secular environment brings temptation to just blend in with the other employees. While integration is important for establishing trustworthy relationships, chaplains must not forget the unique identity and value system from which they evolved. This issue becomes even more entangled when chaplains are asked to minister in an environment that the church is uncomfortable with or that seems too secular.

We often categorize these secular systems and agencies as good, not so good, and even off-limits. For example, many in the church feel that it is okay to send chaplains to the military, to hospitals, even to prisons, but they may question sending a chaplain to a racetrack or a casino. Yet, when we get to the more critical issues, aren't these simply secular institutions? They are neither good nor bad, but simply secular. Therefore, present-day chaplains are found in all of these places: in the military, hospitals, prisons, various industrial settings, churches, and any place people are gathered, are confined, or are simply there to have fun. The theology that undergirds chaplaincy comes from the belief that we must go to *them*, rather than expect them to come to us in our local churches. According to research,[2] a large percentage of individuals experience their initial and continued sense

---

1   This saying comes from the creators of Popeye the Sailorman, 1929. © KFS/ Fleischer TM Hearst/Fleisher. See also http://www.popeye.com.

2   George Barna, *Revolution* (Carol Stream, IL: Tyndale House Publishers, 2005).

of spirituality in relationship with some type of god outside traditional religious institutions; maybe in the workplace, at social events, and in other arenas apart from local churches. Therefore, chaplaincy is a means by which the church trains and sends its very best beyond the gates of the church community.

Jesus had a very clear understanding of this mission—His mission—and where that mission evolved from. The Gospel of John records a lengthy discussion between Jesus and the Pharisees concerning the validity of Jesus's words (8:12-29). Eight times Jesus says He knows where He comes from, and He identifies a purposed path and destination six times. Essentially, Jesus claims both His *pastoral identity* (loosely meaning a pastor's connection to a denomination, education, personality, etc.) as coming from the Father who sent Him, and He thereby claims His *pastoral authority* (given an individual by God and confirmed by a community of believers to act on its behalf) as a minister within a given context.

Claiming Your Pastoral Identity

Those called to pastor may, more specifically, be called to chaplaincy ministry. Chaplains are pastors. They operate out of that same "office." What is the expectation of that pastoral office? John Johnson[3] makes the case that four Old Testament offices underscore the identity of the pastorate: prophet, priest, sage, and king.[4]

As prophets, pastors or chaplains act as the moral conscience of the community they serve. When injustice is present, the chaplain acts as advocate for the affected individuals, families, employees, etc. The tricky part is the chaplain's dual role. Chaplains are employed by an institution, yet they may be called to mediate between the institution and the victims of the alleged injustice. As priests, chaplains provide conflict mediation in hopes of leading individuals towards forgiveness or reconciliation. As sages, chaplains offer instruction and guidance through pastoral counseling, which is one of the most important roles chaplains will play. However, the pastoral identity of chaplains differs from that of traditional pastors in that chaplains primarily offer pastoral care to those who are in the midst of a crisis. Among issues commonly dealt with are grief/loss, marriage and family conflict, sickness, national and natural disasters, and various life transitions.

The last piece of the pastoral identity is "king." No, pastoral figures are

---

3 Though the intended audience of this text is for chaplains/future chaplains, the concept is generalized for use by all pastoral types.

4 John Johnson, "Seeking Pastoral Identity," The Spurgeon Fellowship Journal (Fall 2007), 4. www.thespurgeonfellowship.org. These offices are more fully explored in Volume 2 of this series.

not the "kings of their domain." By this, Johnson is referring to the role of chaplains as administrators and leaders within the context they are called to serve. They oversee and participate in the ethical aspects of how a given context operates. For example, a chaplain may be called upon to advocate for a patient who is receiving poor care because of economic status, or for an employee whose religious rights are violated.

Understanding the role of pastor is only the first part of developing a pastoral identity. While Johnson approaches the topic biblically, most chaplains and pastors will already have an identity in mind based on their particular tradition. They will model, to an extent, what they have seen. This is why it is so important to have a full understanding of who they are as chaplains and ministers; this comes from reflecting on Scripture, personal identity, and specific call. Like Christ, chaplains must possess a certainty that they are called by God to pastor a given setting. They must also have some understanding of what that will look like in a particular setting. Identity is shaped by a particular call and setting; it is shaped by an understanding of a relationship with God; and it is shaped by the church or tradition that confirms this identity.

Maintaining a Unique Faith Identity in a Pluralistic Setting

If I speak with the tongues of men and of angels, but do not have love, I have become a noisy gong or a clanging cymbal. — 1 Cor. 13:1, NASB

Chaplaincy has a long history stemming from its origins in the military. Under the leadership of George Washington, the military ensured that a variety of denominations were represented through chaplaincy. Of course, working side by side with other ministers has its benefits and challenges. For some, the benefits are exposure and a broadened understanding of one's faith. For some, the challenges are self-denial and faith assimilation. In the pastoral care setting, a successful chaplain must validate their unique faith history through balancing three difficult areas: authenticating one's pastoral identity as a chaplain; giving the Holy Spirit a vital, yet appropriate place in ministry; and developing a more integrated view of healing.

The temptation for some chaplains is to deny their unique religious roots. The more mainstream they appear, the more likely it is they will be accepted by their peers, care recipients, and employers. However, self-denial will only make one less effective as a pastoral care provider.

Consider the case of the Protestant chaplain who dressed more like his superior—a Catholic chaplain—than himself. Taking on the identity of a Catholic priest obviously indicated that he was running from his faith. After spending some time with the chaplain, it was discovered that he had carried some shame from his denominational affiliation as a Pentecostal. This is not uncommon for those who have been ridiculed or rejected for their beliefs. However, in trying to constantly conceal their authentic pastoral identity, chaplains may be inadvertently suppressing the identities of those around them. That is, they can never fully see others for who they are. The hope—whether conscious or subconscious—will be to change the other person to be what these chaplains want them to be. In the case of the military chaplain, after several months of working with his denomination's chaplains commission, the man began to more genuinely claim his unique pastoral identity. The significance, personally and professionally, of accepting one's own faith heritage and identity cannot be stressed enough. With such an unclear acceptance of one's own identity, a Catholic cannot be received fully as Catholic; a Southern Baptist cannot be received fully as a Southern Baptist; etc.

Chaplains must also understand the role of the Spirit in ministry experiences. First, the Holy Spirit as guide is an invaluable tool in ministry. The Spirit gives wisdom, direction, and insight. He illuminates and reveals what chaplains cannot discern without His guidance. Because each ministry experience is layered with complexities, chaplains must rely on the wisdom of the Spirit. Stating that God is going to heal a cancer patient or restore a marriage, for example, may only further complicate a situation or impede the healing/grieving process, especially if the chaplain has misheard or misunderstood what the Spirit is saying. While the chaplain may have great faith in God to heal and restore, that may not be how God chooses to respond in this instance. Then, what is the family or the institution left to do as they reconcile the prophetic word given from the pastoral presence that communicated it?

Does this mean that Christians must deny their belief in God's power to heal or restore? Certainly not! However, the chaplain must be able to communicate the work and the will of the Spirit in a way that is not detrimental to the working of God's purposes in a particular situation.

Regardless of background, chaplains must consider the context and allow God to minister appropriately within a particular circumstance. Remember, the desire to bring healing and comfort must precede the familiarity of personal preference as to how the ministry experience occurs. In other words, chaplains are not to glorify a particular spiritual practice; rather, they are to lift up Christ that all men and women may be drawn unto Him (John 12:32).

Christ is lifted up when people are loved, valued, appreciated, validated, and helped. Christ is lifted up when chaplains hear the Word of the Lord and respond in a way that is relevant to the hearer. The Word should never wound or further isolate; that is not the purpose of the Spirit. While the Spirit may operate through revelation and power, Jesus identifies the Spirit primarily as the Comforter. The emphasis is always on loving care for the needy or distressed. Spiritual discernment, service, and giving do not authenticate a life. Faith, hope, and love—the greatest of these love—authenticate the life and the needs of the people served through chaplaincy ministry. First Corinthians 13 describes how this is made relevant. Consider the passage for our discussion:

> [1] If I could speak all the languages of earth and of angels, but didn't love others, I would only be a noisy gong or a clanging cymbal. [2] If I had the gift of prophecy, and if I understood all of God's secret plans and possessed all knowledge, and if I had such faith that I could move mountains, but didn't love others, I would be nothing. [3] If I gave everything I have to the poor and even sacrificed my body, I could boast about it; but if I didn't love others, I would have gained nothing.
>
> [4] Love is patient and kind. Love is not jealous or boastful or proud [5] or rude. It does not demand its own way. It is not irritable, and it keeps no record of being wronged. [6] It does not rejoice about injustice but rejoices whenever the truth wins out.
>
> [7] Love never gives up, never loses faith, is always hopeful, and endures through every circumstance.
>
> [8] Prophecy and speaking in unknown languages and special knowledge will become useless. But love will last forever! [9] Now our knowledge is partial and incomplete, and even the gift of prophecy reveals only part of the whole picture! [10] But when full understanding comes, these partial things will become useless.
>
> [11] When I was a child, I spoke and thought and reasoned as a child. But when I grew up, I put away childish things. [12] Now we see things imperfectly as in a cloudy mirror, but then we will see everything with perfect clarity. All that I know now is partial and incomplete, but then I will know everything completely, just as God now knows me completely.
>
> [13] Three things will last forever—faith, hope, and love—and the greatest of these is love. — 1 Corinthians 13 (NLT)

The chapter can be broken down into four parts. The first teaches that when gifts are emphasized more than the recipient of care, it is meaningless and ineffective—out of balance. It may even be selfish and self-promoting.

The second part defines what love is and is not. Love is patient, kind, hopeful; it rejoices in truth and justice; and it endures through every circumstance. Love is not jealous, boastful, arrogant, demanding, unforgiving, or unjust. Chaplains and ministers alike must operate out of this selfless love, setting aside all personal and/or hidden agendas. This is why good CPE training or other types of clinical training are so important. These courses assist student ministers with weeding out agendas through self-revelation and personal healing.

The third part explains why this kind of love must be at the forefront of Christian action: because we know in part and do not see clearly what God is able to see. Sure, the day will come when our vision and insight are impeccable, but today is not that day. Today, we rely on the Spirit to see what we cannot see, understanding the limitations of our human abilities to fully discern. So we love with the fullness of God's love, leaning and depending on the Spirit's guidance to provide effective and compassionate care.

The final part is a summary of Paul's exhortation to the Corinthian church. Without taking anything away from the relevance of spiritual gifts, he reminds the reader of what is most important and what will have a lasting impact: faith, hope, and love. Chaplains must have faith that God is God, no matter what the outcome. They must have a firm grasp of who God is and who God is not. Chaplains are a symbol of hope for the wounded, dying, and impoverished. They represent both God and the church community who seek to aid them in their distress. Ultimately, chaplains must communicate love through word and deed. Love is what heals wounds, gives life at the end of life, and feeds impoverished souls.

Another area chaplains must come to terms with is their personal and denominational approach to divine healing. Historically, many Christians have held to a narrow understanding of divine healing: that divine healing is *only* a miraculous and instantaneous restoration of one's physical condition. This belief was emphasized over broader understandings of healing; however, a much wider view of healing *did* exist. Healing was, at times, a gradual process; sometimes it did not occur at all; and, at times, healing came through death. Most Christians today more readily accept this comprehensive approach to healing. It comes from the growing understanding that God is God; while He is capable of healing the way we want Him to heal, He may not always choose to do it our way. Therefore, chaplains must learn to still seek the Great Physician, while yielding to the will of the Great I Am. Consider the following example:

> In the late 1960s, I was assigned as the Chaplain at the National Institute of Health, in Bethesda, Maryland. This was a fantastic research hospital, and my assignment was with the

Children's Leukemia Unit, a part of the NIH's Cancer Research Center. The case involved a six-year-old girl who was diagnosed with leukemia. She had gone through bone marrow transplants; however, she came down with pneumonia and died because the "germ-free recovery room" had not been perfected yet. Her thirty-four-year-old mother, a Charismatic, was part of a prayer group that met regularly in the family room adjacent to the ward. These women believed and practiced their Charismatic faith, which included healing and resurrection power.

I was called in during the wee hours of the morning after the young girl had died. The mother, after meeting with her Charismatic friends, insisted that the doctor allow her child to be returned to the ward so that they could pray for her resurrection. I was called in by the doctor who insisted that this was an unusual practice, and he would have nothing to do with it. I tried to explain to the doctor that the child was not his, but the mother's. After much debate, the child was brought into the family room with the mother and six other praying friends. I was there as the chaplain to support this family and as a Pentecostal who believed that God was a God of miracles. We all prayed fervently. After an hour of prayer, reading the Scriptures together, and embracing each other, the mother turned and said to me, "Chaplain, I don't believe that God wants to bring my child back." At that point, all gave God the glory, for He knew best, and we brought closure with prayers and tears, as well as celebration.

That next morning during the doctors' rounds, the young doctor who thought this was an unusual circumstance brought the case to the other doctors. I explained that this was simply a mother practicing her faith, and in allowing her to do so, we brought dignity to the mother and her Pentecostal prayer group. The senior doctor agreed. In this case there was the dignity that was rendered to the mother; there was the redemption of a system that had to learn whose the child was; and at the individual level, these women practiced their faith, even though the outcome had to be left to God.[5]

Scripture teaches that His way is not always our way. And the power over life and death rests with God. This is a most difficult journey for anyone to undertake. Having a more developed view of healing gives a dying care recipient permission to resign from this life and embrace the life

---

5   By Dr. Robert Crick, Director of the Church of God Chaplains Commission, from his personal experiences as a hospital chaplain.

hereafter, and it may give a grieving mother permission to return a beloved child to her Maker. Recognizing that God is sovereign both in miraculous healings and in the sting of death creates an atmosphere where God can be present in both settings, as illustrated in this case.

Establishing Your Pastoral Authority

The other aspect of a calling is pastoral authority. **Pastoral authority** refers to the authority given to ministers by an ecclesiastical body. This is also known as an ecclesiastical endorsement, which is a prerequisite for credentialing. **Endorsement** is given to certain individuals who are already recognized as having general pastoral authority to carry out their ministries through the ministerial licensing process. However, chaplains commissions and other agencies, in addition to offering general pastoral authority, endorse a minister for specific moral/ministerial responsibility and authority. Such endorsement comes after a minister has received specialized training, appears before the Chaplains Commission Board, and has met the requirements (personal, educational and emotional) that would make him/her qualified to carry out this specific ministry, most often categorized as 'chaplaincy,' on behalf of the denomination.

"For as long as you can remember, you have been a pleaser, depending on others to give you an identity. You need not look at that only in a negative way. You wanted to give your heart to others, and you did so quickly and easily. But now you are being asked to let go of all these self-made props and trust that God is enough for you. You must stop being a pleaser and reclaim your identity as a free self." — Henri Nouwen

Of course, all of this means very little if that authority is not internalized. That is, chaplains must own their identity and operate with a measure of confidence in that call. When they can internalize that identity, they will also internalize pastoral authority. This suggests a willing *obedience* to walk in pastoral identity. It is fully realizing Jesus's words in their ministry: "I know where I came from and where I am going." Therefore (John 8:14b, 28b, c), "I am [who] I claim to be, and I do nothing on my own but speak just what the Father has taught me. The one who sent me is with me; he has not left me alone, for I always do what pleases him." Jesus walked and operated out of this central belief about His life. He never parted from it. Even at the cost of His life, He could not deny who He was and what He was called to do.

There are moments when chaplains' pastoral authority is questioned by self or others because of life circumstances. Having a firm sense of identity (writing it down, memorizing it, etc.) will help sustain chaplains when their authority is questioned. In one such scenario, a CPE student found himself holding a small chapel service. That particular day, a woman joined the service and began to debate him regarding his sermon. The young chaplain began to engage in the argument, even trying to sit her down. As the situation progressed, others took her side. After a few moments of this, a janitor poked his head in to see what the commotion was all about. It took the janitor only a few moments to take control of the situation, urging each to hear what the other was saying. Finally, the crowd settled down for a great worship service.

In the young chaplain's notes that week, he had to address the question, "Who has the authority?" Because he had not come to terms with his pastoral authority, the woman reacted accordingly. The janitor took charge of the moment when the young man was incapable. Unlike the young man, Jesus never lost sight of who He was, not even in the most difficult times. Because Jesus had such a firm grasp on His identity, He was able to operate—even in His weakest moments—out of His given authority.

Chaplaincy is a call to minister to people, families, and communities at their weakest moments. While they don't need a superhero with superhuman strength, they do need someone who will lead them through that moment with compassionate and unwavering authority. Jesus certainly possessed the ability to do superhuman tasks, and He did. When John the Baptist asked Jesus if He was the One (Matt. 11:3-5), Jesus responded, "The blind receive sight, the lame walk, those who have leprosy are cleansed, the deaf hear, the dead are raised, and the good news is proclaimed to the poor." However, the world was not changed by His miracles and deliverances; rather, it was transformed by His compassionate and unwavering belief that His ultimate mission was necessary and would yield the Creator God's envisioned result: salvation.

Pastoral authority also comes from taking the time to get equipped for ministry. This may come through specialized training, formal Christian education, and/or years of mentoring by a more mature pastor or chaplain. Whatever the path, individual chaplains must be committed to preparing themselves in spirit, intellect, and practice for this specialized ministry. Paul instructed Timothy (2 Tim. 2:15, ISV), "Do your best to present yourself to God as an approved worker who has nothing to be ashamed of, handling the word of truth with precision." When we consider a person to be an authority on a given subject or practice, we assume he or she knows the subject matter well and can communicate it with integrity. Likewise, chaplains must be well studied in a variety of areas to assist people. Think of military chaplains: they must understand the mindset of servicemen and women. They must understand the special needs of that particular community. Similarly, chaplains who work in an industrialized setting must be familiarized with and equipped to meet the needs of that unique setting. Ultimately, chaplains must be able to counsel, advocate, pray, listen, be present, rightly discern the Word, know the systems they work within, and hear from God. Because the chaplain's arena is so different from the arena of the church, chaplains must take the time to be equipped for their unique and specialized field.

> *But as for you, continue in what you have learned and have become convinced of, because you know those from whom you learned it... All Scripture is God-breathed and is useful... so that the servant of God may be thoroughly equipped for every good work.* — 2 Tim. 3:14-17 NIV

Consider your pastoral identity. What mission has God impassioned you for that is necessary for His work to be carried out through your life's ministry? There is an entire community outside of the self-made, exclusive society that we call church; Jesus had a vision for both. Paul carried that vision to the Gentiles; Peter carried that vision to the Jews. The world (both inside and outside the gates) is full of individuals in crisis who need someone who is certain of their call, equipped to fulfill it, and sent by God and the church to be present, to advocate, to heal, and, ultimately, to love.

Chaplains Have Been Given Moral Authority, not Ultimate Authority

> *Everyone must submit to governing authorities. For all authority comes from God, and those in positions of authority have been placed there by God.*

> — Romans 13:1 NLT

Chaplains find themselves in a distinct ministerial position. They are hired by companies or organizations to be moral authorities, not the ultimate authority. Unlike a church setting, God is not sought for the direction or the continual maintenance/practices of the company (unless it is a religious organization). God may not be given any role at all; chaplaincy is merely a budget issue. Chaplains are hired to offer support and encouragement, often in the form of counseling, to the religious community present within the facility. That religious community is often *pluralistic*, that is, people maintain individual cultural/religious beliefs while fully participating in the dominant culture. Chaplains may provide services to a variety of Christian denominations, as well as to a variety of religious faiths or philosophies. The job is to ensure that all participants have an opportunity to be a person of faith, whatever that faith may look like. In this way, chaplains bear both secular and religious authority. It is religious because they provide ministry or counsel for care recipients; it is secular because they also provide care to non-Christian people in a non-religious setting. They must learn to effectively reach beyond religious boundaries to become acquainted with a variety of faith traditions, values, and political ideologies.

Another challenge that many chaplains will face is the issue of authority. What does that authority look like, and to whom do they answer? If chaplains have been given moral authority, do they have the power to make decisions on behalf of their employers? Probably not, but there will be instances when the answer is yes. Nevertheless, the employer always has ultimate authority; that is, the program is not just the chaplain's program: it is the institution's. Paul wrote in Romans 13 that all authority comes from God, whether we like it or not. The Christian paradigm of ministry is to submit to authorities that God puts over us. However, chaplains must be able to work within the organization without losing a distinctly religious voice. They must resist **assimilation**; they are in the world, not of the world.

> Assimilation—a sociological term referring to the integration of one into the culture of the mainstream society.

The hope is to impact the institution, not vice versa. Both Nehemiah and Joseph were able to do this effectively. Nehemiah served his king faithfully and with a good attitude, but he never lost his authentically Jewish identity. Because of his faithful service to the king, Nehemiah was able to influence the king to release the Jews to go home to Israel. The king even protected them and made provisions for them. Joseph likewise served every image of authority put over him. He had every right to disregard his religious identity and heritage. He had been hurt, rejected, and tossed aside; he had been sold into slavery, falsely accused, and falsely imprisoned. Yet he held to his faith in God, served those over him, and relied on the Lord for guidance. In the end, he was used to implement a policy that would ultimately save an entire race of people and those around them.

While these men were granted authority by the powers over them, Jesus has all authority and power as God incarnate. Yet even Jesus operated only within those powers extended to Him by His Heavenly Father (John 18). What an amazing example of pastoral authority. He did only what the Father instructed Him and spoke as He was instructed. At the same time, Jesus recognized the powers present in this world and submitted to them also.

The authority that chaplains operate out of is their *pastoral authority*. They are not God, and they are not the "lord of their domain." They are *representatives of* their church, their denomination, and the God who sends them to be employees within an organization or business. This may mean very little to some people they work with, and it may mean the world to others. Chaplains in a secular setting must use diplomacy and wisdom. To have authority is to have influence. This must never be misused or confused with having ultimate authority.

CHAPTER FOUR
Questions for Further Reflection

1. In your own words, differentiate between moral authority and ultimate authority in two to three sentences. (5 points)

2. Define pastoral authority, assimilation, and endorsement. (5 points)

3. Identify the four Old Testament offices which underscore the identity of the pastorate and briefly describe each one. (5 points)

CASE STUDIES: The following questions are provided for class discussion. The goal is to get you thinking about how you might approach ministry from the perspective of a chaplain. Carefully reflect on the class materials and prepare/develop a response to the following question:

> A rusty, seasoned sergeant told a newly assigned young chaplain the solution for winning the hearts of his troops. He stated to the chaplain, 'Never get into the chow line to eat until every soldier has been fed; never bunk down to sleep until every soldier has found a warm place to lay his head; and never take care of your personal and family needs until you have adequately taken care of those same needs for your soldiers.' Reflecting on this sergeant's comments, how do you see the chaplain as a servant to his/her ministries?

Chapter Five

Prepare Ye the Way: A Theology of Spiritual, Professional, and Personal Formation for Chaplains

Be diligent to present yourself approved to God, a worker who does not need to be ashamed, rightly dividing the word of truth.

— 2 Timothy 2:15, NKJV

Formation is a necessary condition in the professional field of chaplaincy ministry. Most professionals graduate from an undergraduate and graduate institution equipped with the right information for their future careers in business, medicine, education, etc. In most cases, employers, co-workers, and clientele do not expect them to also be qualified spiritual leaders. While chaplains are highly trained professionals who are equipped as counselors, administrators, policy advisors, teachers, pastors, and advocates/mediators, they are more than informed professionals; their experience, education, and personal spiritual journeys are utilized for the purpose of holistic formation. Holistic formation moves beyond just being skilled and informed about a field; holistic formation occurs when a person chooses to allow the Spirit to use personal and professional experiences and reflections to mold the chaplain into a better conduit of care. In this section, our theological reflection will now move from an ethos of practice to a theology of personal growth that makes possible a spiritually discerning ethos of practice.

Spiritual Formation

Spiritual formation "is the process by which one moves and is moved from self-worship to Christ-centered self-denial as a general condition of life in God's present and eternal kingdom."[1] In this sense, spiritual formation is that intentional pursuit of Christ which moves us beyond personal agendas to knowing the formational love of God. This makes us more receptive of the people we care for and more capable of giving ourselves honestly to care ministry. Without this intentional knowing of God, the practice of

---

1   Dallas Willard, "Spiritual Formation: What It is, and How It is Done." http://www.dwillard.org/articles/artview.asp?artID=58.

chaplaincy is void of the Spirit and the presence of our Holy Creator God, this specialized work is limited to social work or therapy.

Establishing a Theological Core

In chaplaincy, spiritual formation must be balanced with personal and professional formation. While many authors might direct students to begin formation in the practice of specific disciplines, we suggest practical theological reflection as an alternative starting point. For reflection "connects what we believe about God with how we live as disciples of Jesus Christ."[2] That is, to better understand the practices of chaplaincy, chaplains must reflect on those spiritual and theological beliefs that are core to how they live and routinely practice spiritual care. In this way, information becomes formation. Consider Susie, a college chaplain.

Susie's life verse (not to be confused with a favorite verse) is Micah 6:8 (NIV, emphasis added), "He has showed you, O man, what is good. And what does the LORD require of you? To *act justly* and to *love mercy* and to *walk humbly* with your God." It is her constant reflection, and, as a college chaplain, all ministry flows from this paradigm. She seeks to be fair, merciful, and

Spiritual Disciplines:

Prayer, Worship, Evangelism, Serving, Stewardship, Fasting, Silence, Solitude, Journaling, Learning, Celibacy, Meditation, Simplicity, Submission, Confession, Celebration

Richard Foster, "Celebration of Discipline"

Donald Whitney, "Spiritual Disciplines for the Christian Life"

never position herself above those who seek her counsel. A student once visited her office to confess he had cheated on an exam. Because Susie's theological approach to care evolves out of Micah 6:8, her response to this student's issue adequately reflected her beliefs about what is just and merciful. She explained to this student that justice is deciding to do the right thing, and mercy is not found in cover up, but in confession. Furthermore, she had to decide how to communicate humility without letting go of her spiritual authority as chaplain as the student searched for healing in his crisis.

---

2   Kenda C. Dean, et.al, *Starting Right: Thinking Theologically about Youth Ministry* (Grand Rapids, MI: Zondervan Publishing House, 2001).

For this reason, we begin spiritual formation with an understanding of principles and truths that motivate chaplains to be the persons of Christ they are called to be, and frame the thoughts, behaviors, and choices they will make in their pastoral office.

Chaplains must be aware of God's revelation in all situations, regardless of how horrific or destructive the event may be. CPE students are taught to specifically reflect on how Christ is being revealed in every event and every conversation. The very nature of chaplaincy as a critical ministry for individuals, families, and communities demands that chaplains approach theology intentionally and reflectively, personally and professionally, specifically and generally. When a mother reveals her fear of letting go of her dying fifteen-month-old, where is Jesus? What could He possibly be trying to reveal to her... and to the chaplain? These moments force chaplains to reflect on their beliefs about God, justice, theodicy, the world, and themselves. These moments, when approached theologically and intentionally, form—even transform—who they are spiritually.

Critical, theological reflection positions chaplains to hear and to ponder in their hearts the very Word of God. Reflection can bring relevance to practices that define the unique ministry of the chaplain. This is why spiritual formation must begin with understanding *who* they are theologically, as pastors, chaplains, and disciples of Christ.

Becoming the Beloved of God

In a society plagued by self-promotion and personal kingdom building, it is important for chaplains to know and remember who they are as representatives of the church and of Christ. It is most important to know and remember who they are as sons and daughters of Christ. Regardless of what position they hold or how many lives they oversee, chaplains must own their identity as the beloved of God.[3] As such, there are no expectations for them to save, heal, and deliver everyone. His love for His chaplains is not determined or affected by the many accolades or criticisms that may come with leadership responsibilities. Chaplains are loved with the same immeasurable love today as they were prior to call or conviction. Without this revelation, the work of the chaplain can easily become a means of self-indulgence, personal affirmation, and self-seeking glorification. Chaplaincy without personal, spiritual revelation of God's love cannot communicate an authentic care as revealed by the Spirit because the chaplain hasn't fully known that care.

In understanding the love of God, chaplains must free themselves of self-imposed expectations.[4] Chaplains are at the center of crisis situations. They

---

3 Nouwen, *Life of the Beloved*.

4 Mark Yaconelli, *Contemplative Youth Ministry*.

are sought for guidance, support, encouragement, and answers. It can be easy to lapse into the superhero. The problem is that the hero will eventually confront his or her limitations as a mere human being. God does not call chaplains to replace Christ as Savior, but to represent Him before humanity.

In surrendering self-imposed expectations, agendas, self-worship, and need to contain and control the works of the Lord, chaplains can more fully embrace His love and care. It is here they no longer make excuses for His perceived inadequacies and their own; it is here they can more fully accept Him for who He is. He is still God in the midst of great tragedy, like the recent earthquakes in Haiti. He is still God when there are no answers to give a grieving mother or father. And He is still God when others use His name for murderous acts of hatred. It is here that chaplains learn to *not* just passively resign themselves to His will, but actively give themselves and those they serve to His care.

As caregivers, it is very easy to give love—even to God. However, it can be very difficult to receive—especially from God. The Bible describes this amazing and unending love as so vast it is immeasurable. There are no strings attached, no expectations, and no way to separate us from this love. Matthew 7:7 says that if we ask, it shall be given; if we seek, we will find; and if we knock it will be opened unto us. Christ states that in receiving His great love, seekers need only to ask, to seek, and to knock. Spiritual formation is doing just that. It is surrendering the heart, mind, and will to receive from Him a love that is transformative and necessary for the critical context of chaplaincy ministry. By fully receiving their identity as beloved, chaplains can more readily receive and care for the wounded, rejected, sick, grieved, and dying.

Engaging Community

Another essential component to spiritual formation for chaplains is to reconnect or stay connected with the local church. Chaplains are constantly doing the work of the Lord in a variety of settings. They conduct worship services, visit the sick, counsel the brokenhearted, and offer sacraments to care recipients and their immediate community (often this includes family and friends). Consequently, chaplains may not feel the need to offer services within their worshipping community. However, it is imperative to maintain and nurture those relationships. Ephesians 3:16-19 teaches that we more fully and more profoundly experience the transforming love of Christ *within a worshipping body*. It is through corporate worship and fellowship that we come "to know this love that surpasses knowledge—that [we] may be filled to the measure of all the fullness of God."

While we need to seek the opportunity for fellowship and worship, the spiritual formation journey ultimately leads to communion with

God, family, and care recipients. Communion is where we learn each other's language (understanding). In communion, we become more acquainted with each other's passions and personal stories (connection). In communion, we present ourselves to those we commune with as vulnerable and transparent (invitation toward intimacy). And, in communion, we purposefully present ourselves before the holy, transcendent God with the eager expectation of a reciprocated love dialogue (indwelling). Without that dialogue, we have nothing to communicate to those to whom we offer His love.

Spiritual formation is essential in providing excellent spiritual care for families and individuals. The chaplain at rest with God, self, and others is not depleted of those resources necessary for this critical ministry. However, that rest is not obtainable without intentional formational practices, such as personal, theological reflection; time alone with God to refuel and receive of His love and care; and fellowship with family and friends and the local church body.

Professional Formation

Chaplaincy is a unique approach to ministry that has been largely overlooked and undervalued by the church. However, society is growing in its recognition of the need for spiritual care in a variety of secular and pluralistic settings. For individuals called to this ministry, a tension exists between traditional church ministry and the non-traditional, "outside the gates" ministry. The tension within chaplaincy is the shaping of the personhood of chaplains as they attempt to fully represent God and the church, while remaining socially and personally relevant for those they provide with pastoral care. It is the tension of being "in the world and not of the world." This issue is best dealt with through a specialized chaplaincy training called Clinical Pastoral Education (CPE), a required training program for chaplains seeking full-time ministry in most settings. This training not only equips chaplains intellectually, but interpersonally, making them more effective conduits of personal and spiritual care.

Clinical Pastoral Education

Clinical Pastoral Education (CPE) is provided through the Association of Clinical Pastoral Education. It is a special training model whereby chaplains are given an opportunity to develop as pastoral care providers through hands-on ministry experience, theological reflection, and interpersonal growth. It is in this clinical setting that each chaplain's primary issues are confronted and worked through. This includes identity, unresolved anger, intimacy, and loneliness. This training model recognizes the need for caregivers to be healthy conduits from which to offer counsel, guidance, encouragement, and healing. The primary goal is make sure the caregivers' issues do not get in the way of their ability to offer a ministry of healing, restoration, and reconciliation.

In these rigid clinical settings, chaplains must confront the issue of identity—that is, who they are and whether they have come to terms with their own families of origin, their own ethnic/cultural background, their gender, and their call. Second, they focus on any unresolved anger issues. The CPE supervisors confront any issues concerning authority figures, primarily parents and others within and outside the church to whom they answer. This is very important in chaplaincy. As noted, chaplains are always carrying out someone else's religious program, whether a military commander or a hospital administrator. They must learn how to work with and submit to those authorities placed over them. Those who are easily or often offended may want to evaluate what issues lead them to interpret acts as offensive or injurious.

Third, there are the issues of intimacy and anxiety. Intimacy leads student chaplains into a better understanding of the ability to connect with care recipients, to manage healthy boundaries, and to manage anxieties in the care environment. Initially, students will be assessed on the ability to "get close" or connect with care recipients—without violating ethical standards in regards to the opposite sex, his/her own sexuality, and other matters of intimacy. Beyond sexuality, chaplains may have anxiety or intimacy hurdles due to language barriers, cultural/ethnic differences, religious differences, etc. Even the number of family/friends present can cause anxiety and/or an intimacy disconnect. These kinds of issues must be brought to the surface and dealt with so that effective care can be given to individuals and families in every kind of situation. Chaplains must also be able to connect emotionally and spiritually to those they offer spiritual care, such as a dying patient, someone in the midst of a divorce, or other persons in crisis.

Chaplains must be at ease with their environment as well as their ministerial development and journey. If a chaplain is constantly tense about his/her setting or questioning his/her abilities as pastor, the care recipients will sense the uneasiness and therefore alter their interaction and responses to the caregiver. If a chaplain has not worked through and reached a high level of understanding in regards to their own need for biblically centered intimacy, s/he will have problems working and connecting with care recipients in these crisis sites. One CPE student made this discovery the hard way.

> A young, rather energetic "know-it-all" intern was into his head, but needed to plunge more deeply into his heart. That

happened during the wee hours of the morning, when he was the on-call hospital chaplain. Awakened from his sleep, he was asked to give the death notification of a grandfather who did not make it out of surgery. This young man had been raised in the church and thought he had an answer for everything. To his amazement, when he walked into the room, there were many family members present—a sea of faces awaiting news concerning the patriarch of the clan. The young man, with his well-memorized speech, walked toward the man's wife, a grandmother in her late 80s, and passed out. When he came to, the old grandmother had him in her arms humming a song that went something like this, "It's alright; Daddy is with Jesus. It's alright, it's alright."

The young man, a symbol of strength and help, became the care recipient at the hands of the grandmother, a symbol of weakness and frailty. As expressed through the story, if not properly worked through, anxiety will affect the ministry experience. This story, with all its complexities, connects anxiety with the root issue of presuppositions about self, others, and ministry approaches, all of which will lead to either a positive ministry experience or a negative one. The young man obviously made some assumptions about the experience. It could have been the number of people, ethnic barriers, the death notification, or a number of things, whatever the source of his anxiety, the experience teaches a powerful lesson on how presuppositions and assumptions can produce overwhelming anxiety, and how that can potentially hinder an intimate connection between the chaplain and the care recipient.

Finally, chaplains must reach a place in their lives where they can be alone, but not lonely. Here, they will search out peers—not clients, inmates, or soldiers—who can relate to them as peers.

The necessary contribution of professional formation that CPE and other training programs offer is the opportunity to practice care-giving skills while actively engaging the discipline of self-examination. It is an intentional maturing of the chaplain. It is a willingness to learn through self-discovery and other discovery. That is, we learn about ourselves and about God through the stories and life experiences of those we are privileged to walk alongside. While CPE is intense and, for some even, agonizing, it is an invaluable educational tool and model. It creates opportunities for student chaplains to develop the ability to:

- Plan with creativity;
- Choose alternative means of behavior;
- Honestly express a full range of emotions;

- Recognize good supervision without feeling put down;
- Empathize with others;
- Disagree without rebellion;
- Openly express gratitude and disapproval;
- Accept one's own gender/sexuality;
- Be dependent without a loss of identity.

Personal Formation: a Ministry of Integrity

Whatever happens, conduct yourselves in a manner worthy of the gospel of Christ... Continue to work out your salvation with fear and trembling, for it is God who works in you to will and to act according to his good purpose.

— Philippians 1:27, 2:12c-13

Paul, an excellent image of chaplaincy, exhorts the people of Philippi to remain worthy of the gospel of Christ. The Philippian church, predominantly filled with retired military families, had suffered through terrible persecution that caused members to rethink their commitments to the church and to Christ. Like so many chaplains, Paul had the great task of encouraging a wounded and fearful people. His words could have communicated indifference and isolation or compassion and insight. However, before any of his words were made relevant, the recipients needed to trust him to be a person of authority, faith, and integrity. He must be the person he said he was. Because of his long track record (of which they were aware) Paul didn't have to convince them. They knew his character. Having that assurance, his words of exhortation and encouragement were received with love and compassion.

Chaplains are faced with unnerving crises on a daily basis. They find people in the worst of circumstances and sit with them in their pain. These people rely on a presence they believe to be trustworthy, humble, compassionate, and wise. For this reason, it is imperative that chaplains fully embody the goodness of the Lord. Families and individuals in crisis have so much to work through in their dark moments; a chaplain with little integrity or little character can literally destroy an opportunity for the care recipient(s) to begin a healthy recovery process.

For many chaplains, the opportunity to build relationships and "prove" themselves has already occurred at some level. Military, prison, and workplace chaplains work alongside those they care for. Care recipients watch and listen to what chaplains say *and* do. Are they who they say they are? Having character is just that—being who they say they are. Because of the intensity associated with this ministry, the smallest of character flaws can easily be exposed.

Some of the traits that are essential and non-negotiable include integrity, reliability, functionality, compassion, wisdom, and humility. Integrity simply refers to one's steadfast adherence to high moral principles and/or professional standards. In other words, chaplains must be "fair, firm, and consistent." In a sense, this is what professional integrity is. It is operating consistently according to a given standard as derived from the employing organization and the ecclesiastical assembly they represent. Consider the following life example.

> In my latter years of seminary, I found myself on the other side of this motto. During the semester, I gave birth to my second child. I missed only one class; I was in the hospital that day. When I returned, the professor explained to me that I would have to do extra work to make up the hours missed from class. I was so angry. I felt my absence was legitimate and excusable; later he casually explained to the class that while circumstances do occur, his ethical responsibility was to be fair and consistent in the administration of his duties. In other words, he had created a system that valued all persons in the class (even me) and our educational preparedness. For him, it was a matter of integrity. The expectation was clear, and he held to his word, not just in this but in all areas of his life to which we were witnesses. — Brandelan S. Miller

Chaplains who can operate with this kind of integrity will be reliable and functional. By functional, we mean that chaplains have the skills necessary to provide honest and skilled care while maintaining the expectations of the employing organization, as well as the endorsing faith community.

Unfortunately, not every chaplain or every case provides the opportunity to develop trusting relationships with care recipients. In that small, hectic window of opportunity, chaplains must present themselves as persons of character in word and deed and presence. In that small window of opportunity, it is imperative that chaplains follow through on any promises, no matter how small or minimal. It is not only a matter of professional courtesy to do so; it is a matter of personal integrity as a pastoral presence.

Compassion, Wisdom, and Humility

Compassion asks us to go where it hurts, to enter into places of pain, to
share brokenness, fear, confusion, and anguish. Compassion challenges
us to cry out with those in misery, to mourn with those who are lonely,
to weep with those in tears. Compassion requires us to be weak with the
weak, vulnerable with the vulnerable, and powerless with the powerless.
Compassion means full immersion in the condition of being human.

— Henri Nouwen, Compassion: A Reflection on the Christian Life

The last three—compassion, wisdom, and humility—are more inwardly
focused. They are not dependent on job description or professionalism.
They are developed from inward reflection and an honest desire to provide
care for those in need. And they are developed from an awareness of
personal woundedness and reworked through a willingness to reach out by
way of those wounds. Experiences—good, bad, and deeply painful—make
chaplains more humane and more compassionate in their care ministries.

In chaplaincy development, nothing is thrown away. A painful loss can
be a place of divine revelation. This is not the emergence of a theology that
teaches that God brings pain and suffering to our doors for personal good
or for the good of our neighbor; rather, it is a suggestion that—no matter
how or why it came to us—the experience can still possess great value in
personal growth as human beings who hurt and who comfort the hurting.
The great task in this is the willingness and ability to revisit that pain for
the sake of another person. This does not happen without some cost to
the chaplain, since the mind does not distinguish between the emotional
pain of the event and the memory. The pain felt is the same. In ministering
to those in pain, chaplains are inevitably confronted with and experience
anew their own moment of despair, vulnerability, and pain. It is that pain
that makes us more *humane*. It is here that chaplains become the purest
conduit of God's grace, His compassion, and His tender mercies. It is
here that chaplains are most capable of creating an atmosphere of divine
healing, comfort, and restoration.

Compassion. Pastoral caregivers are confronted with all kinds of human
suffering at varying levels, none of which is greater or lesser to those
experiencing the pain of loss, perceived loss, loneliness, rejection, sickness,
or impoverishment. Compassion, literally "to suffer with," does not require
that the caregiver or chaplain understand the totality of a given scenario;
rather, it requires the chaplain to be willing to confront their own fear

58

of pain and suffering in order to suffer with the person, the family, or the community for which they are providing pastoral care. Chaplains who cannot grapple with their own pain will find it very difficult, if not impossible, to be present with others in their time of suffering. As the image of moral and spiritual authority, chaplains who display a compassionate calm and emotional stability can be a lifeline or anchor for those whose lives are in utter chaos. Because of the daunting nature of chaplaincy ministry, those who are unable to have compassion for and patience with those they minister to should consider other avenues of ministry in which they will be more functional.

*And **wisdom** and knowledge shall be the stability of thy times, and strength*

of salvation: the fear of the LORD is his treasure.

— Isaiah 33: 6, KJV (emphasis added)

Wisdom. Scripture makes it clear that wisdom is not something that is inherited or innate. Wisdom is sought; it is pursued. In Jewish tradition, wisdom is slippery, like trying to catch a greased pig. Every time seekers believe they have a hold on the pig, it slips from their grasp. The pursuit of wisdom can be a slippery chase; nevertheless, it is essential in chaplaincy ministry. Lives are dependent upon chaplains who have the wisdom to say, do, and be still, accordingly.

Closely tied to wisdom is discernment, the ability to make good judgments. The wise person is aware that they are always presented with options; the discerning person is wise enough to lean on the Holy Spirit for judgment in that decision-making process when a right choice is unclear. For example, suppose a family desires for their still-born infant to be baptized, but their priest cannot be reached. The potential issue here is two-fold: (1) the on-call chaplain does not believe in infant baptism; (2) this may be a necessary part of the family's path to healing. The unwise chaplain will only see two paths: performing the baptism or not performing the baptism. The wise and discerning person will seek the Lord for an option that does not require the chaplain to perform a religious act that would compromise his or her beliefs while still meeting the needs of the family. For example, the chaplain may suggest that another staff chaplain be called who is more in line with the beliefs of the family. There are several options that can be factored. The point is that wisdom is dependent on the guidance of the Holy Spirit. Chaplains must tune in to what the Spirit is saying to them in any given event or crisis.

Humility. Finally, chaplains must approach this ministry with the greatest humility. Abraham Lincoln wrote, "Nearly all men can stand adversity, but if you want to test a man's character, give him power." Chaplains must refrain from personal agendas motivated by power. It is with humility that they must approach care. Families and persons in crisis may seek counsel, but it is always their choice. Chaplains must not attempt to sway care recipients to adhere to the chaplain's convictions. Families with a history of oppression and poverty will be most vulnerable to such manipulations. Therefore, it is especially important to be cautious when offering counsel to families in need. Manipulation and coercion with the best of intentions is still manipulation. It robs individuals of the freedom to make informed decisions; it robs them of their voice. Approaching chaplaincy with humility is just the opposite. It informs people, encourages people, and affirms them in their ability to make choices that are necessary and are right for them and their families.

Conclusion

Character Maintenance

In all areas of formation, the need for growth and further development never changes. For the chaplain, this does not happen accidentally; it happens intentionally. It is the responsibility of each chaplain to ensure this is happening. Chaplains should seek out peers and trustworthy friends with whom they can establish accountability for the purpose of strengthening their spiritual, professional, and personal formation. For some chaplains, such formation will require professional counseling in order to get to the deeper needs that may block a chaplain's development. In terms of spiritual and personal formation, chaplains may need to meet regularly with a counselor or licensed therapist, and they may meet regularly with peers or trusted friends in order to share personal and spiritual struggles. In terms of professional development, chaplains would do well to be part of professional associations and agencies that require ongoing training, peer evaluation, and other ways to continue to deepen one's professional identity. In addition to academic training, the chaplain must intentionally be a life-long student in skills and personal development. In the words of Paul, "Be diligent to present yourself approved to God, a worker who does not need to be ashamed, rightly dividing the word of truth" (2 Timothy 2:5).

CHAPTER FIVE
Questions for Further Reflections

1. What is spiritual formation and what is its significance in personal and professional development? Respond in three to five sentences. (5 points)

2. Identify and briefly explain the significance of the four issues addressed in clinical pastoral education. (5 points)

3. During the discussion on character development, several traits were identified as non-negotiable. Select one of those traits and examine why it is so important. Also, explain how you have sought or will seek to develop that trait as a chaplain or minister. (5 points)

CASE STUDIES: The following questions are provided for class discussion. The goal is to get you thinking about how you might approach ministry from the perspective of a chaplain. Carefully reflect on the class materials and prepare/develop responses to the following questions.

John, a prison chaplain, comes from a dysfunctional family, with a cruel, dictatorial father. He finds himself now working for a warden who demands long hours, and extensive paperwork regarding the chaplain's duties and the persons he sees. The warden is adamant about the chaplain being on time, and keeping even the most minor of rules (the chaplain got in trouble because his worship service went long; thus creating problems for the guards taking inmates back to their cells, etc). The chaplain responded as he once had to his father, and began to avoid the warden, only meeting with him when it was absolutely necessary and siding with some of the guards who agreed that the warden was overly authoritarian. This internal struggle began to affect the chaplain's ministry, and ultimately, it affected the way he was viewed by the warden and other staff. In light of this case, consider the following:

1. How important is a chaplain's family history? Strengths and weaknesses? To what extent should some of these issues be dealt with and resolved prior to an assignment of this nature?

2. Considering the fact that the chaplain is already assigned to this special ministry, what resources would you envision necessary for him to come to terms with his passive-aggressive behavior?

3. What is at stake for the chaplain to resolve these issues in terms of his relationship with the warden, the inmates, and the staff?

UNIT TWO

A Survey of the History of Pastoral Care and Chaplaincy

Above all, the pastor should maintain his confidence in people, in human possibility. Jesus dealt with real people—harlots, hardened tax collectors, people who were shiftless, failing, sinful, dishonest, unappreciative, and indifferent —but He never lost faith in them, in their worth or in their possibilities.

— Charles Kemp, The History and General Principles of Pastoral Care, in *Pastoral Care*, pg. 22.

Introduction

Pastoral care is a general term used to describe the care given to individuals by spiritual leaders. Traditionally it has been defined as "that branch of Christian theology that deals with care of persons by pastors. It is pastoral because it pertains to the offices, tasks, and duties of the pastor. It is care because it has charge of, and is deliberately attentive to the spiritual growth and destiny of persons."[1] The office, tasks, and duties of the chaplain may look very different in some settings, and the care provided may have little to do with measurable spiritual growth or a plan towards personal destiny. However, this does not mean that the pastoral care provider does not desire for these things to occur. It simply means that the recipients of care are not always looking for a religious experience; they may just be looking for someone to care enough to be present. In doing so, the chaplain is, in fact, providing an "unknowing religious experience" with the potential for a lasting, even eternal, impact. Consider the following reflection:[2]

> Psalm 34:18 (NIV) states, "The Lord is close to the brokenhearted and saves those who are crushed in spirit." As I reflected on this passage, the Spirit urged me to consider how it is that the Lord is close to the brokenhearted. I replied, "Your Spirit presents Himself in the midst of our pain." He replied, "Yes, but how?" I had no reply. He spoke to my spirit, saying, "I am near to the brokenhearted when *you* are a *willing* presence in the midst of their pain." This does not mean that God is not already present, for He is. It simply means that chaplains bring to light God's nearness to those they offer care. In attentive care for the sick and dying, they are a revelation of God's love and compassion to the care recipients. This application of the verse has great relevance on the mission of chaplaincy and pastoral care in general. Pastoral care is more than guidance for a spiritual journey towards a given destiny; it is *being the nearness of God* for the brokenhearted and the crushed in spirit. In this way, chaplains offer an "unknowing religious experience" to someone in the midst of great crisis. Then, as opportunities arise, chaplains can attend to more overt issues such as spiritual growth and personal destiny.

In this second unit, we will briefly survey the history of pastoral care as originally organized by William Clebsch and Charles Jaekle in their text,

---

1   Thomas Oden, *Classical Pastoral Care: Becoming a Minister* (New York: Crossroad Publishing Co., 1987): 5.

2   This reflection was written by Brandelan S. Miller.

Pastoral Care in Historical Perspective[3]. Through our study on the greater context and history of pastoral care, we hope readers will better understand the formation and development of the theology and practice of chaplaincy care as practiced in its present form. While chaplaincy is a rather modern invention as a professional pastoral practice, this evolutionary process in pastoral care has had a long and exhaustive history. In the midst of this evolutionary process, the essence of chaplaincy as a ministry to broken individuals and crushed communities has always been present. From pastoring individuals to pastoring communities, chaplaincy is an ever-shaping model that is sculpted primarily by the culture in which it resides. Please note this is in no way an attempt to complete an exhaustive evaluation of the history of pastoral care.[4] Rather, the goal of this section is to introduce readers to the historical developments and pastoral trends that have contributed to the evolution of the present practices in pastoral care, particularly those which have influenced care practices in chaplaincy; to identify key figures in this evolutionary process; and to familiarize readers with the terminology of pastoral care.

---

3 Clebsch and Jaekle, *Pastoral Care in Historical Perspective*. Note that several contemporaries of Clebsch and Jaekle have also used this breakdown of the eras and movements within pastoral care.

4 See Thomas Oden's series entitled, "Classical Pastoral Care" for a more in-depth evaluation of the history of pastoral care.

Chapter Six

Pastoral Practices from the Days of the Ancient Israelites
through the 17th Century

In this chapter, we will survey the history of pastoral care through the lens of chaplaincy. In doing so, we hope to show that the essence of chaplaincy ministry was embedded in the life and cultic acts of Israel and then translated into the life and practices of the early church and beyond. Throughout history, pastors and laypersons alike have provided care for hurting and wounded people. What this approach provides is a reading of history that suggests chaplaincy has always been evolving. Since we believe that chaplaincy has always been with us in some form, it is our conviction that chaplaincy is an inevitable model in God's vision and mission for the church.

Biblical Model of Pastoral Care

Ancient Israelite Practices

The essence of chaplaincy ministry goes further back in history than most imagine. Traces of this model were present in every ministry or service the ancient Israelite community held. When the poor were fed or the sick cared for, chaplaincy was present. When justice was advocated on behalf of the oppressed and sojourners were given a safe place to rest, chaplaincy was present. The Old Testament provides a glimpse of this ministry in a variety of venues and through a host of individuals and leaders, specifically the priests, the prophets, the sages, and the kings.[1]

The priests, a hereditary class, were responsible for certain acts of worship and ceremony in cultic life. For example, they were called on at different occasions to take the ark, representing the presence of God, outside the tabernacle (later the temple) into the community and even into battle as a means of spiritual support.[2] Priests were mediators between God

---

1   John Johnson, "Seeking Pastoral Identity," *The Spurgeon Fellowship Journal* (Fall 2007): 4. http://www.thespurgeonfellowship.org. Johnson's model includes four leadership roles: priest, prophet, sage, and king. More classical models, such as those by Charles Gerkin and others, only identify the first three as part of the pastoral identity.

2   Charles Gerkin, *An Introduction to Pastoral Care*. (Nashville: Abingdon Press, 1997.): ch. 1.

and humans for provision in times of need, pardon of sin, and offering of various sacrifices.

These priests provided a chaplain-type ministry to God's people in the Old Testament. They were the moral conscience of Israel, and offered spiritual guidance and care to the kings they served (Numbers 10:8-9; Joshua 3:14-17). They understood the human struggle and stood in proxy for sinners as they offered sacrifices for the people and performed other temple duties. In addition, they cared for the sick, lepers, strangers, and many others. These priests provided a "sanctuary" of care for persons often disenfranchised from the community of faith. And they also accompanied the armed forces into battle, reminding the warriors of God's words of truth, integrity, and justice. Like the chaplains of today, the priests were called on to give unconditional care to the hurting.

The prophets were the mouthpiece of God. They spoke to moral issues facing the Israelite community, particularly abuses of power over the powerless and vulnerable (Micah 2:1; 7:3, Amos 2:8). The community had disregarded many of the core tenets of its faith. Prophets such as Isaiah (1:16-17, 3:13-15, 5:8-10), Micah (2:1, 3:3, 6:11, 6:12, 7:3), and Amos (2:6-7a; 5:12; 8: 4, 6) spoke specifically against neglecting orphans, widows, the poor, etc. They were anointed advocates for vulnerable citizens, slaves, and foreigners in Israel. Today, chaplains have a similar "watchman" anointing to speak against injustice and for the fair and humane treatment of patients, prisoners of war, employees, soldiers, inmates, and the disadvantaged. However, chaplains must use wisdom and diplomacy in presenting their cause before unjust powers and authorities.

The sages provided wisdom and counsel regarding issues of daily living. They gave instruction on how to live a "good and virtuous life." They taught about righteousness and right decision making, alongside the value of enjoying the life given by God. The wisdom literature of the Bible emphasized the need to make good decisions that yielded positive results (Proverbs 2:21-22, 3:13-18). The wise person embraces life and is thankful for it (Ecclesiastes 5:18-20, 9:7-10). Instruction was not limited to strict rules of religion. Rather, sages engaged their audience with questions about the meaning and value of life. They delved into the depths of suffering and offered a multitude of responses, all of which brought the audience back to the mystery of the great Creator God. And they exposed those who put doctrine above personal and compassionate care. Like so many chaplains, the sages brought something more than religious offerings (although their actions and counsel were guided by commitment to God's ways as being higher than the ways of man). They brought human touch and personal guidance as an intentional religious experience for those they counseled.

Kings were administrators and helped to lead the people strategically towards fulfilling God's vision for the nation (Psalm 72). They were directly responsible to God for a failed administration. They were keepers and interpreters of justice, and they were responsible for selecting who would serve with them. Approaching chaplaincy as an administrative office is certainly an appropriate designation. Chaplains are administrators. They oversee services, function within a budget, and orchestrate strategies to carry out the vision of the organization while holding on to the vision of God for that community. They play a necessary role in the evaluation of just actions and advocacy for fair treatment and ethical practices.

New Testament Paradigms

In the New Testament, Jesus is the embodiment of the priest, prophet, sage, and king. As priest, He advocates before the Father for all people, and He offers His atoning blood as an eternal sacrifice for the sins of humankind. He came to this world as the living Word of God, spoke against injustice, and communicated the heart of God to all who would receive His prophetic message. As sage, He was the manifest wisdom of God who administrated justice and righteousness through royal and majestic authority. He ministered to men, women, and children, both within the Israelite community and outside. And He did it holistically, as high priest, prophet, sage, and king of kings.

Inherent in these roles is the essence of chaplaincy. Chaplains are priests offering specific religious practices at home and with our military, and they are prophets advocating for the weak and disenfranchised. Chaplains are sages offering a compassionate and intentional religious experience as they provide counsel for life's daily decisions; they are administrators (kings) ensuring justice through the evaluation of company practices and advocacy for fair treatment and ethical practices; and they are evangelists reaching people and systems of all kinds beyond the proverbial temple gates.

The Early Church

The social climate of the first century (post-Christ) was hostile and pessimistic. The Christian church struggled as tension continued to escalate with secular society. In spite of this tension, these early Christians still possessed a great compassion for individuals who were hurting or suffering as a result of poverty, sickness, or spiritual blindness.[3] James even states that a true religious experience will lead to care of orphans and widows (James 1:27). However, due to the changing climate of the day, the emphasis became more focused on Christian living, particularly in the writings and ministry of Paul.[4] Paul dealt with many of the common issues

---

3   Charles F. Kemp, *Physicians of the Soul: A History of Pastoral Counseling* (New York, NY: The Macmillan Company, 1947).

4   Ibid.

that all believers—past and present—face. Furthermore, deacons played a significant role in care of individuals, particularly the care of the poor. This early version of care ministries was essential to the identity of Christianity. Society presents the church many opportunities to present Christ to the world through compassionate care of vulnerable and/or underprivileged citizens. Without organized volunteers (such as the deacons of the first century or the volunteer chaplains of our contemporary context) this work could not be accomplished.

These early church leaders were also forced to deal with questions from those who believed in the imminence of Christ's return. As the years continued, more and more believers struggled with disillusionment because Christ had not returned and because of growing persecution. Pastoral care shifted to helping believers sustain their faith and manage right behavior for fear that sin would cost them access to heaven. [5] This is evident in books such as Hebrews (10:26-39), 1 Timothy (1:20, 1:4, 6, 6:4, 20), and 2 Timothy (2:18, 3). The effects of this notion were evident in pastoral responses to sickness, death, marital issues, etc. The philosophy of pastoral care was to help people endure problems for that season because Christ would surely return soon. [6]

Age of Persecution During the Second and Third Centuries

As the early church neared the turn of the century, tension between Christians and Jews *and* Christians and Gentiles continued to mount. Jews opposed the Christians' insistence they were the "completed Jew." The Jewish people wanted no affiliation with this so-called Jewish movement. Their resistance was lived out in persecution of the early believers. The Christians couldn't get a break. Jews were rarely regarded by the larger society; and, to the Gentile, Christians were a sect within the despised Jewish faith. So, when the Jews had political influence, they persecuted Christians. When the Gentiles turned on the Jews, the Gentiles persecuted Christians because they were Jewish.

During this age of persecution, Christians struggled to maintain their faith and allegiance to Christianity. Slowly, the early believers were forced out of the synagogue—literally outside the gates of the temple—meeting only in the homes of other believers. While still maintaining evangelistic efforts, in many ways they became much more inclusive and protective; yet they were better positioned for God to open ministry opportunities to the

---

5 Gerkin, *An Introduction to Pastoral Care*, ch. 1.

6 Clebsch and Jaekle, *Pastoral Care in Historical Perspective*, ch. 1.

Roman people. By the third century, the separation between the two was more widely recognized, but disdain for Christians still remained. They were, in fact, developing into a new religious group.

Again, the pastoral care practice shifted. As individuals left the church community under the pressures of persecution and then came back, pastoral figures became increasingly focused on helping the community reconcile with those who remained faithful and those who wavered, as well as helping troubled believers reconcile themselves to God.[7] Reconciliation has remained a centerpiece of pastoral care, particularly with chaplains who regularly minister to dying individuals, broken families, wounded believers, inmates, and new/returning believers. Reconciliation is not easily achieved, though. Chaplains accomplish this through skilled pastoral counseling that allows recipients to confess not only sin, but woundedness, fear, and many other issues.

Constantine and the Evolution of the Imperial Church (Early 4th Century through 11th Century)

Perhaps no subsequent era of soul care[8] has so strongly emphasized guiding as did the era of the Imperial Church, and in no other epoch has the function of guiding been cast so completely in its culturally [developed] mode.[9] — Clebsch and Jaekle

There is no question that Constantine[10] played one of the most significant roles in the history of Christianity. Following Constantine's conversion, he ended the ongoing persecution faced by many Christians in

---

7 John T. McNeil, *A History of the Cure of Souls* (New York, NY: Harper & Row, Publishers, Inc.): ch. 5. Gerkin, *An Introduction to Pastoral Care,* ch. 1. Clebsch and Jaekle, Pastoral Care in Historical Perspective, ch. 1.

8 "Soul care" is a term used to identify a specific emphasis on pastoral care during its earliest developments. Pastors were responsible for the spiritual health of the care recipient just as a physician is responsible for the physical health of a patient.

9 Clebsch and Jaekle, *Pastoral Care in Historical Perspective,* 20-21.

10 Constantine was the Roman emperor who took power after rulers like Nero and Diocletian, who heavily persecuted Christians. Constantine ruled from 306 to 337 C.E. (Note: from 306-324 Constantine was entrenched in a battle for the post of emperor). Constantine is best known in Christian history for his role in ending the religious persecution instituted by his predecessors and making Christianity an acceptable and culturally dominant religion.

the previous centuries, giving the religion a more favorable position within society. Roman citizenship began to look to Christendom for the answer to unifying their fragmented society. This new-found favor thrust pastors into the spotlight, and they capitalized on the opportunity.[11] Church leaders instructed people that personal problems and decisions had an immediate impact on the greater culture. And their personal problems had immediate and relevant meaning as followers of the suffering Christ.

Of course, once Christianity became the state religion it lost its once distinctive identity. Over time, Christians began to look and act more Romanesque. Those distinctive principles for Christian living were fused with Greco-Roman social norms. They adopted the high offices and ceremonies of the Roman systems as part of their worship experience, and pastors acted as semiofficial educators.[12] The tension of this era was twofold: leaders had to create and enforce standard church policy on living, etc., in light of cultural influences.

The result of this shift from a minority group to a dominant faith group allowed Christians to indoctrinate the Roman culture in the faith and practices of Christianity, albeit with some measure of impurity. This new position provided the early Christians with the opportunity to work within the systems of Rome as a way to bring sanctification to both the people and their governing systems. One way this was accomplished was through care of the underprivileged; the Christian community expanded its care practices to society as a whole. It was no longer inwardly focused; Christian leaders could more effectively reach the hurting and needy citizens of greater society through programs such as dispensing of state welfare to individuals and families in need.[13] These social efforts allowed for them to instill in people a Christian interpretation of their troubles.[14] However, this did not come without a cost to the community.

As Christianity grew in popularity among the general Roman populace, Christians who had a history and long allegiance to the faith community became dissatisfied with the direction of the once distinct voice of the church. Many left due to the blurring of the boundaries between the dominant culture and their beloved church. Those who left fled to the desert to preserve their religious purity, hence the beginning of Monasticism. The Monastics believed that religious purity could only be

11 Clebsch and Jaekle, *Pastoral Care in Historical Perspective*, 19-21; Gerkin, *An Introduction to Pastoral Care*, 30-34.

12 Ibid.

13 Kemp, *Physicians of the Soul: A History of Pastoral Counseling*; Clebsch and Jaekle, *Pastoral Care in Historical Perspective*; Gerkin, *An Introduction to Pastoral Care*.

14 Clebsch and Jaekle, *Pastoral Care in Historical Perspective*; Gerkin, *An Introduction to Pastoral Care*.

achieved outside the influence of society. Of course, this was due in part to the recognizable influence of the Roman culture on the face of the church, such as the pageantry introduced to worship services.[15] So, Monastics sought refuge in smaller communities where their distinctive lifestyle and beliefs could be embraced without the pressures and influences of a sinful society.

Although there is certainly some concern about the church adapting its principles to fit cultural norms and practices, as Gerkin points out, there is also something noteworthy about it. He notes that the church has benefited throughout history from secular moves, particularly within the areas of social sciences and thought.[16]

> Some of the most significant developments in pastoral care theory and practice during the twentieth century have come of efforts to synthesize traditional Christian pastoral theory and practice with theories about human relationships and behaviors that have origins outside the immediate purview of theology... In meaningful ways, when we in our time work at the task of informing pastoral care practices with non-theological insights, we follow in the footsteps of Quintus Tertullian and John Chrysostom.[17]

In many ways, this tension continues to exist between those who seek to do God's work within the structure of the church and those who seek to do His work within secular society. Most local pastors are limited to working within their congregational context due to the great demands of the pastorate. Chaplains minister within the community. They are employed by the state, federal, or local government, and they are employed by secular, private institutions, not the church. They must value and hold in tension both contexts.

In contrast, local church pastors have in many ways become more segregated from secular society in order to maintain their distinctive religious voice. Nevertheless, in the last decade, the church has made attempts to be vocal on some social issues. The problem is that the church offers philosophical and theological ideals from behind its walled fortresses and "gated community," rather than offering practical care which evolves from serving among the poor and oppressed. This does not mean that all churches are disconnected: many churches engage the secular for ministry purposes. The point is that chaplaincy has broken out of the gates, refusing to isolate or remove itself from society in order to go where Christ went

---

15 Ibid.

16 Gerkin, *An Introduction to Pastoral Care*. 32.

17 Ibid.

and do what Christ did. It is a balancing act; they must not let go of the tenets that define their faith heritage, and they must not let go of their love for the people and cultural systems they serve. Both belong to God. Both are worthy of the ministry of the church.

In spite of which side of the argument these early believers found themselves on, it forced them to define their unique identity regardless of their context. As a result of these defining years, four factors in pastoral care developed:[18] the identification of Christian tradition (core beliefs and practices); the contemporary Christian community (the identity, mission, and specific concerns of the church community); the individual's needs; and the issues/concerns of the contemporary cultural context (example: during an economic meltdown, the concern will be poverty and provision). These four factors are still present in pastoral care practices, particularly in chaplaincy. For example, pastoral care providers must be attentive to the specific needs of the care recipient. If the care recipient needs water, shelter, or food, the pastoral care provider must seek to resolve that particular need. Societal issues may play a role in giving care. For example, the care recipient may be out of work due to a factory shutdown and there may be other families in need of care, or the recipient may be homeless due to mental illness or other personal issues.

John Chrysostom (347–407 C.E.), a Bishop in Constantinople, Rome, also recognized the need to consider the whole person and their particular situation.[19] While his emphasis was on the cure of souls, his approach can certainly be seen as a precursor to the interdisciplinary work of chaplaincy. This method recognizes the many complexities that each individual brings to the ministry experience. In other words, the caregiver must understand and recognize the particular disposition of the recipient so as not to drive them further into the condition from which they need healing. Thus, how chaplains approach care and what they offer in the ministry experience must be shaped—in part—by the recipient.

Chrysostom further instructs that "the decision to receive treatment does not lie with the man who administrates the medicine but actually with the patient (2 Co. 1:24)."[20] Suppose a poor widow complains often about her particular plight; Chrysostom suggests the most appropriate response is to extend her patience, love, and the privilege of being heard. From that starting point, walk with her, be gentle and accessible, and allow her the central role in her healing process. That kind of care was accomplished through a physical pastoral presence, as well as through letter writing,

---

18 Ibid., 35-37.

19 St. John Chrysostom, *St. John Chrysostom: Six Books on the Priesthood*, trans. Graham Neville (Crestwood, NY: ST. Vladimir's Seminary Press, 1964): d. 407.

20 Ibid., pg. 56.

in the case of St. Jerome, an early church father. In 389, Jerome wrote a letter to a woman named Paula whose daughter had died.[21] In the letter he validated the mother's grief, encouraged her to "celebrate her daughter's eternal reward," and encouraged her to "bear her loss with resignation" because it was the Father's will. These kinds of letters were a common form of distant pastoral presence. Their significance to the recipient was undoubtedly a meaningful expression of care ministry.

In re-establishing the personal and intimate dimensions of priestly care, Chrysostom and others fought to preserve the pastoral presence that is necessary as ministers and chaplains care for families and individuals who seek to maintain and sustain their Christian faith during seasons of grief, sickness, personal struggles, and even social pressures.[22] The benefit of his work is most notable when chaplains work in prisons, clinical settings, the military, schools, and many other places to help individuals find renewed strength in their faith during times of overwhelming crisis.

A final development that came out of this era was the area of confidentiality and pastoral confessionals.[23] At the onset of this time period, confessions were still primarily done in public; however, as priests took on a more authoritative role, this began to change. By the fourth century, Basil suggested that the church should approach sin in the same way one approaches sickness: consult someone who knows how to receive confessions and help lead the person toward healing. Basil did not agree that all sin needed to be public knowledge. By the fifth century, Pope Leo the Great took another step forward, stating that public confession was not necessary. Penitents should first seek God, then a bishop. He feared that forced public confession would cause individuals not to repent and instead to remain in a sinful state. Finally, the second synod of Dvin (552-554 C.E.) decided that priests were not allowed to violate the confidence of those who confessed in private their sins. The enormous impact this has had on Christendom is worth noting, since this is a key ethical practice of

---

21 St. Jerome, *To Paula*, "Jerome: The Principal Works of St. Jerome" Letter XXXIX, from the Christian Classics Ethereal Library website. http://www.ccel.org, 2.

22 William Clebsch and Jaekle, Pastoral Care in Historical Perspective and Charles Jaekle, Chapter One in *Pastoral Care in Historical Perspective* (Englewood Cliffs, New Jersey: Prentice-Hall, Inc., 1964). Also, in Chrysostom's book *On the Priesthood*, he writes at length concerning the role of the pastor/priest. He is particularly focused on the great character required to become a minister to individuals: in particular, the one-on-one time spent with those facing difficult times. St. John Chrysostom, trans. Graham Neville, *St. John Chrysostom: Six Books on the Priesthood*, d. 407.

23 Kemp, *Physicians of the Soul: A History of Pastoral Counseling.*

all pastoral caregivers, both chaplains and church pastors.[24]

The Medieval Time Period: The Light of Compassion in a Darkened Age (Late 5ᵗʰ through 15ᵗʰ Centuries)

The Medieval era was plagued by widespread sickness, hunger, and poverty. The description of this time period as the "Dark Ages" is quite revealing, and the church was not exempt as a contributor to its darkness. The combination of superstition, biblical truth, and fear-mongering left the church distant, even calculating. In an era in which pastoral care was stifled by politics and corruption, it was monasteries that sought to guard the purity of the faith and of compassionate Christian action.[25] They did so by establishing orders, both male and female, that provided care for the poor, the orphans, and the sick, and educated young children. As these monasteries developed, they began to build hospitals along trade routes for sick pilgrims. By the tenth century, many parish churches and cathedrals followed this example. They built hospitals and orphanages, they built homes equivalent to today's homeless shelters, and they provided care to lepers.[26]

> Before all things and above all things care must be taken of the sick.
>
> — Rule of Benedict

A central player in this era was a Benedictine monk named Gregory the Great (540-604) who established and refined patterns of pastoral practice.[27]

---

24 The ethical and legal limitations of chaplaincy will be discussed in the last unit of the text.

25 Kemp, *Physicians of the Soul: A History of Pastoral Counseling*. Kemp's evaluation of the monastic life (pp. 35-38), although approving of their many acts of service and compassion, was somewhat cynical of their ascetics. According to Kemp, isolation from the rest of civilization caused these men and women to act in ways that led to psychological issues, such as depression, irritability, and even insanity. He further states that their eccentric behaviors were expressed in visions, illusions, and "self-repression." Essentially, he equates visions with hallucinations, and self-discipline and overcoming temptations with self-repression. It isn't that there weren't those whose piety took on an unhealthy dimension; however, readers must consider the great possibility of such miraculous experiences and the rich heritage of such expressions of religious devotion.

26 Clebsch and Jaekle, *Pastoral Care in Historical Perspective*, 174-75; Kemp, *Physicians of the Soul: A History of Pastoral Counseling*, 35-37.

27 The third section of *Pastoral Care* details how one must approach individuals given their current emotional state, social status, age, gender, and personality. The first chapter of this section includes why this is such a necessary part of the pastoral care approach. Pastors must consider the individual person when approaching their issues. For example, if a person tends to be sensitive, it would not be advantageous for the pastoral caregiver to be heavy-handed.

Gregory, who later became pope, authored one of the most widely read books of the Middle Ages, *Pastoral Care*. Gregory's model of pastoral care emphasized, among other things, caregiving that focused on individual human needs; that is, every care recipient had a particular situation that required an individualized response.[28] According to Gerkin, "We who are the offspring of what has come to be called clinical pastoral care can claim Gregory the Great as one of our most important spiritual ancestors."[29] Gregory recognized the need to operate from a "common doctrine" while simultaneously offering care that is specific to the needs and character of those receiving it.[30] If the poor needed food, then care was focused on this basic need. If the grieving needed encouragement, then care was focused on that particular need. This basic, yet monumental model is central to the praxis of care in chaplaincy. The chaplain should attentively listen, then respond to the recipient's specific[31] and often complex need.

As the Dark Ages progressed, care of the sick took on another form: spiritual and physical healing through the sacraments. This practice centered on believing in God's divine grace to heal spiritual, physical, and mental sicknesses. It is during this era the church expanded its umbrella of care to include medicine. This was because most clergy believed that many physical wounds and ailments were the result of sin. The sacraments embodied the power and grace of God to cure whatever ailed the care recipient. Ordination (as a sacrament) empowered caregivers both to diagnose and to cure the ills of the body. These practices became so commonplace during this era that a manual was actually written to assist the ordained in matters of spiritual and physical cures.[32]

---

28 St. Gregory the Great, *Pastoral Care*, ed. Johannes Quasten and Joseph C. Plumpe, trans. Henry Davis, "Ancient Christian Writers: The Works of the Fathers in Translation," no. 11 (New York, NY: Newman Press, 1950): Part Three.

29 Gerkin, *An Introduction to Pastoral Care*. 39.

30 St. Gregory the Great, *Pastoral Care,* ed. Johannes Quasten and Joseph C. Plumpe, trans. Henry Davis, "Ancient Christian Writers: The Works of the Fathers in Translation", 90.

31 By "specific and complex," we are referring to Gregory's teachings that every care recipient comes to the ministry experience with unique needs and with an individual personal context (personality, emotional state, socio-economic status, etc.). For example, a poor young woman will have issues that a rich older man will not likely face; however, the poor woman might be obstinate while the rich man might be humble. These factors must be considered as part of the minister's care. A brief assessment given at the beginning of the pastoral counseling session might be a helpful tool. Notice that temperament, socio-economic status, and gender are all considered in the evaluation. Remember Gregory's work was being done in the late 6th century!

32 Clebsch and Jaekle identify this manual as *Corrector et Medicus* from Book XIX on church administration. See Clebsch and Jaekle, *An Introduction to Pastoral Care*: 24.

Healing by a minister is notably recounted in an anonymous letter written about St. Francis of Assisi,[33] who was believed to possess healing powers. In the letter, Francis is described as taking on a leprous patient who had physically and verbally assaulted all who attempted to provide him with care. Francis approached the man with great compassion, allowed him to reveal even the darkest and angriest part of his heart against God, and then prayed for him. This excerpt details their conversation following their initial time together:

> "My son, I myself will serve thee, as thou art not satisfied with the others." "Willingly," answered the leper; "but what canst thou do more than they have done?" "Whatsoever thou wishest I will do for thee," answered St. Francis. "I will that thou wash me all over; for I am so disgusting that I cannot bear myself." Then St. Francis heated some water... undressed him, and began to wash him with his own hands..."[34]

This wonderful image of pastoral care reveals several necessary elements of chaplaincy care still present today. First, Francis provided the man with a safe place to bear his emotional, spiritual, and physical afflictions. Second, he prayed for the man. Third, he simply asked the man how he could be served. The result of Francis' ministerial efforts, according to the letter, led to physical and spiritual healing.

Blessed is the person who bears with his neighbor in his weakness to the degree that he would wish to be sustained by him if he were in a similar situation.[35]

— St. Francis of Assisi

Francis lived his life serving the poor and needy citizens of his day. He served through the building of sick houses and shelters for travelers and the poor, and he did so through his teachings. Fortunately, while the church was entrenched in a battle over doctrine and theology, there were those, such as Francis, who still sought to care for society's most vulnerable

---

33 St. Francis of Assisi was a monk whose compassionate and committed work among the poor, the sick, the widow, the orphan, etc. was so profound the church actually declared him a saint before he died. As a result of his and many other examples, this model of ministry blossomed throughout Europe as monasteries created houses for the poor, sick, vulnerable and disenfranchised of society. These men and women (monks/nuns) went to places no one else dared to go. Indeed, they were precursors to what we call chaplaincy ministry today.

34 Anonymous, *A Healing Miracle*, quoted by Clebsch and Jaekle, *Pastoral Care in Historical Perspective*, 176-177.

35 St. Francis of Assisi, trans. Regis J. Armstrong and Ignatius Brady, "Letter XVIII" in *Francis and Mare, the Complete Works*, (New York, NY: Paulist Press, 1983): 33.

citizens—the impoverished and diseased. Among those faithful servants were the Black Friars (Dominican Friars, 14th century) and the Sisters of Charity (17th century France).[36] The Black Friars played a central role in the care of the sick during the widespread epidemic of Bubonic Plague in Europe. According to Charles Kemp,[37] when others were abandoning those riddled with plague, these men chose to care for mothers, daughters, sons, and fathers in spite of the great risk to their own health. In addition, they took on the responsibility for burying the dead. So many people overlook the value of the latter ministry. Burial care is an act that preserves the dignity of those for whom streets, abandoned or crushed buildings, and portable hospitals become mass graves. Burying the dead is one of the many ministry responsibilities for volunteer and immediate responder chaplains who are called upon directly following a natural or national catastrophe, such as Hurricane Katrina, the Haitian earthquake, or the 9/11 terror attacks.

The second group, the Sisters of Charity, began under the direction of Madame Louise Marillae de Gras with only fifteen women.[38] Their mission was to care for and visit the sick of Paris. As a part of their mission, they never refused anyone because of severity of illness or danger to themselves, and they vowed to not "stand in the fear of death."[39] In the language of chaplaincy, they prepared themselves to be a non-anxious presence in death's wake.

In reflecting on the contributions of this era, two questions concerning the development of present chaplaincy care must be asked. First, "How is the care of God and God's people best expressed in the ritual practices of the community?" Second, "How should the Christian community care for the poor and the downtrodden?" Chaplaincy resolves these two issues.[40] Chaplains must be able to find a way to care for God's people through

---

36 Kemp, *Physicians of the Soul: A History of Pastoral Counseling.*

37 Ibid.

38 Ibid.

39 Ibid.

40 Clebsch and Jaekle, in *Pastoral Care in Historical Perspective,* add to this notion by summarizing the work of the Franciscan order in the following way: missionaries, social workers, hospital workers, teachers, and preachers. Without overstating the parallels, the commonality between the early practices of these monks and those of present day chaplains is plain. As missionaries, they venture into the world; as social workers, they network with local services to ensure that proper care is given to those in need; as hospital workers, they participate in the holistic healing of patients; as teachers, they counsel and instruct those under their care through personal life crises, family dysfunctions, Christian discipleship, and mentoring relationships; and as preachers, they pastor individuals, communities, and institutions.

general *and* meaningful ritual practices, not generic worship practices void of the Spirit of God. This is difficult because chaplaincy ministry takes place in such diverse and pluralistic settings. Services must be general enough to accommodate all Christian denominations while still offering something that is meaningful for recipients. Chaplains must also be socially-minded, seeking ways to advocate for, care for, and provide for individuals and families in need of care. This can only be done when the church decides to be an integrated presence among those in need. When this is accomplished, the church can honestly see the plight of the people and hear their specific needs lifted up.

Renaissance and Reformation (14ᵗʰ through 16ᵗʰ Centuries)

The Reformation era, with regard to soul care, belongs with this Renaissance period, for, in fact, the Reformation's great upheaval in doctrine and in ecclesiology never generated a corollary revolution in the cure of the souls.[41]

The Renaissance was influenced in part by the church. Science and theology were still largely controlled by the church, but individualism was on the rise. Individual reconciliation became the primary theme for pastoral practice.[42] This new twist on an old theme forced ministers to better understand the challenges and difficulties faced by their congregants every day.[43] Pastors had to become more integrated into society. The knowledge gained from their experiences led priests to expand the reconciling process to include the mind, body, and soul.[44] For example, unrepentant sin could lead to depression or anxiety, and even physical sickness, as a result of the stress experienced from guilt or shame.

---

41 Clebsch and Jaekle, *Pastoral Care in Historical Perspective*, 13.

42 Andrew Purves, *Pastoral Theology in the Classical Tradition* (Louisville, KY: Westminster John Knox Press, 2001): 76-94; Clebsch and Jaekle, *Pastoral Care in Historical Perspective*, 26-28; John T. McNeil, *A History of the Cure of Souls* (New York, NY: Harper & Row, Publishers, Inc., 1951): 163-168.

43 This new insight opened the door for priests to be more integrated into society and may have paved the way for celibate priests to become married ministers.

44 Clebsch and Jaekle, *Pastoral Care in Historical Perspective*.

According to some scholars,[45] the problem was that other important issues, such as healing and guidance, became subordinate to reconciliation. Many afflictions were believed to be connected to a sin crisis or unresolved sin issues. Of course, the church had become heavily dependent on confessions and acts of penance to resolve these ailments; unfortunately, what began as reconciliatory became mechanical and technical. This moved believers away from heartfelt repentance to formulas and penalties defined by the church, or, more specifically, individual priests given the authority to prescribe such remedies.[46]

Martin Luther (1483-1546)[47] was one of the strongest rivals of this practice. Luther firmly believed in the priesthood of all believers, claiming that all believers shared privileged access to God, not just priests. Therefore, all believers could participate in reconciling the believer to God through confession and healing the sick through prayer. Luther argued that the exclusivity of priestly acts reduced the transformative and healing nature of confessed sin to impersonal and detached acts of religious piety.[48] The reforming nature of this revolutionary approach to ministry and the authority of the church legitimized the ministry of lay ministers, volunteers, and fellow believers who pray with prisoners, hear the confessions of the dying on a battlefield, or pray with a classmate who has just come to saving knowledge of Jesus Christ. It legitimizes the many churches that send laypersons as volunteer chaplains into their communities and around the world.[49]

Luther was likewise concerned for the oppressed and victims of social injustice and poverty.[50] His passion for so-called "victims of the uncaring practices of society" is best rendered in his own words:

> Our Lord and Savior Jesus hath left as a commandment, which concerns all Christians alike—that we should render the

45 Ibid.

46 Priests alone had the official authority of the church to absolve believers of confessed sins.

47 Martin Luther, the father of the Lutheran Church, nailed his Ninety-Five Theses to the doors of the church, resulting in the split between the Catholic Church and what would become the Protestant Church.

48 McNeil, *A History of the Cure of Souls,* 167-168; Clebsch and Jaekle, *Pastoral Care in Historical Perspective,* 27.

49 Models that will be discussed in the third unit of the text are Local Church Chaplaincy and Community Service Chaplains. These volunteers are essential to forward movement of many pastoral care programs. Without them, the great task of the church within organizations and communities could not be accomplished.

50 Kemp, *Physicians of the Soul: A History of Pastoral Counseling*; McNeil, *A History of the Cure of Souls*; Clebsch and Jaekle, *Pastoral Care in Historical Perspective.*

duties of humanity, or (as the Scriptures call them) the works of mercy, to such as are afflicted and under calamity; that we should visit the sick, endeavor to set free the prisoners, and perform other like acts of kindness to our neighbor, whereby the evils of this present time may in some measure be lightened.[51]

These were not just words; Luther cared for the poor, the sick, and imprisoned. He even ministered in the homes of those suffering from the plagues of 1527, 1535, and 1539.[52] Luther's very progressive model was a foreshadowing of what would later become known as chaplaincy. The very essence of chaplaincy is care of the sick, oppressed, prisoner, and fellow neighbor. As advocates and care providers, a chaplain's job reaches beyond spiritual care into the realm of physical, social, and emotional care. By assisting care recipients, chaplains can, in some measure, lighten the load—or at least share the load—that seasons of crisis and change can bring.

One other name is worth noting: Martin Bucer, of the early sixteenth century. Bucer, a former Black Friar, was greatly influenced by Luther's words.[53] According to Bucer, the goal of pastoral care was to help believers understand that all power and authority over the church belonged to Christ alone. The relevance of this is that Christ is truly and actively alive in the church. He feeds his people; He cares for them; He brings in those who are lost; He watches over them; and He leads and provides for them.[54] This image of the ever-present Christ is reminiscent of a question often asked of clinical pastoral education students: where is God in the ministry experience? The presupposition of the question is that He is fully present in all aspects of the ministry experience. It speaks to Christ's rule and authority as the living, personal presence, Immanuel, "the God who is with us," not merely an external, impersonal force.

To be fair, Bucer would not likely be an advocate of the contemporary CPE model, which puts the recipient (the living human documents) at the center of the pastoral care paradigm.[55] Bucer would argue that Scripture must be given the central role in the paradigm. Perhaps what Bucer lends to our reflection on the chaplaincy paradigm is a reminder that Scripture must be the framework that skill and praxis evolve upon.

51 Clebsch and Jaekle, *Pastoral Care in Historical Perspective*, 211, citing Martin Luther, *Fourteen Comforts for the Weary and Heavy Laden*, 1520.

52 Kemp, *Physicians of the Soul: A History of Pastoral Counseling*, 39-50.

53 Purves, *Pastoral Theology in the Classical Tradition*, 76-94.

54 Ibid.

55 Ibid.

The Enlightenment *(17th Century)*

The Enlightenment marks the beginning of modernity and is characterized by the rise of secularism.[56] The church was losing its grasp on the sciences and theology as the intellectuals of the day pursued measurable scientific proofs over immeasurable faith. Once again, pastoral care shifted to a focus on sustaining faithful living in an era riddled with pitfalls.[57] The psychology of religion emerged as a way to bring understanding to the woes of believers as they sought to sustain their Christian experience. Advances in the understanding of the body and mind replaced old beliefs about demon possession and sin as causes of various illnesses. Education and better hygiene practices emerged, reducing many illnesses. The practice of pastoral healing during the Dark Ages subsided during the Enlightenment and returned to its original practice of soul tending.[58]

The 1600s introduced two significant personalities in the area of pastoral care: Richard Baxter, an English Presbyterian pastor, and Thomas Hooker, rector of St. George Church in Esher. Baxter's contributions to pastoral care are many; one specific area worth noting (given the growth of hospice care in our contemporary context) is in the area of death and dying. Baxter considered care for the sick and dying to be a necessary duty of the ministry; however, he wasn't just referring to the physical dimensions of care. He was concerned with preparing recipients for a better life or for the afterlife.[59] This contribution, in particular, is of great value to chaplains as they minister to many who are dying in prisons, hospitals, mental health institutions, on battlefields, and at home under in-home health care.

> I preached as never sure to preach again, and as a dying man to dying men.
>
> — R. Baxter

Hospice is among the most well-known organizations that care for the dying. The value of spiritually mature chaplains who are willing to walk with individuals and families as they embark on the often long journey of death is immeasurable. These chaplains offer the dying an understanding of the process, give it meaning where possible, and provide a

---

56 Gerkin, *An Introduction to Pastoral Care,* ch. 1; Gerkin defines "secularism" as "the belief that human history as well as contemporary life can be understood without speaking of God or assuming divine activity in human affairs" (pg.45).

57 Gerkin, *An Introduction to Pastoral Care.*

58 Clebsch and Jaekle, *Pastoral Care in Historical Perspective.*

59 Richard Baxter, *The Reformed Pastor,* ed. Hugh Martin (Richmond, VA: John Knox Press, 1956).

safe place for the dying to work through their own grieving process as they prepare to let go of life and their families. Chaplains provide a safe place for the dying to work out questions, fears, even anger towards God. This kind of support not only helps the dying to reconcile spiritual issues, but it allows the dying to have opportunities to reconcile personal and relational issues as well.

Baxter also contributed to pastoral care in something commonly known in chaplaincy as presence. In Baxter's writings, he encouraged ministers to take the time to know their flock—to sit with and talk to them.[60] He met with every family in their home each year. The impact of this is recounted by Charles Kemp,[61] who wrote that Baxter was sent to one of the most depraved and immoral communities in that day: Kidderminster, Worstershire. The result of his stay was an entire community transformed by his moral presence. He ministered successfully to the sick, the poor, and the depressed. This may have been due to his ability to empathize with common human struggles as a result of the chronic illness he battled for much of his life.[62]

Thomas Hooker was another prominent religious leader influenced by the Enlightenment. Previously, care practitioners saw pastoral care primarily as spiritual warfare; the Enlightenment changed that.[63] Pastoral care became focused on resolving spiritual conflicts through reason. If an individual was believed to be demonized, the minister would engage the demon in a biblical debate, hoping to bring deliverance through intellectual considerations. One such example is described in E. Brooks Holifields' book, *A History of Pastoral Care in America*.[64]

Holifield[65] described the case of Joan Drake, a woman who was believed to be demonized (she believed she was a reprobate beyond salvation). After three years of care from John Dod, the rector of Fowsley, among others, she was no better off. Dod convinced a colleague, Thomas Hooker, to

---

60 Baxter, 1956.

61 Kemp, *Physicians of the Soul: A History of Pastoral Counseling*.

62 Kemp, *Physicians of the Soul: A History of Pastoral Counseling*; Purves, *Pastoral Theology in the Classical Tradition*.

63 Brooks E. Holifield, *A History of Pastoral Care in America: From Salvation to Self-realization* (Nashville, TN: Abingdon Press, 1983).

64 Ibid., 34-36.

65 John Hart [Jasper Heartwell], *The Firebrand Taken Out of the Fire; or, The Wonderful History, Case, and Cure of Mrs. Joan Drake, Sometime the Wife of Francis Drake of Esher, in the County of Surry* (London, 1654), pp. 4-12, 17, quoted by Holifield, *A History of Pastoral Care in America: From Salvation to Self-realization*, 34-36. To preserve space, we have chosen to only include a paraphrase of the recorded narrative.

assist the woman. Hooker did something revolutionary; rather than trying to win a debate concerning her spiritual disposition (she believed her sins were unpardonable) or religious beliefs, he suggested her trials were an indication of her "chosenness." Hooker sought to help Joan re-approach or reinterpret her present condition of inner conflict as contrition or broken-heartedness. Her broken-heartedness was actually the first step toward spiritual healing, a sort of preparation for grace.

Hooker's example reminds chaplains they are not called to "fix" people; rather, they are called to listen and guide recipients towards healing and reconciliation. Unlike those before him, Hooker did not seek to win an argument with a demon or reason with Joan over unpardonable sins. He validated her struggle and her pain as real in her experience of God. In doing so, he gave her emotional pain meaning, which opened the door for her to receive grace, healing, and reconciliation.

Summary of Significant Pastoral Care
Contributions up through the Age of Voluntarism:

1. *Biblical Era:* The essence of chaplaincy ministry can be traced as far back as the earliest years of Israelite history through the roles of the priest, prophet, sage, and king. In the New Testament, Jesus, as the embodiment of these four roles, ministered to men, women, and children, both within the Israelite community and outside; and He did it holistically, as high priest, prophet, sage, king of kings, *and* evangelist.

2. *Early Church Era:* The emphasis became more focused on Christian living; deacons also played a significant role in care of individuals, particularly in care for the poor.

3. *Evolution of the Imperial Church:* The Church provided and controlled the distribution of social welfare, provided counsel for daily affairs, educated informally, and worked with physicians in diagnosis and healing.

4. *Renaissance and Reformation*: Pastoral care expanded to an intentional advocacy and protection for victims of uncaring societal practices.

5. *Enlightenment*: Pastoral healing (the church's control over medicine) subsided, pastoral care practice expanded to the sick and dying, and caregivers started using patient/client assessment.

CHAPTER SIX
Questions for Further Reflection

1. In this discussion, we theorize that the essence of contemporary chaplaincy has always been present within the Judeo-Christian traditions. In what way was the "essence of chaplaincy" present with ancient Israel's religious leaders, namely, the priest, the prophet, and the sage? Be sure to adequately explain *each* in two to three sentences. (5 points)

2. Explain what Constantine ultimately did for the Christian church and how that opened the door for Christianity to lay the foundations for social ministries. What specifically did the church provide in terms of social care? How does this relate to chaplaincy ministry? Be sure to adequately and completely explain each answer in three to five sentences. (5 points)

3. What impact did the Enlightenment have on the church in the seventeenth century? Identify how it positively and negatively affected pastoral care during this era. Explain why you see these as positive or negative. Be sure to adequately and completely explain each answer in three to five sentences. (5 points)

CASE STUDY: Case studies are provided for class discussion. The goal is to get you thinking about how you might approach ministry from the perspective of a chaplain. Reflect on the class materials and prepare/develop a response to the following case study:

This case study shows the tension between the chaplain's religious identity and his/her role within an institution:

> Chaplain Jones is assigned to a drug rehabilitation center. He learned recently that the director of this center hired a professional hypnotist who will use this technique with addicts. How will this chaplain deal with this institutional practice without violating his own views concerning this or other alternative practices?

CHAPTER 7

Pastoral Practices From the 18th Through the 20th Centuries

Age of Voluntarism *(18th Century)*

The arrival of the Industrial Revolution greatly impacted culture. The church was in disarray, and society was vexed by widespread poverty, criminal activity, ignorance, and immorality.[1] Inner cities were overcrowded, and workers were forced to work long hours for little pay. Citizens were becoming increasingly disgruntled at the few who were made wealthy at the expense of the working class. In addition, the church was losing its imperial control over members to privatization (at the end of the century). The need for an awakening in society and the church was very clear.

That awakening came to North America in the early 1730s. During that time, society experienced a massive revival called the Great Awakening, mainly through the ministry of George Whitefield (1714-1770). Influenced by the works of John Wesley,[2] Whitefield preached a provocative Gospel up and down the eastern coast of North America. While he had a huge impact on the people of the day, and led many to Christ and away from a sin-filled life, his contribution to the contemporary context of chaplaincy was that he legitimized the role of clerical psychology[3] in the "care of souls." His successor, Jonathan Edwards (1703-1758), helped to keep that

> Nothing is more generally known than our duties which belong to Christianity; and yet, how amazing is it, nothing is less practiced?
>
> — George Whitefield

---

1 Kemp, *Physicians of the Soul: A History of Pastoral Counseling*, Ch. 3.

2 John Wesley's ministry was a response to the horrific conditions of residents of inner cities in England. He offered weekly class meetings as an opportunity for men to come together to share their frustrations, struggles, and testimonies of triumph. He preached to the poor working class, holding revivals that gave them a safe place to work through their pain and struggles. Wesley believed firmly in the power of love to heal all human conditions (Kemp, *Physicians of the Soul: A History of Pastoral Counseling*).

3 Clerical psychology is psychology practiced by pastors and ministers.

dialogue going.[4] Though their conclusions have limitations in spiritual care (see footnote), they moved pastoral care practices forward by validating the role of psychology in pastoral care. Chaplains in all contexts give much of their time to ministering to the mental and emotional states of care recipients. They offer care in grief, family, marriage, and relationship counseling, along with moral and spiritual guidance. Whitefield and Edwards brought awareness of these issues for the pastoral care practice and process. Today, chaplains reap the benefits as they seek to provide spiritual care that recognizes the influences of other forces (such as mental, emotional, and physical issues) on the healing and recovery process.

While much of this discussion has focused on the mental health field and care of the poor, it is just as important to report on happenings in the field of medicine. As Walter Bruchhausen[5] pointed out, the Catholic Church has had a central role in medicine. Catholic hospitals still staff nuns who are professionally trained nurses; several of these hospitals are among the most skilled in the world. The point is that medicine and religion have always been intertwined. Even though the influences of the Enlightenment seemed to create a gap between these two interconnected professions/philosophies, the church has continued to have influence on medicine—not just as a contributor to the growth and evolution of medical care, but in setting ethical or moral boundaries as medical staff and scientists expand the frontiers of medical advancement. The medical community has come full circle: hospitals more readily recognize the need for holistic care of patients as practiced through chaplaincy ministries. While chaplains may not prescribe medicines for patients, they do play a vital role in the healing process, such as encouraging acceptance, perseverance, reconciliation, etc.

---

4 According to Gerkin, the problem with the ongoing discussion between these preachers and their opponents was that they still based their practices on the hierarchies of earlier centuries. They believed that certain beliefs or emotions were greater or lesser than others. In terms of depression, a person's *will* could be greater than the emotion of sadness; they could be motivated by what they believed was in their best interest. Edwards claimed that the cure for depression was an active life. Gerkin, *An Introduction to Pastoral Care*, ch. 1.

5 Walter Bruchhausen, "Health Care between Medicine and Religion: The Case of Catholic Western Germany around 1800" in *Hygiea Internationalis* 6(2): 197–194, 2007, http://dx.doi.org/10.3384/hygiea.1403-8668.0771177. (Please note that Bruchhausen was writing about Germany specifically. However, the role of the Catholic Church in medicine has been experienced in many countries.).

An Era of Rapid Change and Transition (19ᵗʰ Century)

The nineteenth century marked great change in Europe and North America. The separation of church and state became clearer; women took on more prominent roles in the church and community; and the emergence of psychology forever changed how churches and ministers approach pastoral care. In this section, we will briefly examine these three areas of transition and how they directly affected the inevitable move towards specialized ministries such as chaplaincy.

Religious Privatism

The privatization of religion forever changed how the church provided care to the local community. Freidrich Schleiermacher,[6] a well-known theologian at the turn of the nineteenth century, was among those who advocated for the separation of social affairs into public and private sectors. Religious and faith practices were moved to the private sector of social life, and church attendance and church life became voluntary. Schleiermacher's goal was to limit the role of the government in religious matters.[7] However, in the early 1800s, church and government were still powerfully intertwined. Almost prophetically, Schleiermacher's concerns were realized in the next century as Hitler's Germany indoctrinated its citizens with hatred and attempted to annihilate its Jewish populace based on supposed Christian principles.

According to Reverend Ichabod Spencer (1850),[8] this social atmosphere had removed much of the church's authority. While the pastoral figure was still the image of church authority, power was ultimately handed over to church members, who were given the freedom to leave the church if offended. This movement empowered parishioners to determine their own path to God. Pastors had to become more diplomatic and understanding about individual needs, both psychologically and spiritually, and as psychology took on a more prominent role in society, pastors discovered they needed to be much more psychologically equipped than their predecessors. This is most notably seen in the ministry of Phillips Brooks.[9]

A study of Brooks's life would prove what most chaplains already know:

---

6   Gerkin, *An Introduction to Pastoral Care*, ch. 1. This idea of separation of church and state had a profound impact in the United States of America.

7   M.K. Smith, "Social pedagogy" in *The Encyclopedia Of Informal Education*, (2009). http://www.infed.org/biblio/b-socped.htm; Michael Forster, "Friedrich Daniel Ernst Schleiermacher", *The Stanford Encyclopedia of Philosophy (Fall 2008 Edition)*, Edward N. Zalta (ed.), http://plato.stanford.edu/archives/fall2008/entries/schleiermacher/.

8   Holifield, *A History of Pastoral Care in America: From Salvation to Self-realization*.

9   Kemp, *Physicians of the Soul: A History of Pastoral Counseling*.

most of the pastoral ministry is given to private counsel. Brooks spent much of his time with people in the midst of their lives, in their crises, and in their homes. He visited sick people of any race, though it was frowned upon at the time. He stopped by the homes of his congregants and took the time to hear people and see their needs. This allowed him precision in care. In Charles Kemp's record of Brooks's life, he recounts this story. Brooks once visited a young mother with a sick baby.[10] She was fatigued from lack of sleep and needed to get away from the house. Brooks took the child and sent the mother out for a reprieve while he tended to the baby. He was a man who understood that a ministry of presence occurs in the midst of life as it happens—at home, in the hospital, on a university campus, and in all areas of the community. His story is not only that of a pastor, but of a precursor to chaplains who pastor whole communities.

The privatization of religion led to a transition in how benevolence and social ministries were carried out.[11] No longer did the church oversee social welfare. Social ministries were handed over to the state, and care or benevolence ministries were overseen by local congregations by the end of the nineteenth century. In many ways, this movement opened the door for a chaplaincy revolution. Trained and skilled chaplains later permeated secular society on many levels and in many contexts, in both paid and volunteer positions. Social ministries were regained in part through the work of chaplains, who were hired by the state or other secular organizations to provide care for individuals, agencies, and communities.

Women in the 19th Century

> What can we do to wake the Church up? Too often those who have its destinies in the palm of their hands are chiefly chosen from those who are mere encyclopedias of the past rather than from those who are distinguished by their possession of Divine Power. For leadership of the Church something more is required.[12] — Catherine Booth

In the 1800s, Catherine Booth and her husband William founded the Salvation Army to reach the poorest people in their community with the message of Jesus Christ.[13] The Booths began as evangelists, benevolent

---

10 Ibid., 62.

11 Holifield, *A History of Pastoral Care in America: From Salvation to Self-realization.*

12 Catherine Booth, *Women's Wisdom Through the Ages,* (New York, NY: Testament Books, 1994), 67: quoted in James and Michal Ann Goll, *Compassion: A Call to Take Action,* Women on the Front Lines Series, (Shippensburg, PA: Destiny Image Publishers, Inc., 2006), 49.

13 Goll, *Compassion: A Call to Take Action.*

givers, and counselors.[14] While their evangelistic efforts were successful, few churches were willing to receive their converts. As a result, a ministry organization was born that has had a profound and continuing influence on care for the poor around the world.

Elizabeth Fry worked to reform the prison system in the 1800s. She reminded communities that prisoners are human beings and deserve to be treated with dignity. She refused to cave in to the stigmas and fearmongering that kept many other ministers at a safe distance. Fry advocated for safe and humane conditions for mothers and their children who stayed with them in the prisons. The impact of her efforts was felt throughout Europe.

Clara Barton took seriously a passage familiar to most chaplains, Matthew 25:40 (KJV): "Inasmuch as ye have done it unto one of the least of these my brethren, ye have done it unto me." Her primary ministry was to wounded soldiers during the Civil War.[15] The impact of her work among these soldiers took her to Europe, where she was introduced to the Red Cross, founded by Florence Nightingale. She was so impressed with this organization that she decided to expand its ministry into the United States. Though her efforts were not recognized right away, she eventually succeeded in leaving the legacy of the Red Cross in the USA.[16]

The Emergence of Modern Psychology

Modern psychology as a legitimate science began in Europe, then gained momentum in America by the late 1800s. Its influence on religion and medicine brought profound change to society. Those who struggled with emotional or nervous conditions finally found a solution to their problems. Modern psychology irrevocably changed how the church approaches care of the mind and soul. Of course, psychology was not the only theme streaming into pastoral care; machismo (stereotypical male images of strength, emotional separation, etc.) and naturalism were also converging on the pastoral scene.

With the growth of industry, powerful moguls, and college athletics, strength became a central virtue of the "real man."[17] This machismo played out in the church through revivalist ministers who were strongly masculine and preached with a bellowing voice. Both these preachers and local ministers taught that church attendance was a source of personal empowerment and iconic strength. As the strong arm of the church,

---

14 Kemp, *Physicians of the Soul: A History of Pastoral Counseling.*

15 Holifield, *A History of Pastoral Care in America: From Salvation to Self-realization.*

16 Ibid.

17 Ibid.

preachers were disciplinarians and enforcers of behavioral boundaries.[18] Ministers who were "real men" called for the elimination of pastoral visits: they were a waste of a man's time. According to Holifield, this dominant male attitude even influenced how ministers portrayed the trinity. God was the powerful judge of the sinner. Common phrases included "the power of the Holy Spirit" (personal empowerment) to carry out the call of God in the life of the believer. Still others spoke in terms of "power to heal" and "power to overcome" adversity and trials.

Not all pastors were so drastic in their abandonment of care ministry. Some replaced it with a form of less formal, more casual care, such as friendship with their parishioners. This new model removed the old hierarchy of the church and placed more importance on intimate relationships with congregants.[19] The emphasis here was on cheerfulness and a positive response to life, relationships, and people. Pastoral care for those in crisis also took on this feeling. For example, Holifield[20] identifies several principles for caring for the sick and dying in this era: the minister should limit investigations into the state of the care recipient's soul; they were not to push for repentance; and guidance should not interfere with recovery. When caring for the bereaved, ministers should approach a loved one's death with hope, focusing on victory through Christ Jesus, and should show concern for recipients through silent presence—not through theology or homilies. This new approach had its roots in the sciences: life and relationships have a natural rhythm which must be allowed to occur. Grief and terminal illnesses have a natural course to follow, and that is acceptable. In fact, the grieving process is not only healthy, but necessary.

Most chaplains often deal with grief and sickness. The most important aspect of pastoral care brought to the ministry experience of the dying or bereaved is allowing people to respond naturally—whether in anger, fear, frustration, hopelessness, comfort, triumph, etc. This is a sort of common grace given to recipients who seek a safe place for self-disclosure and honest emotional processing. This kind of care may not lead to a personal conversion or spiritual reconciliation, but the mere presence of the chaplain is a reminder to the recipient that God is present and available for spiritual processes, too.

The growth and popularity of modern psychology fit easily into the forced changes within the church. Since privatization removed the powerful influence of ministers over parishioners, they needed something else to maintain their congregations: pastoral counseling provided one such

18 Gerkin, *An Introduction to Pastoral Care.*

19 Kemp, *Physicians of the Soul: A History of Pastoral Counseling,* 110-112.

20 Holifield, *A History of Pastoral Care in America: From Salvation to Self-realization,* 180.

opportunity.

In 1879, Wilhelm Wundt established the first psychology lab in Europe. Around the same time, William James began his research in psychology in America.[21] James quickly broadened his studies to include religious experience. His aim was to bring together psychology and religious experience in order to understand the psychology of religious development. Possibly his most important contribution to the psychology of religion was his attention to the healing nature of submission in an era of stereotypical male strength. Men could find relief for their "sick souls" only through submission, not through action or personal effort.[22] The goal was to submit to the natural flow of life, offering reinterpretations of one's circumstances. This is more widely known as "suggestion."

Although James's aim was not to contribute to the growing discussion concerning pastoral practice, his influence on pastoral care is undeniable. Elwood Worcester, who will be discussed shortly, implemented James's concepts into his pastoral counseling as he reached thousands of individuals in the Massachusetts area.

In this next section, we will look at the development of pastoral care in the twentieth century, particularly at contributors such as Anton Boisen, who were foundational in the formalizing of pastoral care outside the walls of the church, i.e., chaplaincy ministry. We must also note that this era had more direct influence on civilian (non-military) chaplaincy than any other.[23] During this era, chaplaincy in secular settings was legitimized in both the workplace and the church. Clinical Pastoral Education (CPE) and pastoral counselors formed their own identity as a bridge between the secular community and the faith community.

---

21 James is considered by many to be the father of the new psychology establishing the first psychological lab in the United States. He is also credited for the popularizing of psychology. Gerkin, *An Introduction to Pastoral Care*; Kemp, *Physicians of the Soul: A History of Pastoral Counseling*; Holifield, *A History of Pastoral Care in America: From Salvation to Self-realization*; Clebsch and Jaekle, *Pastoral Care in Historical Perspective*.

22 Holifield, *A History of Pastoral Care in America: From Salvation to Self-realization*.

23 Please note that chaplaincy ministry in the military was established by our first president, George Washington, in 1775.

The Turn of the Century

The most significant developments in pastoral care at the beginning of the twentieth century were in continuity with the turn toward the self that emerged from rapidly developing privatization of religion in the nineteenth century west.[24]

The turn of the century brought two movements that played a significant role in the formation of pastoral care in the modern era. These movements had very different aims. The Emmanuel Movement built on growing trends in the development of the self; the Social Gospel Movement was a response to the neglected area of community and society in the progresses of the psychological sciences of the day.[25] Of course, both of these movements proved to be necessary components in the care of people.

The Emmanuel Movement made its debut between 1904 and 1906. In 1904, Elwood Worcester, an Episcopal priest of Emmanuel Church in Boston, Mass., returned to the United States after studying in Germany under Wilhelm Wundt and Gustav Fechner, the founders of **physiological psychology**.[26] One of the members of his congregation was a neurologist who encouraged him to "reconsider the therapeutic office of the minister."[27] These conversations led to Worcester meeting and speaking with local doctors. Joined by Samuel McComb, who also studied abnormal psychology, Worcester began working with Joseph Pratt of Massachessetts General Hospital leading small groups for poverty-stricken tuberculosis patients.

According to Holifield,[28] Worcester's success with this early model of group therapy led to other endeavors. For example, in 1906, Worcester organized a group meeting at the parish house for individuals in the

---

24 Gerkin, *An Introduction to Pastoral Care*, ch. 2, pg. 53.

25 Gerkin, *An Introduction to Pastoral Care*, ch. 2.

26 Gerkin, *An Introduction to Pastoral Care*; Kemp, *Physicians of the Soul: A History of Pastoral Counseling*; Holifield, *A History of Pastoral Care in America: From Salvation to Self-realization*; and Clebsch and Jaekle, *Pastoral Care in Historical Perspective*.

27 Holifield, *A History of Pastoral Care in America: From Salvation to Self-realization*, 202; Kemp, *Physicians of the Soul: A History of Pastoral Counseling*.

28 Holifield describes this early hospital practice in the following way: "In effect, they began a program of group therapy modeled on the example of medical practice. Believing that poverty and competition had produced an ominous increase in physical and mental illness, Worcester turned Emmanuel Church into a social settlement offering camps, clubs, and a gymnasium. Group therapy was to be one more tool for the amelioration of social injury." *A History of Pastoral Care in America*, 202.

community suffering from any nervous or spiritual disorders.[29] Two other psychologists assisted him with this meeting. Their expectation was for only a few people to show up, but 198 people came to the parish house seeking psychological help. A movement was birthed which allowed for pastoral care practitioners and psychologically oriented physicians to provide care for people with any type of functional ailment.[30] Over time, tensions grew between physicians and ministers, resulting in a severing of ties between these two professions. However, this movement successfully laid the foundations for pastoral counseling as a professional and effective addition to the healing process.[31]

A parallel study was occurring overseas in the area of psychoanalysis. This field was made famous by the Austrian scientist Sigmund Freud. While Freud originally began his career studying physiological psychology, he eventually moved into the direction of mental, experiential psychology, i.e., examination of the emotional life. Swiss pastor Oskar Pfister found this line of study interesting, particularly Freud's thoughts and experiences with **catharsis**.[32] Pfister saw the potential for religious healing and catharsis to intertwine, enhancing human development. Against Freud's wishes, his work was thrown into the center of the religious world, resulting in the renewal of pastoral care in the United States. Freud's influence continued through the early- to mid-twentieth century, particularly in the area of Clinical Pastoral Education.[33]

The second movement to dominate in the early twentieth century was the Social Gospel Movement. In a sense, the Social Gospel Movement was a response to the imbalance of and heavy emphasis on the individual in restorative health, leaving out the necessary role of cultural influences in healing.[34] Accordingly, the Social Gospel recognized the social forces, such as capitalism and racism, which oppress vulnerable members of society. With its origins in the social sciences and liberal theology, the movement sought to aid victims of social and domestic violence/oppression. In contrast to the Emmanuel Movement, its primary partnership as a social science was with sociology rather than psychology. Members of this movement saw the Emmanuel Movement's emphasis on the individual as the catalyst of systems that segregate and separate communities into classes of the "haves" and "have nots." The Social Gospel Movement

---

29 Gerkin, *An Introduction to Pastoral Care,* ch. 2; Holifield, *A History of Pastoral Care in America: From Salvation to Self-realization,* 202-206.

30 Gerkin, *An Introduction to Pastoral Care.*

31 Holifield, *A History of Pastoral Care in America: From Salvation to Self-realization.*

32 Gerkin, *An Introduction to Pastoral Care.*

33 Ibid.

34 Ibid.

fought against this fragmentation of societal cohesiveness.[35]

The central figure of this movement was Walther Rauschenbusch, a pastor in New York City who witnessed firsthand the atrocities of the worst kinds of poverty.[36] The community Rauschenbusch served was overwhelmed with unemployment, utter poverty, malnutrition, and crime. The terrible state of the members of his community compelled him to respond. In his essay entitled "Christianizing the Social Order,"[37] he addresses the social inequality and injustice of the poor and calls for Christian action. His writings reveal a fervent belief that Christians must be active in politics as a sort of watchman or moral conscience within society. His ultimate goal was to organize a community of believers equipped to redeem society from its immoral and unjust practices.

This task was not easy; Rauschenbusch faced society's fascination with big business, money markets, and consumerism. The powerful were iconic and exemplified the "American Dream;" the weak and vulnerable were forgotten and taken advantage of for personal gain. In a subsection entitled "What to Do,"[38] he advocates specifically for improving the inhumane working conditions of laborers who were grossly underpaid and overworked. Workhouses were an emblem of loss of value for one's neighbor in pursuit of personal prosperity. The unsafe working conditions workhouse owners were willing to put their employees in revealed their depravity. Rauschenbusch sought to remind business owners that their employees were human beings and valuable assets to the community and the company. In a sense, contemporary industrial chaplains work alongside the human resources department as watchmen, protecting the ethical standards that individuals like Rauschenbusch fought for in the early 1900s. Rauschenbusch concluded that the only hope of restoration and healing for these communities was through the workings of the Kingdom of God.[39]

These two historical movements were indicators of the need for a balanced approach to pastoral care that must be a witness to both the individual and the community from which he or she came. As we will

---

35 Ibid.

36 Winthrop, S. Hudson (ed.), *Walter Rauschenbusch: Selected Writings*, (New York, NY: Paulist Press, 1984), Chapter introduction.

37 Walter Rauschenbusch, chapter six in *Walter Rauschenbusch: Selected Writings*, "Christianizing the Social Order (1912)," Winthrop, S. Hudson (ed.), (New York, NY: Paulist Press, 1984), 149-166.

38 Ibid.

39 Gerkin, *An Introduction to Pastoral Care*, ch. 2. Two ideologies evolved from his understanding of the Kingdom of God: (1) the Kingdom of God, as society's only hope, could be realized through human efforts to apply Jesus's teachings; (2) Christian socialism emphasizing God's justice and the social workability of the teachings of Jesus Christ.

discover in the next section, Anton Boisen, the father of CPE, began to move the model for pastoral care into better balance through chaplaincy ministries. As chaplaincy took on a more recognized role in the 1900s, it brought together both the psychological movement (through skilled counseling sessions) and the Social Gospel Movement (through social advocacy and care for the oppressed and vulnerable) as a part of its identity. In the prison setting, chaplains provide counseling to inmates while ensuring their basic civil rights are protected. In the mental health setting, chaplains offer spiritual guidance to residents, as well as a moral consciousness to employees. In all the settings, chaplains must find a balance between being a counselor and an advocate because both are necessary components for holistic healing.

Clinical Pastoral Education and the 1920s

The 1920s marked the beginning of the Clinical Pastoral Education (CPE) movement. The man credited with founding this movement is Anton Boisen, however, William S. Keller, M.D., had provided theological students with exposure to the clinical setting two years earlier. Keller's aim was "to get sheltered students in contact with life including its sufferings."[40] While Boisen shared this perspective with Keller, his ultimate goal was not to expose students to suffering, but to allow students to study theology through the suffering of living human beings. While Boisen's focus was narrowed to the suffering of the mentally ill, it was expanded by the efforts of Richard Cabot to include a variety of health issues such as paralysis, cancer, accidents, and crises of various sorts. In this section, we will look at the life of Anton Boisen and the evolution of this movement. In addition, we will examine his legacy and the impact of CPE on the practice of pastoral care.

The Anton Boisen Story

Boisen's story is fraught with personal tragedy.[41] He came from a family of educators and ministers who were extremely religious. When he was young, his father died suddenly of a heart attack. Consequently, Boisen and his mother moved in with his grandparents. During his early twenties, Boisen's personal struggles led to a bout of severe depression. At the age of twenty-six he fell in love with a woman who would never love him back, though he made great attempts to win her affection. He remained devoted to her

---

40 Seward Hiltner, ed. Glenn H. Asquith, Jr., "The Heritage of Anton Boisen", *A Vision From a Little Known Country: A Boisen Reader* (Journal of Pastoral Care Publications, Inc., 1992), 140.

41 Hiltner, Asquith, Jr., ed., *A Vision From a Little Known Country: A Boisen Reader*, Introduction.

until her death nearly twenty years later. During the course of that time he continued to try to prove his worthiness to her, but he was unsuccessful.

Shortly after her death he suffered from a psychotic breakdown, which led him to be institutionalized at the Westboro State Hospital in Massachusetts for schizophrenia.[42] According to the ACPE,[43] it was during this time of great "human despair and isolation" that he had a life-changing epiphany. Boisen reportedly awakened from his state of mental illness when he realized that his mental image of a moon centered on a cross was actually the wire screen on the hospital porch. "This realization contributed to his recovery; he suddenly came out of the acute disturbance much as one awakens from a bad dream. As he began to reflect on the meaning of his experience, he found a new purpose in life and gained a new understanding of mental illness."[44] Through this experience Boisen recognized that neither physicians nor ministers were equipped to deal with the religious aspects of mental illness. His goal was to address this gap through a practicum-based educational process. He thought that time spent with the mentally ill in their environment should remove some of the ministers' uncertainties and fears while allowing them the opportunity to critically reflect on theology through human conflict and suffering. Boisen's experiences led to the creation of a formal educational approach to chaplaincy ministry.

After his release from Westboro, Boisen was appointed chaplain of Worcester State Hospital. In 1925 he brought his first small group of theological students to study at the hospital with him. There they expanded their theological studies from written documents and recorded theological findings to a study of what Boisen called **the living human documents**."[45] Boisen believed the only way to truly learn how to be a pastoral care provider was to study human personalities in their environment and/or crisis; hospitals and mental institutions provided this opportunity for

---

42 Ibid.

43 ACPE stands for the Association of Clinical Pastoral Education. See also: www. acpe.edu

44 Hiltner, ed. Asquith, Jr., "The Heritage of Anton Boisen", 6.

45 Ibid., 6; Holifield, *A History of Pastoral Care in America: From Salvation to Self-realization*; ACPE, Anton Theophilus Boisen, Association for Clinical Pastoral Education, Inc. www.acpe.edu/networks/boisen_bio.htm.

students.[46] Boisen's teaching style evolved into a **case study** methodology[47] with the help of physician and co-laborer Richard Cabot. They later founded the Association for Clinical Pastoral Education (ACPE).[48]

Cabot played a central role in the inception of this movement. Boisen and Cabot worked closely together, and it was Cabot who influenced Boisen to enlarge his vision of the living human documents to include patients of all kinds in their training. The experience of CPE training includes rotation through all units available within a hospital setting: NICU, emergency room, oncology, ICU, psychiatric unit, and general population.

In 1930, Boisen and Cabot joined together with others to form the Council for the Clinical Training of Theological Students. Within two years, the group separated due to irreconcilable differences.[49] The Boston group (Cabot's) wanted more focus on the creation and study of ethics. Cabot believed that spiritual growth was the result of a purposed individual plan; therefore pastoral care helped patients accept and move towards that divinely instituted plan. The praxis focused on two skills: listening to the care recipient's words and discerning what he or she is communicating nonverbally (including body language, facial expression, tone of voice, etc.). The New York group (Boisen's) focused more on the psychology of religion and was largely influenced by popular psychology of the day. For Boisen, moments of mental breakdown were a prelude to conversion or a deeper religious experience with God if directed properly.[50]

---

46 "But of any such possibility the Church is utterly oblivious. She takes no interest in cases of profound mental disorder... We have... this truly remarkable situation—a Church which has always been interested in the care of the [physically] sick, confining her efforts to the types of cases in which religion has least concern and least to contribute, while in those types in which it is impossible to tell where the domain of the medical worker leaves off and that of the religious worker begins, there the Church is doing nothing." Reprinted from Christian Work, Vol. 120 (January 23, 1926), 110-112, in *The Journal of Pastoral Care*, Vol. 5 (1951), 8-12.

47 Boisen's case study methodology included both research and teaching. Students researched on the medical and theological side; their care recipients were a part of their research. Later this was replaced by *verbatims*, a word-by-word account of the activities of pastoral care. These accounts were then reflected upon during class time as a part of the learning process, aiding personal and professional growth.

48 Hiltner, ed. Asquith, Jr., "The Heritage of Anton Boisen"; Kemp, *Physicians of the Soul: A History of Pastoral Counseling*; Gerkin, *An Introduction to Pastoral Care*. Note that Cabot and Boisen would eventually part ways due to contrary beliefs about the organic nature of mental illness. The break came shortly after Boisen had his second psychotic episode.

49 Holifield, *A History of Pastoral Care in America: From Salvation to Self-realization*.

50 Ibid.

The Birth of Pastoral Care Specialists

Pastoral care, from the New Testament era right down to the early twentieth century, has been viewed as the responsibility of the local church. In other words, the majority of pastoral care was not performed by full-time pastoral care specialists, i.e. chaplains, pastoral counselors, etc., but by ministers who were part of the mainstream of traditional ministry.[51] The church pastor nearest to the mental hospital, prison, etc., served as a volunteer chaplain, primarily offering only worship and similar rituals. Individuals like Boisen saw the need for paid, full-time chaplains who were trained for specialized areas. Their legacy and impact on specialized ministry has been great. According to Boisen, what was missing from the church ministry model was chaplaincy. This specialized ministry required its ministers to be mature pastoral care providers, have the specialized training necessary to work with families in crisis, and be a part of the system they served in order to know how to serve a specific institution.

Boisen understood that chaplains could provide a necessary dimension to the hospital setting (or, for our purposes, any setting). These chaplains had to be persons of personal and spiritual maturity. The courses devised by Boisen provided student ministers with more than intellectual knowledge of various models of ministry and psychology; they forced students to reflect on their own personal and spiritual journeys as a pathway to maturity. Students were better conduits of care because their own issues were not impeding their judgment. Training was not only required for issues the chaplain might have, but also for helping the chaplain cope with issues in their workplace.

Chaplains need special training to understand the pluralistic environment of the settings in which they work. This training allows student ministers to effectively address the complex layers of issues that arise in ministry settings. This requires sensitivity and some knowledge of the various cultural, ethnic, and religious groups represented in a designated setting. For example, a chaplain working in an area with a large Hispanic population might try to be better informed about the cultural and religious norms of that demographic. This can weed out stereotypes and generalities while cultivating an understanding of the rich dynamics that the care recipient brings to the ministry relationship.

Chaplains have to be individuals who can work within the system, not apart from it. For a long time, ministry to these institutions was limited to the church offering services at the institution. Ministry was not part

---

51 This does not negate the necessary role of the many volunteers throughout history who have given spiritual care to persons in critical life moments, such as the men and women who visited and cared for the poor, the imprisoned, and the sick.

of the internal process of these institutions. The ministry was primarily a ministry to the patients in a hospital, the inmates in a prison, etc. People like Boisen began to see that if the church was going to have an impact on these secular institutions, its ministers had to be "insiders," not "outsiders." The privilege of being an "insider" allows the minister to serve as a reminder to staff and administrators of their moral and ethical responsibilities. The chaplain can also offer this same moral conscience to administrators as they lead the staff.

The following example identifies how all these things come together through the CPE experience:

> At Grady Memorial Hospital in Atlanta, Georgia, a young, very bright white student from South Africa was brought to the Intensive Care Unit where an African-American baby was dying. He felt led to take the child into his arms as the parents observed, and, even before he began his prayer, he stated, "The Lord seemed to say to me, 'Loving this child is the entryway into my deeper love for you.'" Leaving that scene, this young man declared that his life had been changed forever. He went back to South Africa and became one of the white Pentecostal leaders to join the revolutionary cause to give human rights and dignity to persons of all races. That experience seemed to solidify the missing link between what he had felt with his head and what he incorporated into his heart. It also addressed and resolved a race issue within him as a white African ministering care to an African-American family. Finally, he took from the experience a willingness to work within the systems of Africa to bring change. Often these moments are essential for bringing our faith heritage into the larger context of the cultural systems we serve.[52]

Impact of CPE on Education: 1950s and 1960s

CPE continued to grow through the 1930s and '40s; by the end of the '40s, pastoral care was a "recognized member of the family of practical theological disciplines."[53] According to Gerkin, this is due in large part to the impact of the mental health movement on American culture and the psychological impact of World War II on returning soldiers. Pastoral care practitioners, both military and civilian, joined with other mental health professionals in response to these needs. Pastoral care began to be recognized as a specialized ministry to individuals with multitude of care

---

52 This personal case study is by Robert Crick, Director of the COG Chaplains Commission.

53 Gerkin, *An Introduction to Pastoral Care*, ch. 2.

needs. By 1950-1960, CPE was *the* dominating force both in and outside traditional theological schools.

The newest member of the CPE movement was Russell Dicks. Dicks's major contribution to pastoral care education was the **verbatim**.[54] Verbatims allowed for students to record their pastoral conversations with care recipients for the purpose of further group discussion with their peers and supervisor. They have become a central part of the learning paradigm in CPE as they force students to consider their responses, their emotions, and their theological positions on particular issues which may arise.

In his book *Principles and Practices of Pastoral Care*, Dicks summed up six basic principles pastors and chaplains must consider when providing care to recipients: to do no harm, to practice supportive listening, to practice pastoral prayer, to make another appointment, to refer to someone else, and to share your concern.[55]

Dicks paralleled the primary principle of pastoral care with that of the medical profession—do no harm. The chaplain must seek to help to the best of his or her ability without causing further damage to the recipient. Of course, skills training and formal education equips chaplains better for this task.

The second principle is supportive listening. We have often referred to this as *presence* in this text. Supportive listening allows the recipient to confess their concerns, fears, frustrations, etc. without interruption or judgment. There is much to be said for the healing power of confession (James 5:16).

The third principle is pastoral prayer. For Dicks, this was the expression of the "longing, the doubts, the hopes of the suffering person"[56] through the prayers of the pastor.

The fourth principle was to make another appointment. The goal was not only follow-up, but to use that first meeting as an opportunity to assess the recipient's need and build a rapport. If the chaplain decided the recipient's issues were outside of his or her expertise, they referred the recipients to someone better equipped in that area—the fifth principle.

The final principle is to share your concern. Dicks suggested that chaplains/ministers, after listening to recipients, respond with care and concern. If the care recipient has suffered great loss, acknowledge that; if the recipient has been wounded by a friend or family member,

---

54 Ibid.

55 Russell L. Dicks, *Principles and Practices of Pastoral Care* (Englewood Cliffs, NJ: Prentice-Hall, Inc., 1963), 24.

56 Dicks, *Principles and Practices of Pastoral Care*, 25.

acknowledge their wound. This not only lets recipients know that they have been heard, but that you care about them. Dick's supportive listening parallels the work of a famous therapist named Carl Rogers.

Carl Rogers is most known for his **"client-centered" therapy**.[57] This new methodology was rooted in the belief that the answer to most relationship problems rests within the client. The role of the therapist was to help bring these solutions to light. This was done through **reflective listening**, i.e., the therapist repeated back the client's own thoughts through paraphrasing. Reflective listening not only ensured clarity for the therapist, but it also allowed for clients to make their own way towards personal revelation and healing. As noted in the works of Russell Dicks, this method of therapy soon became a favorite for the CPE community.[58]

Throughout this era, Boisen remained committed to patient advocacy as a central component of his "care of persons."[59] This is still a key component in the pastoral care model of chaplaincy. "In these and other ways, the emerging interest in pastoral care took hold of a primary criterion: pastoral care meant a response to persons experiencing particular forms of human need."[60] As a result, the concern to provide skilled care for the neglected and vulnerable carried over into other areas of pastoral care ministries, such as hospitals, psychiatry/mental health facilities, correctional institutions, sporting arenas, schools, and the marketplace.

Among the many contributors to pastoral care and counseling in the 1950s was Wayne E. Oates, a professor of pastoral care and the psychology of religion at Southern Baptist Theological Seminary.[61] Oates is "noted for pioneering an academic body of literature in the fields of pastoral care and pastoral counseling."[62] His literature predicted that the moral system of Western society, particularly its emphasis on competition and social classes, would lead us away from a biblically-centered moral construct and toward a socially-centered morality. This is certainly a danger area for many chaplains working in pluralistic settings. The temptation is to blend in order to be accepted, however, the need is to maintain an authentic, biblically-based faith and commitment to Christ. For Oates, the pastoral care provider's role was representing Christ's care and acceptance for those

---

57 Gerkin, *An Introduction to Pastoral Care*.

58 Ibid.

59 Ibid.

60 Ibid., 66.

61 Holifield, *A History of Pastoral Care in America: From Salvation to Self-realization*.

62 Wayne E. Oates Institute, "Dr. Wayne E. Oates: A Living Legacy", http://www. oates.org/learn-more/wayne-oates-legacy.

in need of His saving grace.[63] Recipients are not in need of more pop-culture psychology or ambiguous spirituality; they need a caregiver who is willing to authentically represent the love of Christ, and a moral system that, at its core, values human life more than personal agendas, schedules, and self-promotion.

63 Gerkin, *An Introduction to Pastoral Care*.

CHAPTER SEVEN

Questions for Further Reflection

1. Define *voluntarism* and *religious privatism*. Explain why you see them as positive or negative. Be sure to adequately and completely explain each answer in two to four sentences. (5 points).

2. Describe the aims of the Social Gospel movement and the Emmanuel movement in two to three sentences each. (5 points)

3. In a three- to five-sentence response, identify the elements of chaplaincy that can be found in BOTH of these movements. (5 points)

4. Who is the founder of the CPE movement, and in what ways is CPE different from seminary training? Be sure to include a discussion on the "living documents." (5 points)

Class Discussion: The goal is to get you thinking about how you might approach ministry from the perspective of a chaplain. Reflect on the class materials and prepare/develop a response to the following questions:

> As we (chaplains/chaplain candidates) gain more training and skills and begin to move beyond the local, worshipping, and reflecting community, *how* will we keep alive the supernatural potency of our faith? Is there a need to develop a process of accountability which forces us to continue to raise the right questions and plug into the larger, more profound issues of personal faith?

CHAPTER EIGHT

The Contemporary Context Of Pastoral Care and Chaplaincy

This last era of the twentieth century brought significant changes to pastoral care on three levels: the individual, the Christian community, and society.[1] Individual care could be accomplished through group care, rather than the historical model of one-on-one pastoral care. Christian communities were invited to share in the healing process by connecting through common histories and tragedies. As awareness of cultural and social issues grew, the caregivers in the church once again emerged as social ministers whose mission was care for the oppressed.

In this last look at the twentieth century, we will examine insights from Charles Gerkin, one of the leading authors of pastoral care and chaplaincy ministries of this era. In his book,[2] he identifies and explores the shift in pastoral care that becomes a much more inclusive care practice. In the past, we have seen a variety of pendulum swings that have focused on individual care, church community care, and social movements. Gerkin presents a model that integrates all of these layers as necessary components in chaplaincy ministries.

According to Gerkin,[3] a broad range of developments occurred at the level of individual care. As care for the individual continued to progress, churches and pastors responded with centers for pastoral counseling. These counseling services were held in the church, outside the church as non-profit organizations, and in community-based centers that were connected to a church or pastorate. These agencies worked through a cooperative effort of therapists, social workers, and physicians. As time and practices progressed, pastoral counseling services were also seen as referral services in which pastors could "refer out" individual cases that were beyond their expertise.

---

1   Gerkin, *An Introduction to Pastoral Care*

2   Ibid.

3   Ibid.

The church also began to recognize the power of the people of the community to reach out and help one another. Influenced by the successes of group-based care programs such as Alcoholics Anonymous, churches developed other help groups largely formed and led by lay leaders.[4] This shift marked a move away from the individual psychology of the WWII era. Pastors became more interested in the care of the community as a whole. Lay leaders took on a more dominant role as communities and pastors understood the magnitude of the community's contributions to individual healing.

In Gerkin's final analysis,[5] he asserted the cultural climate had suffered a serious moral decline by the mid-1970s and '80s. The impact of this change on pastoral care meant that pastors could no longer assume that care recipients shared a common moral and ethical belief with the pastoral care provider. Previously, care providers could focus on the recipients' needs with little focus on moral issues; however, this was no longer the case. Gerkin concluded that, due to the moral decline of society, both issues needed to be met as a part of pastoral care.

A number of issues surfaced during this era as awareness of many societal inequities and societal problems revealed a need for care greater than what pastors could effectively provide. This social awareness prompted yet another resurgence of the Social Gospel movement, this time with greater force.[6] Pastoral care providers were better informed about the multi-dimensional issues facing AIDS victims, equality in the workforce, and many other challenges that plagued American culture. With this came awareness of the vast cultures that comprise this great nation. Consequently, chaplains and ministers had to become more accepting and understanding of these ethnic groups and their political, religious, and cultural practices and beliefs.[7]

An Integrative Model of Chaplaincy

As the 21st century has dawned, the pastoral care conversation has become much more focused on the multi-disciplinary approach often used in chaplaincy ministries. This approach calls for chaplains to intertwine theological reflection with personal experience. It demands that all pastoral care recognize the multi-dimensional issues of individuals and families. Every care recipient will have a unique crisis experience related to family

---

4 Ibid.

5 Ibid.

6 Ibid.

7 Ibid.

history, personal history, and cultural dynamics, along with medical history, mental history, and cognition (ability to fully understand what is occurring and how that will affect them and those around them).

In this final historical section, we will briefly examine this multi-disciplinary approach as a summation of the various pastoral care contributions, *both past and present*, which have led to our postmodern approach.

An Adaptation of Andrew Root's Interdisciplinary Model of Ministry

As we look back on various historical contributions, it is our belief that Andrew Root's Representative Model[8] best illustrates the purposes and practices of chaplaincy. While there are many noteworthy models that illustrate a chaplaincy care modality, Root's model aptly brings together the distinctive elements already present in chaplaincy ministry, such as bringing the suffering of Christ into the human experience and approaching that experience through understanding the various external influences of the crisis.[9] The key to ministry is the ability to fully represent the wounded and vulnerable Christ to a broken and troubled family or individual. This cannot happen through a detached and impersonal model, and it cannot happen through a one-dimensional approach which clings to personal theology while denying the realities of socio-cultural context, medical and mental history, and the recipient's personal narrative.

One way this is accomplished is through becoming representatives of the suffering and victorious Christ. Let us pause for a moment before moving into Root's Representative Model to briefly review what is most commonly understood as a "theology of the cross." Understanding this concept is crucial to understanding Root's model.

The theology of the cross "bravely enters into the darkest corners of human hells claiming God's presence there through the cross of Christ."[10] By way of the cross, Jesus is the ultimate representative of both God and humanity. However, as a pastoral care model for chaplaincy, the chaplain—as follower of the crucified Christ—shares in His life by

---

8 Andrew Root, "Youth Ministry as an Integrative Theological Task", *The Journal of Youth Ministry* 5, no. 2, (2007): 33-50. ALTA Religion Database. ©*The Journal of Youth Ministry*. Used with permission. A few notes should be made concerning Root's model: (1) while the Representative Model evolved out of Luther's *theologia crucis* (theology of the Cross), Root adds to Luther's model by inviting the pastoral presence to engage in a multi-disciplinary approach to ministry; (2) Root's model was constructed for the purpose of youth ministry; and (3) this model represents a chaplaincy model that has been practiced since the mid- to late-twentieth century.

9 Root, "Youth Ministry as an Integrative Theological Task".

10 Ibid.

becoming Christ's representative to the care recipients in both celebration and crisis. This begins with the living God who reveals Himself to be known in the crucified humanity of Jesus. The cross and resurrection of Christ is an invitation to live in the "deep relational life of God."[11] He is not calling this an invitation to be in a deep relationship *with* God; rather, it is an invitation to share in the relational life *of* God. It is moving from a one-dimensional relationship with God alone to a three-dimensional relationship that includes one's neighbor. It is a relationship that must be measured vertically and horizontally. It is the mutual and reciprocal love relationship with the Creator God and the continual extending of that love—even sacrificially—to others.

The relational life of God is more than practitioner/client based. The relational life hears the whole story in order to better relate and better assist in providing godly care to individuals and families. In order for this to happen, chaplains must *call it what it is*. They must be brave enough to make their way deep into human suffering. And, as Root points out, chaplains must recognize that the care recipient's suffering is not just a spiritual reality; chaplains must embrace the historical reality of the event.

For example, reflect upon the case of a chaplain whose young relative took his own life in the basement of his home while his family was at church. Immediately the issue of suicide and its spiritual consequences was discussed within that family. When a crisis of this magnitude happens, we are tempted to deal with certain issues while neglecting others, a practice often called "spiritualizing." This person is far more than a single issue; he has a history, which includes multi-layered relationships within his family, emotional struggles that may have included depression and other mental disorders, and some issues that he may have carried painfully and secretly for years. We can cite ample real-life examples of triumph and Scriptures that offer valid interpretations for difficult times, but if those are the only things offered to the family, church, and community, the opportunity to bring wholeness to an otherwise fragmented and meaningless crisis may be missed. During a crisis like 9/11 or Hurricane Katrina, chaplains are what Root calls "the Representatives" who draw these fragmented parts into a whole. Chaplains acknowledge the spiritual (in this example, the theological ramifications of suicide and the hope of Christ), the physical (depression, hopelessness, fear, guilt, shame, etc), and the social (the order or disorder of the family and community). Let us examine more closely Root's Representative Model.

The Representative Model requires ministers to play a dual role in the ministry experience. As chaplains, they simultaneously embody the suffering of the care recipients before God and the suffering Christ, who

---

11 Ibid., 42.

is present in the human struggle before the care recipient (the theology of the cross). According to Root, this happens when the chaplain does three things: the chaplain is willing to acknowledge the recipient's pain, he or she defines it, or "calls it what it is," and then he or she engages it through the chaplain's own personal suffering and the suffering of Christ.

The first aspect of this model is to acknowledge the care recipient's pain. This occurs on three different levels: (1) the pain is validated: it is real to the chaplain because it is real to the recipient; (2) the recipient is assured that they are significant to God *and* to the chaplain; and (3) the recipient is given the opportunity to voice their concerns, frustrations, and/or struggles. In reflecting on the young family member's suicide, the chaplain and other ministers who offered a path towards healing created a space for the family and community to engage all of the pain—not just the obvious loss of life. A suicide is complicated. A very real part of the pain was wrapped in shame and the need to protect the young man from taboo and idle talk; guilt by certain members of the family who felt responsible for his life and well-being; and the hurt for family and friends who were also working through their own complex responses to his death. In the midst of these overwhelming feelings, those involved needed to be reminded that the young man is (and all who suffer are) still beloved by God and by those who gave their time and energy to sit for hours and help the grieving process their pain. In those moments, the chaplain served as a catalyst to help create a space where pain, fear, anger, etc. could be voiced without judgment and in spite of perfect theology.

After the struggle is given a space, the chaplain must define it or "call it what it is." Here they seek "God's unveiling in the grittiness of the broken humanity of Jesus... [T]here is no fear to speak about sin or evil, or to face the crushed or mangled humanity of another."[12] At the core of the experience is a theology of the cross that fearlessly enters into all aspects of human pain. This occurs through assessment; chaplains must ask questions to better understand the concrete situation. In Paul's letter to the Philippians, he urged them to be interested in one another's lives. We must be willing to ask the necessary questions compassionately and wisely. Chaplains, as "Representatives," help individuals to put words to their most feared and protected feelings; this is why listening skills are so important for chaplains to develop.

Asking questions about recipients' particular situations may open the door for them to share the bigger picture of the loss. Once the struggle is defined, chaplains can better assist families and individuals by offering care that is specific and relevant to their particular need. Chaplains will do an injustice to the care recipients if care is limited to spiritual and theological

---

12 Ibid., 41.

realities; yet, as chaplains, the recognition of this core element to holistic healing is undeniable.

In the above example, defining the struggle required the chaplain to ask questions, inquire, and assess the whole picture before making generalized assumptions about the complexities of this specific situation. This approach must be compassionately scientific; that is, it must seek to better understand needs by considering social context, family dynamics, cultural issues, education, etc; these are areas of training covered in Clinical Pastoral Education. Once the situation has been fully assessed, chaplains can graciously and gently enter into the recipients' pain with them.

Through this model, we recognize that the care recipient is at the center of the ministry experience. The role of the chaplain as representative is to bring a revelation of Christ into the moment. The chaplain enters by way of Christ's suffering and his or her own suffering as a means of authentically engaging the recipient. Then, through discernment and compassion, s/he asks evaluative questions which allow the chaplain to better understand the bigger situation the recipient is facing. During this process, s/he must continually ask what methodologies and disciplines (sociology, psychology) will help him/her better define the need ("call it what it is") and engage the person.

Conclusion

The traditional pastoral care paradigm, defined by Thomas Oden[13] at the beginning of this unit, is rapidly changing as families seek alternatives to traditional pastoral care. The reality is that fewer people are seeking out churches as America moves toward being less Christianized. In recent years, this shift has caused churches to be more missional, but the postmodern culture more readily rejects *the institution* of the church as a means to finding Truth and knowing God. Institutions and large, powerful structures are viewed as suspicious or untrustworthy. This is why the old model, which is still widely used (seizing opportunities to tell individuals, families, and communities what they need, i.e., jobs, Jesus, and us) fails. This old model of outreach does not work in a postmodern world because the weak and the vulnerable have a long history of abuse at the hands of such powers.

In contrast, chaplaincy presents a model that goes where the people are, asks permission to enter into their crisis, listens to their needs, and then, together with the care recipients, works toward resolving the present crisis

---

13 Oden, *"Classical Pastoral Care: Becoming a Minister"*, 5. Bracketed information added.

through an understanding of it in its context.

This kind of ministry doesn't just happen in a church buildings; it happens in ghettos, hospital rooms, war zones, casinos, and at large social events, such as NASCAR. It happens in the midst of living and to individuals who have a specific story tied to a specific socio-cultural context. Ministry experienced "outside the gates" has to be shaped in a way that the traditional church has not done. It is "ministry without walls" (pulpits, pews, etc.); it is "ministry on the go." It could not occur without an intentional understanding of the life experiences and culture of those who chaplains serve. It is the military chaplain conducting a service out in the field, a hospital chaplain serving communion at the bedside of a dying patient, and other non-conventional means of religious practice. It is a rediscovery of the New Testament model of Jesus; on a hillside, on the backside of a desert, in a sinner's home, and on a criminal's cross.

Definitions for Further Review:

Physiological Psychology: a branch of psychology that studies the interactions between physical or chemical processes in the body and mental states or behavior (North American English Dictionary).

Christian Science: a religious group that believes illness should be overcome or managed through religious faith alone; no medical intervention is allowed.

Catharsis: an intense emotional release.

"Living Human Documents": a phrase coined by A. Boisen, referring to the care recipients studied by his students (as opposed to written documents).

Case study: a record of a client or care recipient over a period of time for the purpose of study or analysis.

Verbatim: a word by word account of the activities of pastoral care.

"Client-centered" therapy: a humanistic therapy model that emphasizes the role of the client in bringing about their own healing.

Reflective Listening: repeating back to clients their thoughts through paraphrasing or parroting.

CHAPTER EIGHT
Questions for Further Reflection

1. In a two to three sentences each, provide a brief description of the development of the three levels of pastoral care examined in the last section of the chapter. (5 points)

2. In two to three sentences, explain how Root is using "Representative" in his model. (5 points)

3. In what ways does a "scientific approach" aid in the provision of care for families/individuals in crisis? Explain your answer in two to three sentences. (5 points)

Class Discussion: The goal is to get you thinking about how you might approach ministry from the perspective of a chaplain. Reflect on the class materials and prepare/develop a response to the following question:

A wife just lost her husband, who was the sole bread-winner of the household and oversaw all financial decisions for the family. All of her children live out of state with their own families. What obvious concern might the chaplain address with this widow? Using Root's model, create a list of questions that might help better assess her needs.

UNIT THREE

Understanding the Practice of Chaplaincy

The chaplain serves the needs of the community; therefore, s/he must find a way to reach secular society.

— Chaplain Robert Crick

Introduction

A chaplain, as pastoral caregiver, crosses institutional, economic, cultural and ecclesiastical boundaries to present the God who demonstrates a desire for healing and wholeness in life. Because they have access to the entire community, pastoral caregivers are in a unique position to embody a harmonious healing environment for those being served.[1]

History of Chaplaincy

The origins of the word "chaplain" can be traced back to Saint Martin of Tours. According to biographer Sulpitius Severus,[2] St. Martin was born into a military family; his father was a senior officer in the Roman cavalry. At the age of ten, Martin attended a Christian church and became a catechumen (candidate for baptism); however, he did so against his parents' wishes. At the age of fifteen, he was required to join the cavalry according to recruiting laws. Soon after he joined, his regiment was sent to Amiens in Gaul.[195]

It is here that Martin's life would forever change. According to Severus,[3] Martin met a half-naked beggar one severely cold morning outside the city gate. His immediate response was to cut his cloak into two parts, giving one to the beggar. Because of the Christian influence on his life as a catechumen, Martin's actions were fitting. Severus records that Martin lived a very simple life, giving to those in need what little he was given; he served his fellow soldiers, and he even served the man elected to be his servant. So when Martin saw this beggar who had been rejected by so many, he did what was natural to him: he shared what little cover he had from the treacherous cold. Severus[4] further records that Martin had a dream in which Jesus visited him wearing the cloak he had given the beggar. In the dream, Jesus turned to the angelic host surrounding him and said, "Martin, who is still but a catechumen, clothed me with this

---

1   Mountain States Health Alliance, *Spiritual and Pastoral Care*, http://www.msha.com/body02.cfm?id=342.

2   Sulpitius Severus, "Life of St. Martin", trans by Alexander Roberts, A Selected Library of Nicene and Post-Nicene Fathers of the Christian Church, 2, no. 11, (1984). http://www.users.csbsju.edu/~eknuth/npnf2-11/sulpitiu/lifeofst.html#tp.

3   Ibid.

4   Ibid.

robe."[5] Immediately after this encounter, Martin was baptized, and he felt compelled to lay down his sword. Martin told the Emperor that he could no longer fight for the Roman army; he was now a soldier of God. The response was not good: he was deemed a coward by the guard in front of the Emperor and imprisoned. Martin declared he was no coward, but a man of faith, and he would go to battle unarmed if that is what the emperor chose. They agreed; however, the next morning, the barbarians declared peace surrendering and forfeiting all their possessions to Rome. It was declared that this victory was the result of Martin's faith. Thereafter, "his cloak came to symbolize care and compassion for those in need. The strength and conviction of his compassion was so great that kings carried the cloak into battle, accompanied by priests who tended to the king's religious needs. These priests came to be known as the 'keepers of the cloak' or cappellanus—and today are known as chaplains."[6]

Since the days of St. Martin of Tours, chaplaincy has maintained its mission of service and compassion to "the least of these." While this distinct tradition was originally begun in the military, it has expanded into a multitude of settings. These settings include, but are not limited to, various clinical settings, prisons and local jails, the marketplace, educational institutions, and emergency responses to catastrophic events.[7] Please note, given the space limitations of this book, it is not possible to provide an all-inclusive list of the various fields within chaplaincy; it is a rapidly growing discipline with subsections creating their own subsections. For example, in the field of clinical chaplaincy there are several specialized areas, such as mental institutions, hospice, long-term care, etc. While each of these settings possesses necessary requirements and contribution to the field of chaplaincy, chaplaincy itself has a common thread—a common humanity—present in all of its particular settings. Each strand of this common (Christian) thread seeks to reveal the presence of the incarnate Christ, who is already present in the pain and the sufferings of His creation. Chaplains, in all of their specialized settings, are compelled by compassion for individuals, families, and communities in crisis. So how do chaplains approach that ministry holistically, practically, and reflectively?

---

5 Severus, "Life of St. Martin", trans. Alexander Roberts, ch 2. http://www.users. csbsju.edu/~eknuth/npnf2-11/sulpitiu/lifeofst.html#tp.

6 http://www.cogchaplains.com/ministry/about/history-of-chaplaincy/.

7 See also the Commission for Ministries in Specialized Settings: http:// comissnetwork.org/default.aspx.

An Approach to Chaplaincy: Chaplaincy as Covenant, Character, and Commission[8]

This approach grew out of a call to examine some of the historical patterns of meaning, conviction, and image that shape our understanding of care given in a historical, ministerial context. Paul Pruyser says (concerning pastors who do clinical work), they would do well to consider that "body of theological and practical knowledge which evolved over years of practice by themselves and their forebears." Otherwise, he warns, while meeting the needs of the community at large, the caregiver may very well become a stranger in his/her own *agapic* community.

Chaplains must stay connected to their local faith community. In this section, we present an approach to chaplaincy care that takes into account this common, critical issue. The model encompasses three areas: covenant, character, and commission, which seek to bring balance to a ministry which often finds its story developing outside the gates of the local church community.

Chaplaincy as Covenant (Shared Faith)

Staying connected to your local church and faith context through worship

and critical dialogue

A chaplaincy model of ministry must be based upon a biblical, covenantal view of individual and corporate accountability. While individual and group growth is a primary issue in the covenant, such growth should always be judged and legitimized by the overarching covenant of God extended to all humanity. Chaplains of all types seem to find their focus within a congregation that has a deep sense of responsibility to the larger Christian community and to the world.

Because chaplaincy is a ministry outside the gates, chaplains run the risk of focusing almost totally on individual growth outside the boundaries of the historical church. In such models of care, chaplains may lose their authentic pastoral identity as it has evolved within their specific faith tradition and local church body. It is important to maintain a connection to the local body and pursue individual growth; this is accomplished

---

8 Chaplain Robert D. Crick, "Drinking From Our Own Wells: Search for a Pentecostal Care and Counseling Paradigm in the Development of Contemporary Caregivers." This paper was originally presented by Pentecostal Caregivers' Conference, Cleveland, TN. However, Dr. Crick's paper has been reworked to meet the purposes of this text.

through care which takes into account both the human experience and historical tradition. In essence, the process shifts focus from "who I am" to "Whose I am." Such a process is dependent on two activities: worship and critical reflection.

> *Without meaningful and purposeful rituals, daily life cannot be made or kept human. Humanizing rituals humanizes all of life... Conflicting rituals result in alienation and dehumanization. On the other hand, common meaningful rituals result in the gift of community.*[9]

> — John H. Westerhoff

Jacob Firet[10] states that by keeping pastoral care focused within the life and spirit of the worshipping community, pastoral care providers guard against the professional arrogance that categorizes individuals into chaplain/care recipient, counselor/client, doctor/patient, and teacher/ student. Such arrogance often keeps chaplains from being fellow travelers in an "equihuman" process. God's original intention for humanity was mutuality. As an extension of the worshipping community, the dignity of humanity takes on a new dimension. "A human being is never, even as a child, only an object which can be taught, commanded, spoken to; he or she is always an equal who is and has to be himself or herself an agent, and, as such, has to be dealt with."[11] This radical privilege of equality is only protected in a worship-centered environment where the Holy Spirit empowers each person, whether recipient of care or caregiver, as possessors of special gifts, but neither of them possessors of the whole truth.

In this context, we are reminded, as was the Apostle Paul, that though we are conscious of having authority as believers, we still know ourselves to be equal to our fellow human beings, regardless of how wounded they may be at the moment of encounter. Paul longed to worship with Roman Christians in order to "impart some spiritual gifts;" but also for the encouragement and admonition that he would receive from them as one believer among others (Romans 1:1-11).

While a worship-centered environment is a context that generates a confession of shared faith, critical theological reflection in this process is the means by which such a covenant is maintained and strengthened. Like our forefathers who regularly came together in Christian conference to reveal and search their souls, chaplains must have dialogue partners and

---

9 John H. Westerhoff, "The Church and Family", Religious Education, 78 no. 2 Spr 1983 (ATLA religion Database with ATLASerials), 249-274.

10 Jacob Firet, *Dynamics in Pastoring* (Grand Rapids: William B. Eerdmans Publishing, 1986), 193.

11 Firet, *Dynamics in Pastoring,* 188.

groups. It is inconceivable that a chaplain would ever try to minister apart from a reflective process.

Chaplaincy, like all ministry, is "theology in the making." In and through a critical, dialogical process we cleanse ourselves of any hidden agendas that may corrupt or distort the ministry. This must happen in an environment where critical dialogue is valued, where co-laborers share a common mission, and where the Spirit is given permission to enter into the dialogue. In such a context, theology is described as reflective moments in practice; stated and affirmed theology arises from that practice to yield further practice. This takes place within a community of reflection, and decreases the gap between the faith we claim and the one we live. Reflection of this type will see that the personal and corporate issues of chaplaincy ministry stay in dialogue with the larger mission of the church.

In summary, chaplaincy is most effective within one's personal faith context that allows for the Holy Spirit to lead, illuminate, and correct. Otherwise, chaplains can become captive to an over-emphasis on competency and refinement of skills.

Chaplaincy as Character (Shared Love)

Character development moves one toward a "new identity in Christ";

character as shared love is staying connected to your story and God's story,

and remaining open to connect with their story as it is woven into your story.

— Henri Nauwen

It goes without saying that chaplains must be persons of deep devotion and prayer. Consequently, their ministry must be more than mere knowledge or technique; it must grow out of and be an extension of the spiritual life of the caregiver. The natural tendency of pastoral caregivers is to leave behind their sense of human powerlessness and lean more on the skills and techniques of their trade. While training and insights are necessary, only as the "powerless healer" (wounded healer) are chaplains able to become acquainted with God in an intimate, personal way.[12]

As chaplains, we regularly deal with suffering people who yearn for God's presence; yet we are all too frequently out of touch with the presence of God. Our forefathers, with their limited training, knew that without prayer pastoral care quickly degenerates into mere programs and human skills. Prayer helps us to see clients not just as a set of problems, but as faces in

---

12   Nouwen, *The Wounded Healer*, 102.

the very heart of God. By keeping these faces in our hearts through prayer, we discover clients to be more than problems which can exhaust us; they become brothers and sisters who mysteriously touch our afflictions with their own suffering and pain, and they enable us to experience anew the presence of a merciful God.

In addition to a personal devotional life of prayer and continued training and skill development, chaplains must incorporate into their lives a model allowing their story with its many dimensions to be available to their peers. When fellow laborers get together and share their stories, they leave with new healing resources.

Chaplaincy as Commission (Shared Hope)

The commission is to become living documents and read by all men; telling our

story with the vision towards hearing that grand narrative which addresses

our future participation in the story of the broader Christian community.

The pastoral care model is a practice of change, always in the light of the kingdom that is coming and that is at work among us. Chaplains might best be described as the *pneumatikos pater,* or "spiritual guide," whose deep perceptions and insights enable those under their charge to discover their own future possibilities. Two qualifications are necessary in the development of these persons.

First, chaplains must have encountered and reconciled their own deep passions and conflicts, both personal and corporate. In doing so, they will be able to discern between the impulse to care and the gift of caring, the drive to provide limits for others and the fear of their own freedom. After they have focused on their own internal processes, spiritual guides acquire the ability to discern and help interpret the conflicting stories of others.

Second, chaplains must connect these distresses to the larger community. The connectedness between personal struggles and the struggles of the world is described by the Apostle Paul:

> [B]ecause the creation itself also will be delivered from the bondage of corruption into the glorious liberty of the children of God. For we know that the whole creation groans and labors with birth pangs together until now. Not only that, but we also who have the firstfruits of the Spirit, even we ourselves groan within ourselves, eagerly waiting for the adoption, the redemption of our body. — Romans 8:21-23 (NKJV)

This is a process in which the caregiver's eyes are opened to the reality of the world and his/her ability to bring transformation to that reality. In essence, chaplains take that revelation and join it with action.[13] And they do so in many corners of the world, fully prepared to impact the lives of communities, individuals, and institutions.

Conclusion

Because of the great task of this ministry, all full-time chaplains in any field must undergo much training and certification in order to be fully prepared to meet people in their time of need. Even volunteers go through a series of certifications and endorsements to ensure their care recipients are being offered the very best. They are not only trained to handle critical life moments, but to offer more common or traditional services, such as worship services, communion, administrative work/documentation, etc.

In this final unit our study will turn to common areas of chaplaincy practice, such as military, clinical, prison, and the marketplace. The goal is to provide the reader with a closer look into each of these specialized areas with emphasis on training, duties, and critical issues that are specific to each field of chaplaincy. We have also included a chapter on volunteer chaplaincy, which is the life source of many of the above programs. As we will discover, without volunteers, chaplaincy programs could not offer the level of professional and spiritual care that is necessary in dealing with human tragedies. In addition, we devote an entire chapter to the study of ethics with an emphasis on both religious and legal issues that must be understood in order to effectively offer pastoral care in pluralistic settings. The goal is to give a comprehensive overview of the many dimensions that accompany both spiritual and professional practice.

---

13 Sheryl Bridges Johns, *Pentecostal Formation: A Pedagogy Among the Oppressed* (Sheffield, England: Sheffield Academic Press, 1993), 13.

Chapter 9

Military Chaplaincy

Evidence of the philosophy and history of military chaplaincy can be found even in the Ancient Near East. In the Old Testament, special priests were assigned to military units as indicators that the war was a special, spiritual one. Texts such as Deuteronomy 20:2 identify the expectation of these priests in battle. They were commissioned by God and the community leader (often a king) to go out onto the battlefield ahead of the army. In 2 Chronicles 13, Abijah confronts the rebellious Israelite army concerning the sins of Israel. In verse 12 he states, "God is with us; He is our leader. His priests with their trumpets will sound the battle cry against you. People of Israel, do not fight against the LORD, the God of your ancestors, for you will not succeed." Here and in many instances, the priests would blow their trumpets before their enemy at the command of the King as a siren, a battle cry to intimidate the enemy and send forth the army. It was an indicator that YHWH was with them.

One of the greatest stories of the New Testament is that of the military officer Cornelius, who was brought to the Lord and filled with the Spirit through the efforts of Peter, the Apostle. Jesus himself ministered to a centurion in need. Furthermore, the Letter to the Philippians was written primarily to a group of Christians who were retired veterans. These texts are beautiful affirmations of the ministry of the early believers to the military. It is obvious from this and other stories that the military was not considered "off-limits" to the church. It was simply another area of secular society to be evangelized.

"The modern chaplaincy's roots are essentially medieval Catholic in origin. The Council of Ratisbon (742 AD) first officially authorized the use of chaplains for armies, but prohibited 'the servants of God' from bearing arms or fighting."[1] Following the era of the early church, the Roman Catholic Church and the commanders of military forces were in what one may call a "partnership of equals." The church felt that it had been and should be an integral part of all of government life; therefore, kings and commanders ultimately had to have the blessing and anointing of the church.

In the United States, even before the country was officially established in 1776, chaplaincy had already been incorporated into the armed forces.[2]

---

1 http://www.nationalguard.com/chaplaincandidate/chaplainhistory.php
2 Ibid.

The colonial people fought many battles against the Native Americans and the French. Prior to the establishment of the United States, chaplains were commissioned by governors and courts. Others volunteered as chaplains for the militia.[3] Later, under the direction of Commander-in-Chief George Washington, chaplains received an official place in the armed forces during the Continental Congress on July 29, 1775. Some say that General Washington saw the war not only as a physical break from England, but a spiritual one. Many documents and articles speak of General Washington's dependence upon his chaplains, who represented many different groups. Articles list Congregational, Quakers, Puritans, Catholics and other faith groups as part of this early chaplaincy team.

Since 1775, chaplains have been assigned to the US Armed Forces.[4] They were prominent in all wars and conflicts, and represented most of the major faith groups. Since US military chaplaincy began, "approximately 40,000 chaplains have served in the military forces of the United States as dual professionals, certified religious leaders and commissioned staff officers. Four hundred chaplains have lost their lives in the course of eight major wars. Eight chaplains, six from the Army and two from the Navy, have been awarded the Medal of Honor."[5] There are two principles from this early history that are paramount to chaplaincy assignments. First, chaplains must not lose their identity as ordained ministers and representatives of a particular faith group when they put on a uniform. Regardless of their allegiance to the armed forces, they are still Presbyterian, Baptist, Methodist, etc. Second, chaplains are expected to respect the great religious diversity that comprises the vast military personnel, thus making provision for all those who wish to celebrate their faith traditions. "Cooperation without compromise" is a major aspect of US chaplaincy operations.[6]

---

3   Mickey Jett. *Prospectus* presented to the staff of the Pentecostal School of Theology, Summer 2009.

4   Countries around the world offer chaplaincy ministries to members of their military. The presence of the church in military settings is not a contemporary invention; it is a historical reality dating back to the Ancient Israelites. The formalization of chaplaincy occurred as a result of St. Martin's contributions. The general requirements identified in this section are USA-specific, yet they are typical of the standards followed by most nations. Standards include (but are not limited to): receiving ordination/ministerial license, denominational endorsement (or equivalent), bachelor's degree, theological degree, CPE units, and ministerial experience. In addition, international chaplains are similar to their US counterparts in most ethical practices, such as providing spiritual care to people of all faiths/no faith. Chaplains are considered non-combatant military officers.

5   Ibid., 5.

6   See the following website for a full account of the history of chaplaincy in the

Education, Training, and Endorsement

The military depends upon the churches to send trained male and female chaplains. Because of the nature of chaplaincy ministry—ministry to a pluralistic society, with multiple needs—training has always been an integral part of chaplains' development. While the military normally wants individuals with a Master of Divinity degree, they also want the denomination to send them chaplains that are prepared with special skills needed in military service. In addition to the normal seminary track/courses, these skills include preaching, counseling, crisis intervention, divorce and remarriage, addictions, and other emotional and spiritual needs that are present in a vast pluralistic environment. A high percentage of those who serve in the armed forces do not come out of strong church environments, and many come from dysfunctional families. Therefore, chaplains must have the appropriate training to meet the emotional and spiritual needs of their care recipients. The requirements set by the military, in cooperation with the denominations, are:

- Mature, well-balanced chaplain and family;
- Ministerial credentials from a denomination that is authorized to send chaplains to the armed forces;
- Graduate theological degrees;
- Clinical Pastoral Education, or equivalent clinical training;
- Two years of pastoral ministry beyond seminary training;
- The completion of military chaplaincy schools.

In recent years, the Army, Navy, and Air Force Chief of Chaplains Offices have developed special "seminarian programs." This allows students at the beginning of seminary training to be commissioned as officers in a special military reserve program. While there are restrictions as to what officers commissioned as a "seminarian" can do, it does allow them to attend basic chaplains' school with seminary credit and to have short-term chaplaincy assignments. Students are not classified as "chaplains;" rather, they are "chaplain candidates." These candidates receive vital training in preparation for either full-time, National Guard, or Reserve chaplaincy assignments. Shortly after chaplains graduate from seminary training, "seminarian" status is removed, and chaplains are given the oath of office either as full-time military chaplains, National Guard chaplains, or Reserve chaplains.

United States Navy: http://www.tpub.com/content/religion/14227/css/14227_13. htm. See the following website for a history of chaplaincy in the United States Air Force: http://www.usafhc.af.mil/history/index.asp. See the following website for a history of chaplaincy in the United States Army: http://www.usachcs.army. mil/HISTORY/Brief/TitlePage.htm

The National Guard chaplains are not full-time; they meet with National Guard units on the weekends, in the summers, and during critical times. On occasion, they can be called to active duty for special assignments. When the special assignment is over, they go back to regular National Guard status. The Reserve chaplain, similar to the National Guard chaplain, only serves at particular times, either on weekends with Reserve units, during summers, or other extended times for special assignments. Full-time chaplains, if they stay on active duty, may retire with a minimum of twenty years of service. Most active duty chaplains remain beyond twenty years. The National Guard and Reserve chaplains also have a twenty-year retirement program; however, they do not receive retirement pay until they reach the age of sixty. Of course, all these rules and programs change periodically.

> ### DEFINITION
>
> Chaplains Commission—an approved agency within the denomination that serves as the denomination's official and legal endorsing agency.
>
> Endorsement—the official approval of or permission for one to represent an ecclesiastical body as a member of their clergy.

In short, whether Army, Navy, Air Force, National Guard, or Reserve, the duties of the military chaplain are similar. The chaplains' responsibilities are to carry out the command's religious programs, both in the areas of spirituality and morale. The ministries are extended not just to the military person, but also to his/her family. It should be noted that the Marine Corps and the Coast Guard do not have their own chaplains; Navy chaplains are given special assignments to these units. When a Navy chaplain is serving the Marines or the Coast Guard, they wear the uniforms of that respected corps. Most Navy chaplains will have the opportunity, during their twenty- or more-year career, to be assigned to one or both of these units.

Endorsement

Since 1775, the military required some form of endorsement by the sending denomination of the assigned chaplain. This endorsement comes from that denomination, normally through the **Chaplains Commission**. A Chaplains Commission is an approved agency within the denomination that serves as the denomination's official and legal endorsing agency. **Endorsement** is simply the legal process whereby the US can bridge our long history of "separation of church and state." In other words, the church, in partnership with the military, endorses chaplains for special assignment to the military knowing that they are both under the authority of the military commander with whom they are assigned and at the same time under the authority of their endorsing faith group. Technically, both the military (for justifiable reasons) and the endorsing church can recall chaplains back to civilian ministerial service.

A national organization brings all endorsers together, along with Chief of Chaplains personnel, for an annual conference in Washington, DC, to ensure a thorough understanding of the special relationship between the church and the military, under the banner of endorsement. This organization is called the National Conference for Ministry to the Armed Forces, and it includes most of the denominations that are authorized to endorse ministers as chaplains to the military armed forces. This organization, along with the Department of Defense, has established standards and procedures that allow our chaplains to operate fully within the military.

Functions of the Military Chaplain

When I entered into the military chaplaincy in 1961, I will never forget the words of wisdom that I received from my Sergeant Major. He stated, 'If you want to succeed, Chaplain, never get into the chow line until every one of your troops have been fed; don't open your letters from home until you have observed your soldiers who got letters, those who did not, and their reactions when they open the letters; and never tuck yourself in at night until you have been assured that every soldier has a warm, clean place to rest.' — Chaplain Robert D. Crick, D.Min.

Arriving in Bagram, Afghanistan, we all hit the deck running. It was long days of counseling, Bible studies, collateral duties, Sunday Chapel sermons and bulletins, the constant paperwork and administration, Red Cross messages from home, community relations programs with the local population, an on-going ministry of presence and a myriad of other functions that push chaplains to the limit every day in combat. Yet, our troops have a feeling of accomplishment in the mission, and their spirits

remain high as does mine in carrying out this tremendous ministry

— Chaplain Terry Simmons, US Army

Generally, military chaplains are thought of as "pastors in uniform." Most of what is done in civilian life will be practiced and carried out as common religious practices in the military also. This includes preaching, counseling, dealing with finances, leadership and administration, Sunday school programs, youth groups, revivals, choirs, etc. The difference is the community's diversity of faith backgrounds. Chaplains must always take into consideration the current context, the military personnel and family members and their diverse faith backgrounds, and individual spiritual needs. That is why the military—in partnership with the sending denominations—seeks individuals who are well-balanced and mature; have a strong theological understanding and practice; and are able to work, without prejudices, with individuals from various backgrounds and faiths. Chaplains must also rid themselves of racial and sexual biases. The military, even more strongly than society as a whole, will not tolerate biases and narrowly-defined thinking about people and their needs. The best chaplains are those who are very secure in their faith persuasions, yet have a deep appreciation for the faith development of other individuals, their history, and their beliefs. The best chaplains are those who see pluralism as an opportunity, not a problem, are interested in people of different persuasions, and can creatively minister to and with them without violating their own religious doctrines and practices. Let us briefly survey some of the practices with these basic guidelines:[7]

(1) Worship/Preaching/Etc.

While a chaplain from a particular faith group may have an occasional opportunity to establish worship similar to what he/she would establish in a civilian church; normally this is the exception and not the rule. Normally, chaplains conduct general worship services, categorized under three major Christian groups (Protestant, Catholic, or Orthodox) in a general worship environment. That does not mean that chaplains become generic in their theology or preaching; rather, the preaching and worship should flow out of the deep tenets of the chaplains' faith, while always taking into consideration that their language, illustrations, and even Scriptures should

---

7 For complete descriptions of the duties of chaplains in the Air Force or Navy, see the following websites:
Air Force: http://www.usafhc.af.mil/whatwedo/index.asp.
Navy: http://www.tpub.com/content/religion/14230/css/14230_17.htm.

create an environment of cooperation, not defensiveness. Chaplains must always take into consideration their recipients or congregation. Common topics of salvation, the Spirit-led life, the mission of the church, and other scriptural themes are probably a more appropriate way to gain the confidence of military personnel and their family members. After that confidence is gained, the deeper tenets of a personal faith tradition can be shared, such as water baptism, holiness, baptism in the Spirit, etc.

Baptism in a Jungle

In 1967, our Mess Sergeant, who weighed more than 300 pounds, came forward to accept Jesus Christ as his Savior. As was typical with our services in Vietnam, we prepared to baptize this new convert. The only place to baptize him was a river adjacent to our base camp, which could be a danger to anyone who took the chance to cross the strong currents. To protect the soldier, we tied a strong rope around him. When he stepped into the river, to our surprise, he was caught by the currents and went downstream rather quickly. Fortunately, with plenty of strong young men, we eventually pulled him back in, and my good friend the Lutheran chaplain and I laid our hands on him and said, "In the name of the Father, the Son, and the Holy Spirit, we baptize you." The soldier's reply was, "Thank God we only have to do this once."

— Chaplain Robert Crick

(2) Pastoral Care

Most of the pastoral care in military settings begins around various needs that are identified initially as social or relational, not religious. For example, couples may seek help for marital difficulties, a soldier may be depressed, or may have gone AWOL and been required by the First Sergeant to seek counseling, etc. Chaplains are considered to be one of the first lines of defense when a military person or their family gets into trouble, even though the care recipients may not attend services or be a member of the chaplains' denomination. The best rule of thumb for the practice of pastoral care in the military is to receive them unconditionally. By giving good pastoral care to their human dilemmas and problems, chaplains establish credibility, and eventually they will be able to pass on to care recipients the deep spiritual tenets of their faith. Because pastoral care and counseling are a major component of the military chaplain's role, chaplains are encouraged to get clinical training, take marriage and family courses, and gain an understanding of suicide and suicide prevention, domestic violence, depression, and other human struggles.

Commanders and other leaders in the military generally think of the chaplains first when a member of their unit is struggling with a problem. While this is a heavy load for chaplains to bear, it is the best opportunity for them to establish the integrity of their own call to be a missionary in a military environment.

> It's everything you can imagine—pastoral ministry, missions work, counseling, critical ministry, teaching, combat patrols, and practically everything in between. For a ministry that is hands-on, this is the place—in Iraq with the troops. Every day is a reality check. Soldiers in a war zone have neither interest in, nor time for theological philosophizing. There is a kind of stern realism to their faith and an earnestness in their seeking God—tempered no doubt by the ever-present danger of their environment. I love serving with and ministering to these soldiers. — Chaplain Jeff Roberson, US Army

(3) Ministry Presence

Among the many duties of a military chaplain, chaplains must not forget that "presence" is one of their greatest spiritual tools. We have already considered in the theological section one aspect of presence: being physically, spiritually, and emotionally present with care recipients.[8] However, there is another sense of ministry presence that we must consider. Chaplaincy presence can also be understood as having established relationships with persons of all levels in the command, to the extent that even when chaplains are absent, their presence is felt. That is why chaplains must establish good relationships with their commanders, key officers, military personnel, and others who are in the leadership chain. As relationships establish, trust will develop. This is so important considering the high stress levels of military personnel, particularly in war zones. Having trustworthy chaplains present during extreme stress or in the middle of a terrible crisis is a reminder that the Lord is present in our deepest crises.

The Immeasurable Presence

> Church of God Army Chaplain, Barron Wester was seriously wounded in Iraq by sniper fire. Though his wounds were not

---

8   See "Ministry of Presence" in Unit one, chapter 3.

life-threatening, he required emergency evacuation to a major military hospital in Germany. Upon arriving in Germany, he was met by two Church of God Army chaplains—Joe Melvin and David Hall. "When we arrived, we found Barron ministering to another soldier from his unit who was wounded in the same attack. It was obvious this wounded soldier greatly respected his chaplain, and he was reaching out to one who could readily identify with the pain of loss and the devastating experience.

— Chaplain Joe Melvin, US Army

The value of the presence of a chaplain in crisis situations is immeasurable. They are reminders of the sacredness of the participants in great and terrible life events. They are a reminder that God is still present, even in the most catastrophic moments.

The same principle applies to soldiers and their family members. Chaplains must think of themselves as the chaplain to every soldier and every family member of their unit. Even though soldiers and families may go to other denominational chapels or services, or even off-base to a civilian church, the chaplain still must consider everyone within that unit as their flock. Everyone in the unit can get in touch with the chaplain for normal or emergency relationships, and other opportunities that enhance this special role as chaplain to the entire unit.

(4) Special Duties

In addition to normal, more traditional duties, chaplains conduct couples' and family retreats, oversee special youth assignments, serve as finance officers for the command chaplain's office, and have other special duties. Normally, before being assigned special duties, the chaplains are given the opportunity to receive additional training.

Air Force Chaplain, Gloria Tyner (CPT) was in Iraq at a large combat hospital. Both the dead and the severely wounded were brought into this intensive medical care area where Chaplain Tyner served as the First Respondent chaplain. She struggled with what her role should be in this medical unit: would she minister outside the surgical suite, or would she be called in after the doctors had finished their work? In correspondence with her MD director, it was decided that she would change into scrubs with the doctors and work/minister right in the middle of that crisis center as they dealt with seriously wounded and dying soldiers. Here, she brought God right into the middle of the medical mess. In her description of one day's activities (dealing with many seriously wounded soldiers and preparing the dead for proper shipment to the mortuary unit), the stark reality of her ministry of presence was most vivid in the blood-covered medical gown she wore. Later that day, before she left the surgical suite, she gathered a physically and emotionally exhausted staff around her to remind them that they had handled the very sacred bodies of individuals who were connected with moms and dads, sisters and brothers, and a church or community back home. Long before clean-up, they had a memorial service; and, as she related this experience she described it as a reenactment of how our Lord is personally involved in our deepest crisis.[9]

Critical Issues

1. How do you maintain the deep tenets of your own faith while serving in a vast, pluralistic environment?

"The blending of our American society with other cultures, traditions, and beliefs extends to our military and presents another difference between [military] chaplains and civilian ministers... Presently, the chaplaincy is a ministry made up of Christian pastors [and priests], Jewish Rabbis, Muslim Imams, and Buddhist chaplains, truly reflecting the diverse cultures of the chaplain's community of service. This diverse culture of the clergyman in the [military] chaplaincy is a pluralistic setting for ministry, and it demands that the chaplain minister under certain cultural restraints."[10]

These cultural restraints are bound by the legal system that guarantees all citizens the right to freely exercise or to refrain from personal religious practices. Furthermore, chaplains' responses to this issue stem from their personal and spiritual identity. If the chaplains are strong in their personal and faith identity, they have few problems working in a vast pluralistic environment. It is only when this identity is distorted that a chaplain

---

9   Chaplain Tyner's story is contributed to this chapter by way of the Chaplains Commission under the direction of Dr. Robert Crick, a retired and decorated Army Chaplain.

10   Mickey Jett. *Prospectus* presented to the staff of the Pentecostal School of Theology, Summer 2009, p.6. Bracketed information added.

will either approach pluralism in a defensive matter or will embrace it uncritically.

2. Whose religious program is it?

Chaplains must remember that as a military chaplain, this is not just their religious program, but the command's religious program. While commanders do not expect chaplains to dilute their own faith, they will very quickly let them know that it is the command's program, not theirs. In a legal way, this is carried out through an annual rating by supervisory chaplains and/or commanders. Mature chaplains will make sure that they understand the program to be the command's, and integrate their own goals and passions in a way that the command and the commander will claim them as their own. It all stems from how the chaplain approaches this special ministry in this special setting.

3. What is the code of ethics?

It should be noted that the military now recognizes more than 200 different faith groups who are legally eligible to send chaplains. It should also be pointed out that not only are all large and small Protestant denominations represented, but also Roman Catholics, Orthodox, Hindus, Buddhists, Muslims, Mormons and many other groups. Some of the critical issues involve the fact that a country which prides itself on the "separation of church and state," must also recognize groups that are not part of the mainstream of religious life in the US, such as Wiccans, Native American religions, and other religious groups. While these are a small minority, chaplains must remember that a democratic nation such as the U.S. cannot show preference for one group over others. That is both one of America's struggles and one of its great democratic successes.

While endorsements are rendered on a good faith basis between the military and the sending denomination, there are times when the endorsement has to be withdrawn. The withdrawal of an endorsement by a faith group happens when (1) the chaplain no longer is adhering to the principles, policies, and theology of that endorsing denomination, (2) the chaplain is charged and found guilty by the military for an indiscretion warranting such action, or (3) when a chaplain, for various reasons, desires to seek endorsement from another denomination. Often, that chaplain will either be withdrawn from the military or be asked to seek an endorsement from a denomination similar to the way in which s/he now practices his/ her faith. (In those cases, both endorsing groups talk about the desire for a transfer and reach some level of understanding and acceptance. If the two endorsing groups agree with the change of endorsement, the military reserves the right to review and approve the transfer based on their need for certain denominational chaplains.).

For the Sake of the Cause

Army Chaplain (CPT) Barron Wester, the only Church of God Chaplain to be wounded during the Persian Gulf conflict (to date), was hit by a sniper's bullet as he was attempting to give a final blessing to a Catholic soldier, apparently already dead, but trapped in his Humvee.

Chaplain Wester insisted, in the absence of his priest colleagues, "I just felt led to carry out, to the best of my abilities, the final prayers of one of my troopers." It should be noted that Chaplain Wester's life was saved, even though he did take a bullet, because his Chaplain's Assistant threw himself over Chaplain Wester, protecting him from any further injuries.

— COG Chaplains Commission

Conclusion

Military chaplaincy is an invaluable resource for our soldiers and their command. They are not just representatives of another religious institution; they are men and women who walk alongside the wounded, who sit with the bed-ridden, and who are present with the suffering of soldiers and their families. Chaplains celebrate life among the living and the dead; they represent hope beyond war, internal and international conflict, and natural disasters. Called by God to this setting, they are a constant reminder of the moral consciousness which is necessary even in times of war. For this reason, chaplains are an essential component of the military community.

CHAPTER NINE

Questions for Further Reflection

1. In the introduction to this section, the various fields of chaplaincy are briefly described. Provide a brief description of all three. Provide a well-developed sentence for each. (5 points)

2. Explain the origins of the word "chaplain" in a well-developed paragraph. (5 points)

3. Who began the use of military chaplains in the United States? When and why did he deem it necessary? Please submit a well-developed paragraph. (5 points)

4. Select one of the functions of a military chaplain, and, in one to two sentences, summarize that function. Describe how this particular function would be challenging for you and why. How might you resolve that issue? Your answer should be a well-developed paragraph. (5 points)

Case Study: Case studies are provided for class discussion. The goal is to get you thinking about how you might approach ministry from the perspective of a chaplain. Reflect on the class materials and prepare/develop a response to the following case study:

> Joe Smith is assigned to an army military unit, and his commander is Roman Catholic. Therefore, most likely, the commander will not be attending the worship services of his/her assigned chaplain. What is the best approach by the chaplain, working with this Roman Catholic Colonel, in understanding and assimilating the commander's ideas concerning the unit's religious program? List several things you think would be important to the chaplain, first, in establishing a relationship with his/her commander, and second, in finding out what the commander expects out of his/her chaplain. How should he develop a language that bridges these two religious traditions, which must work together towards the development of a common religious program that serves the soldiers and family members of that unit?

CHAPTER TEN

Clinical Chaplaincy[1]

I was sick and you visited me... —Matthew 25:36 (NASB)

The role of a clinical chaplain—whether in a hospital setting, a Hospice setting[2], a pastoral counseling setting, or any other clinical setting—stems from the belief that God cares for His creation. He cares for those who are experiencing sickness, disease, distress, marriage and family break-ups, and all the other human traumas that impact individuals and families. God's long interest in the care of people is well documented through scriptural writings, professional documents of the church, and the personal writings of the church fathers.

The Old Testament provides many examples of God caring for those going through pain and struggles. Our first example is Adam, whose struggle was not physical, but emotional. Adam was alone. God responded by creating Eve. The Psalms, like other Scriptures, deal with grief, emotional trauma, and even specific illnesses like venereal disease, leprosy, loneliness, disillusionment, and grief. In Mowinckel's[3] analysis of the Psalms, he contends that many of the Psalms were written specifically *for* individuals with specific problems and *by* individuals with specific problems. These ancient prayers and proclamations are honest and transparent disclosures of those in great crisis. While the specific ailment—

---

1   While this chapter is labeled "Clinical Chaplaincy," the principles in it can be expanded to the more general area of clinical pastoral care. Clinical pastoral care is a general term that describes any setting within the health-care system. This includes short-term hospital settings, mental health facilities, long-term care facilities (nursing homes), rehabilitation, hospice, etc. Clinical pastoral care is predominantly spiritual care for families and individuals who have mental, emotional, or physical needs.

2   "Hospice is generally considered a philosophy or program of care rather than a place. Hospice is a unique blend of services that address the physical, emotional, and spiritual needs of the terminally ill person and his/her family." Marcia Lattanzi-Licht, John L. Mahoney, and Galen W. Miller, *The Hospice Choice: In Pursuit of a Peaceful Death* (New York, NY: Simon and Shuster, 1998), 44. When a physician determines that a terminally ill person has less than six months to live, hospice is an option for specialized terminal care and guidance in the home, facility, or healthcare institution.

3   Sigmund Mowinckel, *The Psalms in Israel's Worship*, Vol.1-2, Translated by D.R. AP-Thomas in 1962 (Nashville, TN: Abingdon Press, 1967 revised).

> ## PSALM 6:1-10 (NIV)
>
> 1 O LORD, do not rebuke me in your anger or discipline me in your wrath.
>
> 2 Have mercy on me, LORD, for I am faint; heal me, LORD, for my bones are in agony.
>
> 3 My soul is in deep anguish. How long, LORD, how long?
>
> 4 Turn, LORD, and deliver me; save me because of your unfailing love.
>
> 5 Among the dead no one proclaims your name. Who praises you from the grave?
>
> 6 I am worn out from my groaning;
> all night long I flood my bed with weeping and drench my couch with tears.
>
> 7 My eyes grow weak with sorrow; they fail because of all my foes.
>
> 8 Away from me, all you who do evil, for the LORD has heard my weeping.
>
> 9 The LORD has heard my cry for mercy; the LORD accepts my prayer.
>
> 10 All my enemies will be overwhelmed with shame and anguish; they will turn back and suddenly be put to shame.

whether emotional, spiritual, or physical—is known only to the author, the experience of pain and internal conflict are universal.

Consider Psalm 6. We read about a man coming to terms with his own death. He expresses anger through his accusation (v. 1-3); he is desperate enough to bargain with God (v. 4-5); he gives in to his sadness (v. 6-7); he then accepts God's will for his life (v. 8-10). This psalm, written approximately 3,000 years ago, is textbook Elizabeth Kubler-Ross.[4] This psalm gives an inside look at an individual coming to terms with the dying process (denial, anger, bargaining, depression, and acceptance). The reader is witness to all but the first stage of grief in this psalm. The author gives word and expression to internalized pain. Chaplains who allow patients to speak give them the gift of validating their fears and pain. Chaplains do not force acceptance; they create an atmosphere that gives patients permission to move towards that place of acceptance at their own pace. Hospice chaplains are most familiar with this process, as they are present

---

4   Elisabeth Kubler-Ross, *On Death and Dying* (New York, NY: Scribner, 1969). Kubler-Ross studied the internalization of one's death process. In her studies, she discovered five stages that her patients experienced in their dying process: denial, anger, bargaining, depression, and acceptance.

with the family and the dying in their final stages of life.

The New Testament, like the Old Testament, lifts up a wide range of illnesses and distresses. Jesus showed great concern and compassion for individuals as He tended to the distressed, the lonely, and widows; those suffering imprisonment; those struggling with doubts, fears, and losses of all types; and other human experiences.

The spirit of the church as a "lighthouse of care" for individuals and families in need has been carried faithfully since the beginning of the early church. Special orders were developed through the Roman Catholic and Orthodox churches to care for lepers, orphans (creating orphanages of all types), the mentally ill, and widows. There seems to be no separation between physical and emotional needs. Out of a sense of compassion, food was provided for the poor, clothing for the naked, medical services for those with physical problems, and, most especially, compassion and counsel for those with emotional trauma. Francis of Assisi and other early church fathers were looked upon as those who underscored the need for the church to be compassionate.

Naturally, as the world became more sophisticated in its scientific and medical developments, these needs became more focused and categorized. In the early development of ministry in the United States, seminary candidates for pastoral ministries from schools such as William and Mary, Harvard, Yale, and other seminaries and Bible colleges were given special training in taking care of emergency physical needs, first-aid services, and those suffering emotional stresses. In fact, candidates for the ministry during the late 1600s and early 1700s were expected to be able to do emergency care like setting a broken bone. In addition, they were trained to deal with mental distresses. It is interesting that these candidates were trained to provide minor medical services, counsel those with special emotional and mental problems, and exorcise those with evil spirits. They did not see a disassociation from these various tasks. In a sense, they were probably more integrated in the role of pastor/care counselor than we are today. While priests and ministers have historically been equipped to care for these physical and emotional needs, the formal role of chaplain in these clinical areas did not get solidified until the late 1800s and early 1900s.

A shift in care occurred in the 1800s as secular agents arose that began to replace those services (medical and psychological care, welfare, etc.) that had been primarily rendered by the church. This included the rise of secular medical centers, the developing social work movement, psychology, and other agencies and programs now primarily operating apart from the church. Freud, in his work from the 1900s forward, began to identify the need for those specially trained people within a secular context. Some would say that the church gave up its prominent role as social organizations replaced the care services of the church.

In the 1920s to 1930s, seminaries, church agencies, and local churches shifted again towards social ministries. This movement brought about clinical organizations such as the Association of Clinical Pastoral Education, the American Protestant Hospital Association (later called the Association of Professional Chaplains[5]), and other organizations that began to emphasize putting chaplains into medical, counseling, and other clinical settings. Today, medical, psychological, and other agencies are required, in order to be accredited, to have chaplains and other spiritual specialists to ensure that the patient is treated holistically—physically, socially, and spiritually.

Legitimacy: An Illustration of a Worthy Ministry

The constant pace of a Long Term Care facility (LTC) is abrasive to the emotions of the caregiver. Often, personnel have chosen to be emotionally distant from residents due to previous personal hurt. The tragedy is the isolation that happens to the person who truly needs care and support on an individual level. Staff and family members can walk away when times are difficult, but residents are often left alone. Without the commitment of people who are willing to contribute hope for each day, the LTC facility becomes a lonely place.

> I personally experienced miracles at a facility that did not give up on tomorrow, and which was willing to join together to make things better for each patient. One blessing I received came from a 97-year-old blind, Catholic woman, named Lillian. One busy day, she grabbed my arm as I was passing her in the hallway. I was late for a meeting, but she insisted that I stop for a moment so that she could pray for me as she "felt that God wanted to provide strength." Although I needed to hurry on and deal with two deaths that had occurred that day, I responded to her request and knelt beside her wheelchair. She was neither brief, nor quiet with her prayer, yet something wonderful happened to me as she prayed. God's Spirit renewed my inner man, right there in the middle of the hall. Lillian called on me many times for prayer that was directed towards the chaplain (me), and I found her timing very accurate. I remember participating in her funeral, and feeling the peace of knowing that this child of God, who was a partner in bringing hope to this LTC, was now

---

5 For a more in-depth look at the history of this professional organization, its creators, and its work in training and educating chaplains since the 1940s, see the Association of Professional Chaplains' website: www.professionalchaplains.org.

home with God. Residents (and chaplains) are spiritually and emotionally uplifted when hope for tomorrow becomes real to them. How will they hear this message of hope without a messenger? — *Chaplain Bill Broughton*

Education, Training, and Endorsement

Like military chaplains, those assigned to hospitals, hospice centers, pastoral counseling centers, and other agencies that provide physical and emotional care must be endorsed by a faith group. While these clinical settings set their own standards for hiring chaplains and other pastoral specialists, they normally include:

- A Masters of Divinity degree or an equivalent theological degree from an accredited institution. Candidates should have had (through seminary and other specialized programs) courses and internships that provide an understanding of individuals with physical and emotional problems and understanding of the way in which these clinical institutions function.

- Beyond seminary, most clinical settings want chaplaincy candidates who have had some clinical training, either through the Association of Clinical Pastoral Education or an equivalent training agency. For those going into pastoral counseling ministries in these centers, there also must be training and understanding of family systems, family problems, drug and alcohol addictions, divorce and remarriage, and other issues that are characteristic of those seeking services through these agencies.

- Endorsement from a recognized faith group.

Religious/denominational endorsement means the following:

- The chaplains commission attests to the fact that a person meets the standards necessary for ministry within clinical settings.

- The candidate understands the rights of individuals who are confined to hospitals and other similar clinical agencies.

- He/she knows how to work with chaplains of other denominations and with other professionally trained persons in these clinical settings.

- The chaplain has clinical training that has allowed him/her to flush out any "hidden agendas" or personal dysfunctions that would limit the ability to work with people with serious physical and emotional problems. A good example of this level of maturity is the way Jesus Christ dealt with hurting people. He allowed them to pass their stories through His spiritual conduit without His problems becoming entangled with theirs. A mature and healthy chaplain can work with individuals, accept them and their stories unconditionally, and process that through his/her own experiences and training in a highly professional manner.

- A chaplain is held accountable in two areas: first, he/she represents a particular faith group and is true to the tenets of that faith; second, he/she has the professional training/posture to approach work as a clinical chaplain at the high level that is maintained by other professionals in different disciplines.

The Functions of the Clinical Chaplain

Like in the military, when chaplains are hired at a hospital, they come to understand that their ministry mission is subordinate to the greater mission of the hospital. While these clinical settings want chaplains who are firmly committed to their own faith persuasions, they must be mature enough to understand that faith is worked and lived out in a pluralistic environment representing people of many different faith backgrounds. One way this and many other issues are kept accountable is through a *code of ethics* that chaplains, like other professionals, must adhere to on a regular basis. This code includes: (1) respect for the patient's rights to either accept the chaplain's spiritual offerings or reject them; (2) the chaplain is there to give pastoral care, not proselytize. Evangelism is not restricted, but it must be initiated on the part of the patient, not imposed by the chaplain; and, (3) in giving pastoral care, chaplains respect the care recipient's faith history. Chaplains give pastoral care, but have an understanding and respect for the context in which they find the patient. If care recipients want particular religious rites—such as baptism or communion—chaplains must be able to either provide them without violation of their own denominational principles and practices or find someone of that faith persuasion that can carry out the spiritual rituals. The following is a more detailed description of each of these functions.

Worship within the Clinical Setting:

Again, like military chaplains, clinical chaplains must not leave behind any of their faith principles and practices, and must be mature enough to practice them in a way that is not offensive to the pluralistic audience of their particular clinical setting. Hospital settings provide for many worship opportunities. Chaplains, out of their own deep faith and convictions, preach sermons and lead worship in a way that keeps their spiritual relationship alive with people of many different persuasions.

Pastoral Care:

While clinical chaplains draw from their deep religious traditions and understanding of people in need, they realize that they are talking and sharing with individuals who come from an entirely different context. The key is to draw from these tenets, but also to have a common language and approach that keeps them in a good pastoral relationship with the care recipient. In the following example, that common language came in the form of a beloved hymn shared by Christians beyond denominational lines:

> I recently had one of those "Oh yes, Lord, you *are* using me" moments. I was called to the emergency room to be with a woman because her mother was dying. At a point after we had spoken and I had been listening to her, I felt the Lord prompt me to ask her if she would like for me to sing a hymn to her mother. She enthusiastically said "Oh yes, please sing Amazing Grace." She began to weep, along with others, including nurses, who had come into the room. As the end drew near for her mother, she asked me to sing to her again as she went home to be with the Lord. — Keena Cox, Hospital Chaplain

Confidentiality is one of the most cherished and essential elements of the pastoral care relationship. Beyond the security of personal, emotional disclosure, chaplains protect patients' personal information, whether medical history, family history, current needs, and critical issuess, which they must handle in a mature, confidential matter. There are special circumstances in which they must tell the patient that this information has to be shared; generally in the area of some type of child or spousal abuse, or some other area that legally requires them to disclose that information to another professional.[6]

Administration in Clinical Settings:

Chaplains, while in a primary role of giving care to patients and staff, are also expected to be mature, professional administrators. Chaplains will often serve on various clinical committees: ethics, medical options, family support, and the like. In these administrative roles, chaplains must draw from deep faith and specialized training as valuable members of the clinical staff. In a sense, they bring a moral consciousness to medical services by ensuring that all individuals receive quality care regardless of economic status, religious preference, or any other factor that may require a spiritual spokesperson to represent the patient's needs and concerns.

6　The general rule of thumb for an ethical and legal breach of confidentiality is if the patient is a threat to themselves, others, or their country.

Critical Issues

The Integration of Theology and Practice

How do chaplains bring together deep spiritual history/training with clinical training and the insight necessary to serve in clinical settings? And how are these integrated into the practice of ministry? A central issue that student chaplains face is the integration of personal theology and professional practice. As they come to understand and embrace clinical processes and gain critical thinking skills, they often struggle with how these skills factor into the tenets of their faith. This may lead to some internal conflicts when ministering to families who want divine healing—which the chaplain believes in—but the reality of death is impending. While chaplains must not let go of their theological identity, they must find a way to make room within that theology for practice in a clinical setting. In this way, death and healing, divine authority v. corporate authority, and personal practice v. public practice can be issues that lead to a deepened sense of both spiritual practice and divine presence.

Death and Healing

Ministering to the dying and to grieving families is a daunting, challenging, but rewarding task for any minister of the Lord who truly prays to be a strength and a blessing. In some traditions, chaplains believe that the power of the Holy Spirit can supernaturally heal any manner of disease or illness at any time or place. Many sick persons and their families look to chaplains for the prayers or the touch of supernatural faith that will move God to remove or rebuke the painful or destructive physical symptoms that lead to death, to avert death itself, and sometimes, to reverse death when it has happened. In addition, the dying persons and their families or friends desperately seek comfort and consolation from the minister that will ease emotional and spiritual pain and calm their anxious souls. The problem is we often assume that patients who are sick are powerless. The opposite is true.

> During one of my hospital assignments, a group of dying female cancer patients requested, at Easter, to discuss their death. As they gathered together, some too weak to get out of bed, they talked about their impending death, and asked all those questions one would expect. What happens after death? To what extent will I know when I am in the arms of the Lord? And, most especially, what can I do to prepare my family for this critical moment? This taught me that patients were more ready to discuss impending death than their family, and sometimes, even their chaplains. — *Chaplain Robert D. Crick*

146

If chaplains are truly honest in their experiences, more often, God does not answer the prayers for physical or emotional healing in the manner that they (we) would like; rather, He allows the dying ones and their families to walk through the valley of the shadow of death at the time God chooses for His purposes and for His glory. — Chaplain Susan Harper[7]

Who Has What Authority?

Ministers assigned as chaplains in clinical settings are confronted with the reality that this is not just their program, but the hospital's or the hospital administrator's. How does a chaplain, who is used to being in charge of a local church, work as a subordinate team member under the authority of a hospital administrator? This happens first as a result of a submissive and humble heart that seeks to serve. Second, it happens successfully when the pastor/chaplain recognizes and validates secular authority as directed by God. These systems play a necessary role in the privilege of having a pastoral care unit provided as a part of patient care. These systems ensure the rights of the patient and the patient's family and keep us in check even when our intentions are good and charitable.

In the late 1960s, I was doing a one-year residency at the National Institute of Health. My assignment was with the Children's Leukemia Unit. One of the patients, a bright fifteen-year-old, was diagnosed with advanced stages of leukemia. In visiting her room almost daily, we formed a very good pastor-patient relationship. In our conversations, she said she wanted to recommit her life to Christ.

This sounded rather standard to me as a chaplain. But, a couple of days later, I was called in by my CPE Supervisor, who said, "The family has requested that you not be allowed to visit their daughter any longer." I was devastated. My spiritual and pastoral authority seemed to be violated. In processing this with my supervisor, he finally said, "It is their daughter; you must honor this request. But there is nothing that keeps you from visiting the parents." After smoothing my ruffled spiritual feathers, I began to visit the parents on a regular basis. As you might suspect, after a week or so, the father said to

---

7   Dr. Susan Harper is currently the Director of Pastoral Care at Hutcheson Medical Center in Fort Oglethorpe, Georgia. An ordained minister and seasoned clinical chaplain, Susan writes about ministry to the dying from over forty years of health and spiritual care experience in a variety of settings. This passage was taken from an unpublished essay entitled, A *Pentecostal Perspective on Ministry to the Dying,* submitted to the Church of God Chaplains Commission, 2009.

me, "You can visit our daughter now if you would like." In a baptismal service, led by me with the family's Reformed pastor, we celebrated the re-affirmation of her faith. She died a few weeks after the service. Forty year later, I still correspond with her family.[8]

There are several lessons to be learned in this case. First, it is important to recognize the girl's faith context, her family, and her tradition, which was the Reformed tradition. Secondly, it is important to recognize the wise supervision resulting in not just considering my faith and her faith, but "their faith" and "our faith." Third, this is a case that positions the church in the marketplace, beyond the gates and beyond our comfort zones, into many crisis areas.

Personal Practice and Pluralism

This issue examines how chaplains can and must maintain an authentic faith tradition while serving those who have very different faith beliefs. For example, Chaplain Grey, a Presbyterian, may be called to provide pastoral care to a Muslim in the absence of an Imam. The question she will face is how to fulfill her calling as a Presbyterian chaplain while working with these individuals, respecting their faith stories, and at the same time being a genuine Presbyterian caregiver? Denying her faith tradition will not make her more capable; rather, it may hinder her work as the chaplain and as a genuine conduit of care. In other words, Chaplain Grey's denial of her authentic identity may create an atmosphere that denies the recipient's faith tradition/identity by trying to maintain a more mainstream feel. However, the recipient may need to rely on his/her own tradition for comfort and encouragement. The other side of this is that Chaplain Grey's acceptance of her faith identity gives the recipient permission to find healing and encouragement through his/her own specific faith tradition. It is very important, however, for chaplains to remember that their goal is not to proselytize, but to provide spiritual care for individuals amidst their faith traditions.

Conclusion

Many psalms have been written about the afflictions and sicknesses of God's people. These writers, tormented by their physical or mental anguish, sought some kind of answer or resolution. Yet, none are as memorable as Psalm 23:4, "Though I walk through the valley of the shadow of death, I will fear no evil, for you are with me; your rod and your staff, they comfort me." What is the resolve this psalmist comes to? Presence. The psalmist finds rest in the revelation that he is not alone—not outside God's reach—even in the

---

8 This case study is by Robert Crick, Director of the COG Chaplains Commission.

valley of the shadow of death. For those facing insurmountable health issues, that valley is reality. The good news is that, even in fear and despair, they are not alone. Chaplains can be the presence of God, the presence of comfort, that helps patients and their families discover hope and healing amidst the most devastating circumstances. While chaplains may have little to do with the medicines administered or the vitals that are catalogued, their presence is undoubtedly a significant part of the healing process that takes place every day in hospitals all over this country and others. They speak to the spirit of those they sit with and offer a balm that can only come from the hand of a merciful God.

Excursus

Mental Health Chaplains

Clinical chaplaincy has grown into a field as diverse as the medical profession it serves. Part of the field is the growing ministry of chaplains within the mental health community. As Americans become more aware of the devastating effects of mental disorders on individuals, families, and communities, the recognition of the need for holistic care in this area becomes more apparent. According to the National Institute of Mental Health (NIMH),[9] approximately one in every four adults (25%) suffers from some kind of diagnosable mental disorder each year. This includes depression, anxiety, Critical Incident Stress, and even Post Traumatic Stress Disorder (PTSD). While most individuals can still function on a daily basis, there are those—about one in seventeen individuals—who suffer from serious mental illness.[10] Many of those who are not institutionalized will find themselves living homeless on the streets or caught up in criminal activity (such as drug abuse or petty theft) in order to survive. The burden of mental illness on society, according to research by NIMH, is greater than that caused by *all* cancers.[11] There is no doubt the need for an effective and caring response is great.

Legitimacy

Although Anton Boisen's CPE model evolved out of his experience with a mental disorder and institutionalization, clinical chaplains have predominantly made their impact in the medical community, such as hospitals, hospice, etc. The ongoing hurdle for some is still the stigma attached to mental illness. Chaplain Craig Rennebohm captures this in his

---

9   National Institute of Mental Health, "Statstics", NIMH website. http://www. nimh.nih.gov/health/topics/statistics/index.shtml.

10 Ibid.

11 Ibid.

essay "Spiritual Care with Psychiatric Patients."[12] Rennebohm explains how in his early years of chaplaincy (approximately twenty years ago), he decided to include the psychiatric ward in his clinical rounds. He was finally called into a meeting by resident psychiatrists who asked him, "What are you doing here?" The question speaks volumes about how society approaches (or doesn't approach) spiritual care with the mentally ill. While great strides have been made to overcome these stigmas, chaplains must recognize the magnitude of care for this often forgotten segment of our society. In understanding this, two questions must be addressed.

First, why do mental health patients need spiritual care? "The most powerful antidote for the internal effects of stigma and discrimination is spiritual strength. Reinforcement of the conviction that God loves us and is with us even in our most difficult times is of utmost importance."[13] Second, what role do chaplains play in the healing process? Gunnar Christiansen of the National Alliance on Mental Illness (NAMI) notes,

> "Scripture repeatedly tells us that God wants us to come to him... He wants us to have a place of refuge... He wants us to have peace. He also wants his voice of love and compassion to be heard and he wants us to do the talking just as he directed Moses... in Exodus 4:11-12... David makes it clear in Psalm 37 that God wants us to aid in advocating for that which is just."[14]

In other words, "[Chaplains are] here to care for the spiritual concerns which arise for [their] patients in the course of their illness and healing." Holistic healing is not reserved for patients who are suffering from physical health issues. It is a necessary part of the ongoing healing process for patients who suffer from all kinds of sickness and disease, including mental illness.

The Model

Rennebohm offers a four-part approach to this vital, chaplaincy ministry: discernment, understanding, meaningful spiritual practice, and a supportive faith community.[15] As a spiritual care provider, Rennebohm helps his care recipients discern what part of their experience is the result of illness and what part is an authentic spiritual experience. Second, he assists the care recipient in understanding the illness experience in light of their faith background. Third, he helps care recipients consider spiritual practices that

---

12 Craig Rennebohm, "Spiritual Care with Psychiatric Patients," The Mental Health Chaplain website. http://www.mentalhealthchaplain.org/index.htm, p.1.

13 Gunnar Christiansen, M.D., "Stigma of Mental Illness: The Role of the Faith Community," National Alliance on Mental Illness website. http://www.nami.org/Content/ContentGroups/Faith/Stigma_The_Role_of_the_Faith_Community.htm

14 Ibid.

15 Ibid.

are meaningful and helpful, not detrimental, to their well-being. Fourth, Rennebohm helps the recipient find a faith community where they are accepted, understood, and supported. These communities must foster an atmosphere in which their life is recognized as meaningful and purposed.

Myrtle and Her Flower Garden

I was Chaplain at a large mental hospital in Nashville, Tennessee, with well over 1,000 patients. The only way we could get Myrtle, a 70 year-old patient, out of her depressed state was with the words, "Myrtle, if you don't get up, your flowers will die in your garden." That little sense of responsibility, of taking care of her small flower garden, would often motivate her to get out of bed, and to go through, though painfully, the daily chores of life. At her funeral and burial, I was happy to let the congregation of staff and patients know that, "This morning, as we celebrate this worship, Myrtle's flowers occupy our altar to the glory of God."

— Chaplain Robert Crick, D.Min.

The Mental Health Chaplain's DNA

The vision to care for society's most vulnerable citizens must include those made vulnerable by mental illness. Mental illness can be devastating for families and individuals, and mental health chaplains can offer direction, hope and even formation during these terribly trying times. Whether as a paid chaplain in a mental hospital or a volunteer working with those on the streets, this is a vital ministry for our communities.[16]

---

16 For more information on mental health chaplaincy, see: http://www. mentalhealthchaplain.org/index.htm or www.pathway2promise.org.

CHAPTER TEN:

Questions for Further Reflection

1. Spiritual care providers in the clinical setting have a code of ethics that the chaplain, like other professionals, must adhere to on a regular basis. In a well-developed paragraph, describe the three parts of this code as listed in this chapter. (5 points)

2. Read Psalm 42 and 43. Reflect on what the writer is trying to communicate. What is his struggle? How is he attempting to deal with it? What is his view of God? In what way is God present? Please submit a well-developed answer. (5 points)

3. Read Psalm 137. Reflect on what the writer is trying to communicate. Generally, we like issues to be resolved and the writer (or care recipient) to be in a better place by the end. That is not the case in this psalm. What is the author's struggle? What role does the psalmist give God in his crisis? Please use only the information given in the passage. Your role as chaplain is not to fix his problem. So, what is your role in this visit? Please submit a well-developed response, answering all of the questions listed fully. (5 points)

4. According to Chaplain Crick, when did the role of chaplain become formalized in the clinical setting? At the same time, the church was losing its dominant "care" role in society. What was taking place that led to these changes? Be specific in your answer. (5 points)

Case Study: Case studies are provided for class discussion. The goal is to get you thinking about how you might approach ministry from the perspective of a chaplain. Reflect on the class materials and prepare/develop a response to the following case study:

> You are a Pentecostal chaplain assigned to a 200-bed hospital. You have been at this hospital for a number of years, and are a well-respected member of the staff. A 16-year-old girl who has been raped is a patient at the hospital, facing the decision whether to keep her child or abort it. You have been asked by the staff to work with her so that she reaches the right decision "for her." How will you approach her, and how will you deal with the staff, most of whom basically favor an abortion, in your counseling/consultations?

152

CHAPTER ELEVEN
Correctional Chaplaincy

Correctional chaplains, similar to their counterparts in the military and in hospitals, provide spiritual care to those who are disconnected from the general community by certain circumstances. This is the case with those who are incarcerated and with correctional staff and their families who often find themselves isolated. Each correctional chaplain is also a representative of his or her particular faith group and is required to be endorsed by a religious body in order to become a chaplain.[1] — Paul Rogers, President ACCA

Prisoners and their families have been receiving spiritual care as early as biblical times. In the First Century, Timothy tended to Paul's needs while Paul was imprisoned. Since the first century, preachers have visited prisons seeking to feed and convert their captive audiences. Ministry has been so prevalent in these settings that prison chaplaincy has come to be seen by the state and wardens as a regular part of the rehabilitation process. However, this by no means suggests that religious pursuits are a mandatory part of prisoner rehabilitation in the United States. Freedom of religion is still a sacred right to be protected for all those who choose and refuse to practice religion. Nevertheless, the presence of ministers offering hope, basic essentials, prayer, education, etc., has been a common and essential part of prison life since its recognition by wardens as an official state position in June of 1886.[2] At this time, three New England chaplains came together to form the American Correctional Association. Today, that group is known as the American Correctional Chaplains Association.[3]

---

1   Paul Rogers, "Correctional Chaplains Calming the Storms of Life for Staff and Inmates" *Corrections Today*, February 2003. (*Editor's Note: This article is the first of a three-part series written by members of the American Correctional Chaplains Association about the role of chaplains in the corrections community. The other two articles are available via the American Correctional Chaplains Association's website.*)

2   Ibid.

3   Ibid.

Legitimacy of the Prison Chaplain

"Five million people in the United States are under the supervision of the criminal justice system. Two million are in prisons or jails while the rest are on probation or parole. Over 500,000 Americans on any given day are arrested and locked up for a variety of criminal activity. If it continues to increase, and it will, this number will soon rival the six million students that are enrolled in the nation's higher education systems.

Five billion dollars each year is spent to operate prisons and jails in the United States. Yet, crime and the uncertainty of what to do with those who commit crime remains."[4]

Given the already staggering number of individuals in the criminal justice system, the value of prison ministry is undeniable. The hope of the prison experience is beyond segregating offenders from the rest of society; it is rehabilitation and transformation through sanctification and regeneration. God is still a God who is present in all places, including prisons. There is no place we can conceive of that is so horrific that it is outside of His ability to be present and to be revealed. These men, women, and young people—like us—are in desperate need of a savior to help them overcome the woes, the cycle of generational sins, and the mindset that this is their purposed destination. Truth in love is what prison ministry must communicate. They must know there is still hope, and they must know there is still a purposed existence for their life. And they must know that nothing—not even the most heinous crime—will separate them from the love of Christ.

I was in prison, and you came to me. — Matthew 25:36

This excerpt from Matthew 25 speaks of God's affirmation and blessing on those who minister to all people in all conditions. This example in particular, is an indicator of God's love for those mothers, sons, friends, and fathers who are currently in our prison systems. God does not forget the hungry, the thirsty, the naked, or the imprisoned, nor does God forget

---

4 Quote is taken from the *Jail and Prison Volunteer Ministry and Chaplaincy* training manual for the Church of God Chaplains Commission, p.2, by Dean Yancey of "Prison Ministry." For the most current statistics on the criminal justice system's occupancy, consult the National Criminal Justice Reference Service website, particularly the "Bureau of Justice Statistics." These statistics are submitted annually.

those who care for individuals and families in need. Hebrews 6:10 states, "God is not unjust; he will not forget your work and the love you have shown him as you have helped his people and continue to help them." In Matthew 25, Jesus teaches that care for the needy is not just an Old Testament practice; rather, it is the mandate of every believer who seeks to please God. Thus, the ministry of prison chaplaincy is an imperative. The author of Hebrews writes, "Keep on loving each other as brothers... Remember those in prison as if you were their fellow prisoners, and those who are mistreated as if you yourselves were suffering."[5] This passage is a stark reminder that we must not love with empty emotions, but with action. How do we love our brothers and sisters in prison? We must go to them and offer care, support, guidance, encouragement, and hope that a greater life (in Christ) awaits them.

> Practical reasons must be considered when developing the need to minister to prisoners and their families. Everyone wants a safe, crime-free environment in which to live. The rapid rise in crime is underscored by the equally rapid rise in prison population which has grown at a rate of more than six times that of the overall U.S. population. Inmate population today is estimated at approximately 1.9 million souls, including local, state, and federal institutions. The rising threat of violence can only be stemmed by the work of God in the hearts of men. Rehabilitation does not seem to work, but regeneration, true regeneration works every time. The Gospel of Jesus Christ must be proclaimed to those behind bars. Responsible behavior can develop as one is made new by the resurrection power of the Savior.[6]

The church has a responsibility to serve and tend to the physical and spiritual needs of those imprisoned. Of course, laws and facility regulations determine to what degree this can take place. However, laws and regulations must not be an excuse for neglect. What makes this ministry legitimate is the same thing that makes all chaplaincy ministries legitimate: human beings are in need of care. They suffer from brokenness, fear, loneliness, unforgiveness, personal and emotional limitations, broken relationships, loss, and so many other things that all people suffer through. Chaplains can offer a better, alternative approach to responding to these personal trials.

---

5   Hebrews 13:1, 3, New International Version.

6   Dean Yancey, *Prison Ministry: The Responsibility of all Christians is to Minister to Inmates and Their Families*, Introduction. Publishing information is not available.

Educational, Training, and Endorsement Requirements

Professional Requirements

Specific training and requirements vary according to the particular prison facility.[7] Private institutions may follow the state guidelines or federal guidelines; both can be found online. The following is a description of the qualifications for employment at a federal facility:[8]

> **Qualifications:** GS-12: must have successfully completed an undergraduate degree from an accredited college or university and a Master of Divinity degree or the equivalent (20 graduate hours of theology, 20 graduate hours of sacred writings, 20 graduate hours of church history or comparative religions, and 20 graduate hours of ministry courses) from an American Theological School (ATS) accredited residential seminary or school of theology; ordination or membership in an ecclesiastically recognized religious institute of vowed men or women; at least 2 years of autonomous experience as a religious/spiritual leader in a parish or specialized ministry setting; current ecclesiastical endorsement by the recognized endorsing body of the faith tradition; willingness to provide and coordinate programs for inmates of all faiths; and the necessary credentials and the ability to provide worship services in his/her faith tradition.[9]

Person of the Chaplain

The person of the chaplain must be considered, also. While training and educational preparations are necessary indicators of professional skill and religious commitment, they are not the only indicators of pastoral effectiveness. Prison chaplains must be able to function within the unique and intense environment of the prison setting.[10] This requires an awareness of the many social and cultural dimensions that are interwoven into the fabric of the institution, including an awareness of the mindset, learned behaviors, and survival mode of prisoners. An appropriate awareness of

---

7   Naomi K. Paget and Janet R. McCormack, Chapter 7 in *The Work of the Chaplain* (Valley Forge, PA: Judson Press, 2006).

8   Paget and McCormack (2006, chapter 7) suggest using the federal guidelines for qualifications as a starting point, since states and private institutions may look to this criterion for guidance.

9   This job description is taken directly from the Federal Department of Corrections' website at http://www.bop.gov/jobs/job_descriptions/chaplain.jsp.

10 Naomi K. Paget and Janet R. McCormack, chapter 7 in *The Work of the Chaplain* (Valley Forge, PA: Judson Press, 2006).

these issues and wisdom in how to interact with the prison population are essential elements to being effective in this specialized ministry.

Another aspect is character. Chaplains must be who they say they are and aware of who they represent at all times.[11] Both inmates and staff are watching. Integrity, acceptance, wisdom, and fairness must be at the core of the person of the chaplain. One important rule to internalize is "firm, fair, and consistent."[12] Prisoners will try staff on this by watching for favoritism and lack of integrity. And when they waiver inmates will let them know. The mark of a good chaplain, then, is the ability to love as God loves: unequivocally, indiscriminately, and judiciously.

Functions of the Prison Chaplain

Prison chaplains have become necessary participants in the life and function of the prison system. This is due in part to their function on two levels: first, they seek to accommodate every prisoner's rights, as a US citizen, in the free pursuit of religious expression; second, in doing so, they are participating in the rehabilitation of these prisoners. In this section we will explore the many roles and functions that a prison chaplain will have to fulfill, including pastor, teacher, counselor, administrator, and advocate.[13]

Pastor

"The primary role of the Chaplain is to be a minister performing pastoral care for committed offenders. His/her ministry is that of preacher, shepherd, spiritual leader, and personal witness."[14]As preachers, prison chaplains perform the liturgical duties which are consistent with their own broad religious affiliation, such as leading a worship service or offering prayer to participants. These services are often geared to a broad spectrum of participants; for example, chaplains may hold Protestant worship services that focus on the commonalities of their branch of Christianity, rather than a specific denomination within it. Volunteers are then brought

---

11 Yancey, *Prison Ministry: The Responsibility of all Christians is to Minister to Inmates and Their Families.*

12 This is one of several core principles taken from Cornell Abraxas, a juvenile drug and alcohol rehabilitation center.

13 See also the job description as defined by the Federal Department of Corrections: Chaplain—GS-060-12. Chaplains administer, supervise, and perform work involved in a program of spiritual welfare and religious guidance for inmates in a correctional setting. http://www.bop.gov/jobs/job_descriptions/chaplain.jsp.

14 Yancey, *Prison Ministry: The Responsibility of all Christians is to Minister to Inmates and Their Families .*

in for the many services and religious ceremonies that occur outside of their specific religious affiliation. Priests will oversee Catholic services; rabbis will oversee Jewish ceremonies and services; etc.

Prison chaplains shepherd the community of the institution offering spiritual care to both staff and inmates. As shepherds and spiritual leaders, they are present with the community of the institution in daily matters and in times of crisis. It is in the little tasks of the day to day that they have the opportunity to build trusting relationships and to be a personal witness about Christ to prisoners and staff alike. Here, they are called on to assist inmates in very practical ways. They assist prisoners with completing legal documents or letter writing/reading; as shepherds, they may even visit the families of prisoners; and wait with inmates before surgery, trial, and parole hearings.[15] The mere presence of these shepherds can change the atmosphere of a room. They don't demand order; they are witnesses to the ordering power of the holy, Creator God. While a certain reverence is natural, much of this comes from developed and invested relationships with the inmates and staff.

The pastoral role must also present opportunities for the inmates to be reconciled with their past as part of the process of reconciling with God, society, and any others who shared in the criminal event, such as the victim(s). It cannot be stressed enough how pivotal it is for this to be done without judgment of crime or the inmate's personal history. These men and women are beloved and valued sons and daughters of God. Please note: this is not always easy. Chaplains come to the ministry experience with their own life experiences too. For example,

> When I was about 19 years old, I used to hold services on Saturday nights for women in the city jail. One night an old friend and former classmate attended our meeting. I had not expected to see her there, and I had no idea why this friend had found herself in jail. Near the end of the service, she approached me in tears because she was there for stealing my mother's checkbook, which amounted to merely a few hundred dollars stolen (I had actually forgotten about this event). Thankfully, the Lord extended to me wisdom beyond my young years. My goal that night was to offer reconciliation to these women with God; but that night my dear friend and I experienced another— often forgotten—dimension of reconciliation, that with self and with victim. Had there been any judgment in my heart towards her she could not have fully received that inner healing that is found only in forgiveness by God, of self, and of victim.

---

15 Naomi K. Paget and Janet R. McCormack, Chapter 7 in *The Work of the Chaplain* (Valley Forge, PA: Judson Press, 2006).

This story is from my ministry experience as a young, untrained woman in jail ministry. Although I couldn't have understood the significance of such an opportunity, I am truly thankful that God's Spirit guided me in His desire to extend love and reconciliation to a friend in great need. Isn't that the heart of chaplaincy? These men and women and young people are not faceless numbers simply recorded on our monthly ministerial records; they are friends worthy of being valued; autonomous human beings with personal history and narrative.

— Brandelan S. Miller

Chaplains must be aware of their own issues they bring to the ministry experience so they are never a hindrance for those inmates who are seeking a dynamic transformation through salvation and forgiveness.

Teacher

As teachers, prison chaplains have the awesome responsibility of discipling inmates who desire a mature relationship with Jesus Christ. This may be done through a regular Bible study or class. In addition to religious education, they provide moral instruction on how to make good decisions and how to be good citizens, fathers, mothers, etc. The most effective means of communicating these truths, though, is through modeling positive behaviors to both inmates and staff.

We have a special coffee house ministry at our prison that operates similar to other coffee house programs on the streets. It is a time where our inmates can simply open up. One of our Christian inmates told me that he was born two months premature to parents who were 'permanent drunks.' Over the years, his mother told him how much she hated him, how much money he was costing them, taking away from their liquor needs. She beat him, and one time chained him to the washing machine with a dog collar around his neck. By the time he was five years old, he learned to hate her passionately. He stated that, in his anger, he would cut the throats of puppies and kittens, and each time would picture his mother in his mind. At the age of fifteen, he was riding with a well-known motorcycle gang who made him the 'enforcer' (hired killer). One night, while attending our Mug-Shot Café, he had a long talk with a Christian inmate, and, by his own reports, went back to his cell, laid on his bed, and cried out for God to save him. He has never been the same since. After I baptized him, he wrote his mother a letter forgiving her. He told me this story with the greatest and most sincere smile I had ever witnessed.[16]

— Prison Chaplain Joseph Miller, Newland, NC

Counselor

As discussed many times in this study, a major component to chaplaincy in all areas is that of counselor. Since families are separated due to incarceration, chaplains may be called upon to provide marital counseling, pre-marital counseling, family counseling, etc. During their stay, inmates may also experience the loss of loved ones or friends. Thus, chaplains are responsible for "death notifications" and the aftermath of emotions that come with those notifications. Adding to the complexity and layers of issues, too often families and friends disconnect—intentionally or unintentionally—from the inmate. This too is a personal loss, and the inmate will have to work through the layers of grief, separation, and loneliness associated with it. Prison chaplains provide necessary care for those wounded individuals who, while still going through all the same crises as any other "free world"[17] individual, are also isolated from their families and from their support systems.

Prisoners are not the only recipients of pastoral counseling; chaplains are also available to the staff and administration. Prison work is very stressful, to say the least. Guards must always be on watch for their own safety and that of co-workers and inmates. One wrong move or bad decision can cost the worker greatly—even wrong decisions with good motives. Chaplains are present for staff dealing with stress, transition, family crisis, work-related issues, etc.

The most difficult and complicated aspect of prison chaplaincy is playing the role of "dual advocate," i.e., being a voice and care provider for both sides of the fence, so-to-speak. An invisible "wall" or "line" exists between staff and inmates; it is an "us and them" mentality. As dual advocate, chaplains must be a neutral party to both sides of this equation, providing excellent and non-preferential care to both sides of that invisible "line."

Administrator

As administrators, chaplains oversee the entire functioning of the religious program with little or no funds for religious or worship materials. Because of budget issues, much of the legwork is done by an entire

---

16 This testimony was posted in the May 2009 Weekly update. See also www. cogchaplains.com.

17 The phrase "free world" is how author, Dean Yancey, differentiates between prisoners and workers. See his text, *"Prison Ministry."*

network of volunteers who bring in their own materials. For example, if they offer communion, they must both supply the materials and remove what is left. The task of the administrator is to ensure these volunteers are well trained in this specialized area of chaplaincy ministry.[18] Part of that training is to educate the volunteers on the complexities of the prison setting. For example, the volunteer must understand how important it is to work within the institution's strict schedules. Therefore, a service that is scheduled to begin at 6:30 must begin promptly at 6:30. A service that is due to conclude at 7:45 must end at 7:45. Prisons are managed and maintained according to rigid schedules. While these schedules may appear to be cumbersome to outsiders, they are a necessary part of the security system that is in place for both prisoners and staff.

As a young minister, time meant very little to me. The corrections officers at the juvenile facility were extremely flexible and patient with my team of volunteers. We would pray and counsel the teenage females as long as it took. When we would leave, the male juvenile offenders were lined up outside waiting for us to finish so they could complete their nightly routine. In retrospect, we did a disservice to the institution and these young offenders. Over time, relations became strained as a result. The most significant and preventable problem in this scenario was lack of training and understanding. I was raised with a limited view of the practice of a Christian service. In my narrowed understanding, services were not limited to the confinements of schedules designed by men and women. Services were governed by God and the move of His Spirit. If it took an hour, great; but, if it took two hours, that was even better. My narrowed scope suggested that in God's infinite ability to act on the behalf of His people, He was in fact incapable of meeting the needs of these young ladies within the hour time frame allotted. I lost track of the greater picture. It is an honor to communicate a Christian lifestyle that values a sense of social order and organizational authority. By disregarding the institution's guidelines, I communicated the opposite to the inmates. Instead of working with the institution to rehabilitate these individuals on effectively living in society with clear expectations to be law-biding citizens, I taught them that laws which hinder personal agendas can be broken and disregarded.[19] — Brandelan S. Miller

18 Yancey, *Prison Ministry: The Responsibility of all Christians is to Minister to Inmates and Their Families*.

19 This example is from Brandelan S. Miller's personal experience as a minister to young female offenders at the Richland County Juvenile Detention Center in Mansfield, Ohio.

Administrators are also responsible for identifying, organizing, and utilizing all available resources to meet the needs of the inmates.[20] This means that prison chaplains must make themselves aware of the various spiritual care needs of the inmate population. It is their responsibility to ensure, legally, that all inmates have the opportunity and freedom to worship. Prison chaplains must be aware, then, of the rituals and practices that define a given faith group or cult. Provisions are then made for this segment of the population. For example, space and opportunity must be made available for worship according to the ritual and practices of each represented faith group regardless of size. Muslims must be afforded the opportunity to worship three times per day; Catholics must have access to mass and a catholic priest; Jews must be allowed to observe the Jewish Sabbath. Along with these specific worship gatherings, the administration may also be asked to provide materials for these to occur, such as grape juice or wine and unleavened bread for communion. There may be dietary restrictions that are ongoing or localized to specific holy days. All matters of the faith must be considered in the organization and development of spiritual care. It may be important to remember that issues of faith include medical treatment and dietary regulations. The delicate balance between reasonable provisions, population safety, and personal, religious freedom can be very complex.

In 1993 this very important point became national news as three prison groups[21] rioted at the Lucasville Prison in Ohio for eleven days.[22] One of the issues, besides the ongoing poor conditions of the prisoners, was the forced vaccination of Muslim prisoners. This was a direct violation of their strict religious codes; however, tuberculosis is a highly contagious and deadly illness. Many constitutional rights were forsaken by this institution; as a result, several groups came together to fight for their human rights. The terrible nature of those crimes committed by these prisoners and those committed by the administration has forever impacted the protocol of prisons in Ohio. Had this just been an issue of vaccinations, this may have had a completely different outcome. The issue then becomes one of the health of the population verses the right to practice faith.

Prison chaplains are not simply advocates of their own faith. They are providers of spiritual care for all those who seek to engage their specific religious heritage. They have a responsibility to protect the religious rights

20 Yancey, *Prison Ministry: The Responsibility of all Christians is to Minister to Inmates and Their Families.*

21 The three "gangs" that united for this riot included an Aryan Brotherhood, a "gangster" group, and a Muslim group.

22 Ohio Historical Society, "Lucasville Prison Riot," Ohio Historical Central, http://www.ohiohistorycentral.org/entry.php?rec=1634. (Accessed November 2009).

of inmates including those who choose not to practice any faith.

Other aspects of the administration of prison chaplaincy include planning programs; developing policies; maintaining adequate and accurate records; recruiting, training, and supervising volunteers; acting as a liaison between the institution and the community by attending community-based meetings; and informing religious communities of the needs represented by the inmates.

Advocate

Prison chaplains are advocates for inmates and employees. They do this by ensuring that the needs of both the inmates and staff are met appropriately. For example, they may act as the voice of the prison community in regards to policies and procedures enacted by the prison administration or they may act in smaller, more personal ways on behalf of the care recipient.

Little Daddy

The young offender stood at my door and asked, "Chap, you got a minute?" When invited in, he came in and sat hunched over like a basketball player awaiting his next shot. He asked me to help him get in touch with his "baby's momma." He had phone numbers but no one answered or took the call collect. He began to tell his story, because he knew I needed to be convinced that this was an emergency. He called the baby, only six months old, Little Daddy—born just as he came to prison. Now he sat in a maximum-security prison and wanted to know how his baby was doing, and no one seemed to care.

— Eugene Wigelsworth, Correctional Chaplain

While chaplains do not have ultimate authority in decision- and policy-making, they are moral witnesses to an institution which seeks to provide a vital service to society. This moral witness can lend invaluable wisdom and guidance to issues of faith, tolerance, and awareness. Chaplains help to protect the rights of individuals both as members of a faith community and citizens of the United States, even individuals seen as hateful or menacing to society.

Critical Issues

The prison is an intense and complex system. Chaplains in this specialized area must be prepared for such a stay. The inmates and the staff look to chaplains for moral, spiritual, and emotional support. They are essential participants in the inner workings of the facility. However, success is largely dependent on the ability to understand and work within this complex system. Among the issues are its pluralistic setting, First Amendment rights, the prisoners, and ministry pitfalls.

Pluralism

Correctional chaplains, like most other chaplains, must work within a pluralistic setting. However, since we have already touched on this issue several times, we need only briefly revisit the topic in the context of prison ministries. It is important to remember the primary objective is to minister to individuals of all faiths (and those with no faith) equally. Since all individuals are worthy of the chaplain's time and resources, no one must be forgotten or dismissed.

Likewise, chaplains must not enter the prison setting with the goal of Christianizing the prisoners and/or staff. This does not mean the chaplain shouldn't take advantage of the many opportunities to be a Christian witness. Having an appreciation for a pluralistic setting does not demand a chaplain compromise his or her pastoral identity; this is the beauty of pluralistic environments.

Prison Chaplaincy At Work

By Judith Coleman

An inmate named Joe had been incarcerated in many prisons throughout Pennsylvania for about 20 years before he was transferred to SCI Muncy as a lifer. He made an appointment with the chaplain to discuss his faith needs. The chaplain was startled to learn that Joe considered himself a Satan worshipper and was requesting a satanic bible, which the facility did not have. Having concerns about Joe's faith, the chaplain questioned his views but Joe insisted it was his right and he wanted a satanic bible.

According to the state's commissioner of corrections, the Pennsylvania Supreme Court recognized Satanism as a legitimate religion, and as long as the practice of his faith did not interfere with or harm others, he could practice it, so the facility placed a satanic bible in the library. In response to the chaplain's interactions with Joe, petitions filed by other inmates went to the administration complaining that the chaplain was a witch because she was counseling him. They said that the chaplain was holding secret coven meetings and that she should be removed from her position. The inmates' petitions proved unsuccessful and the chaplain continued to relate positively to Joe and counseled him several times about family matters.

During one of the counseling sessions with the chaplain, Joe was beginning to question Satanism and later admitted that he had been a Roman Catholic as a child. The chaplain suggested that he attend Yokefellow, a small Christian discussion group in the prison led by outside volunteers. After attending for one month, he joined Yokefellow, began to attend church, and became a strong Christian. One day, the chaplain asked him what had happened over the past month, and he whispered, "I never was a Satan worshipper. But it scared... the other inmates on the yard when they thought I was. It was a great protection."

Had the chaplain not shown him respect, had she revealed to others that his satanist views were made-up, and strongly confronted his views or thrown scriptures at him when he first came to see her, he may never have found a positive faith. There could have been a power struggle, he might have pressed a lawsuit or it could have drawn more attention to his cause. Joe's case forced the chaplain to use diplomacy, counseling, legal knowledge and teaching skills. She had to rely on her faith for every move and word. The chaplain believes that these techniques caused Joe to change his views. However, had Joe's journey led him deeper into Satanism, as a professional chaplain, she would have had to respect his rights and provide for them, as long as it did not interfere with the freedom and faith of others.

Joe was one of only five inmates who had his life sentence commuted by Pennsylvania Gov. Bob Casey in the late 1980s. After he was released from prison, he visited the chaplain often and became an active church member and trustee of the Harris Street United Methodist Church in Harrisburg, PA. He and several other ex-inmates have helped the chaplain with prison ministry, assisting in the establishment of two halfway houses and a program for inmate families.[23]

Reprinted with permission of the American Correctional Association, Alexandria, VA.

---

23 Judith Coleman is the former chaplain at State Correctional Institution in Muncy, PA. Currently, she is chaplain at two state youth facilities—Youth Forestry Camp 2 in Whitehaven, PA., and Loysville Youth Detention Center in Loysville, PA. Coleman is also vice president of the American Correctional Chaplains Association. This is an excerpt from an article written by Judith Coleman for the American Correctional Chaplains Association in *Corrections Today*, August 2003. Reprinted with permission of the American Correctional Association, Alexandria, VA.

First Amendment Rights: Religious Freedom

As citizens of the United States, all prisoners are guaranteed under the Constitution the freedom to practice their religious beliefs. Prison chaplains, then, have the responsibility to ensure that all prisoners have the opportunity and freedom to practice a recognized faith tradition. Since there are so many religious beliefs, chaplains must be aware of those belief systems represented by the prison community. While chaplains are not expected to be rabbi, pastor, priest, Imam, and Brahman, they are expected to make arrangements for the appropriate representatives of each religious group to conduct services. Above all, chaplains must make sure that no one is denied the right to practice their particular religious beliefs.

Earlier in this chapter, we made reference to the Lucasville riot in Ohio. That riot, among other examples, is a heart wrenching reminder of what happens when people are denied their religious freedoms. The issue here, however, isn't just the need to ensure the inmates' religious freedoms; it's also about security. This issue becomes critical when a specific religious practice threatens the security and well-being of the prison community. Security is of the greatest importance. According to an article from the May 3rd, 2009 edition of the *News Sentinel*, Tennessee, a follower of the Christian identity white supremacy group (Aryan Brotherhood) believed he was being denied his religious freedoms. This case was taken all the way to the US district court where the lawsuit was overturned. According to the judge, the prison facility has the right to ensure the safety and security of prisoners and staff first. The judge also stated, "Prisoners have a First Amendment right to practice their religious beliefs. This right is not unlimited, however."[24] As you can see, the balancing act between what is a human right protected by the US Constitution and which religious practices lead to issues of people's security is a delicate one. This issue also applies to health concerns, such as vaccinations. As witnessed in Lucasville, Ohio, leaning just a little too far either way can have dire consequences.

The Prison Community in Context

Paget and McCormack[25] provide some necessary insights into this issue. The authors remind readers that chaplains must be aware of the criminal mindset and manipulation tactics that permeate many of the relationships within the correctional facility. The authors further warn, chaplains must not see these men and women as simply criminals.[26] They are mothers,

---

24 Jamie Satterfield, "Tennessee: Chaplains Facing Challenges," *News Sentinel*, via *Chattanooga Times Free Press*, (May 3, 2009). www.timesfreepress.com.

25 Naomi Paget and Janet McCormack, *The Work of the Chaplain* (Valley Forge, PA: Judson Press, 2006.)

26 Paget and McCormack, 2006.

fathers, daughters, sons, friends, etc. They are human beings who have been deeply wounded by personal histories, social injustices, and/or cultural cycles. They are people who once dreamed of great things for their lives, like our own children. Like us, they were future firemen, princesses, and doctors. Chaplains must not forget the humanity of these inmates. To see these people as simply murderers, molesters, addicts, and "gang bangers" is to forget they are people. It is too easy to dehumanize and depersonalize the inmates. The best safeguard against this is to personalize them through authentic relationships and humanize them through their personal stories and validated circumstances.[27] Volunteer Chaplain Betty Standifer has done this successfully with the women she ministers to at a female prison. On Mother's Day, 2010, she asked the female inmates to bring pictures of their children. On that special day, she recognized these women as more than inmates identified by numbers; she recognized them as mothers who loved and valued their children. The women wept for their children, and they wept in prayer on behalf of their children—the only offering they were able to now give them. Of course, this must be balanced with the awareness that this approach can make well-intentioned chaplains vulnerable to manipulation by staff and prisoners.

Conclusion

Prison ministry is a necessary and fulfilling ministry that requires individuals with the professional skills, religious insight, and godly wisdom to navigate through the complexities of the correctional field. This is an awesome responsibility. As the moral conscience of the institution, the chaplain has an opportunity to provide care for staff members and administration as they seek to provide this service to citizens. As spiritual care administrator, chaplains also provide care to incarcerated individuals whose life choices have left them isolated, afraid, and alone. Validated by its long history, the value of care for individuals caught in the cycle of crime has both present and future relevance.

---

27 Paget and McCormack, *The Work of the Chaplain* (Vally Forge, PA: Judson Press, 2006)..

CHAPTER ELEVEN

Questions for Further Reflection

1. Read the article by Judith Coleman. Identify at least three ways in which chaplaincy has changed since its beginnings. Provide a two- to three-sentence explanation for each as to why these changes were necessary. (5 points)

2. Explain in your own words the value of offering pastoral care to both the prisoners AND the staff. Also, what precautions should a chaplain take in caring for both groups? Provide a two-to-three sentence response. (5 points)

3. Define "pluralism." Then, in your own words, explain why "pluralism" is such a critical issue in the prison setting. Submit a three-to-five sentence response. (5 points)

4. Since it is unlawful and unethical to proselytize in a prison setting, how might one be a Christian witness in this setting? Be specific. Create a one- to two-paragraph scenario to illustrate your point (5 points)

Case Study: Case studies are provided for class discussion. The goal is to get you thinking about how you might approach ministry from the perspective of a chaplain. Reflect on the class materials and prepare/develop a response to the following case study:

> Jenny B. is new to the prison setting. This is her first incarceration for a non-violent offense. She appears withdrawn from the rest of the community. As is common with many incarcerated individuals, the loss of family and friends as a support is devastating. In addition, a complex and dysfunctional family background may make it difficult for Jenny B. to trust anyone, including the chaplain. How should the chaplain approach Jenny B.'s situation? What can the chaplain do to help Jenny B. create a healthy and supportive community during her imprisonment? What pitfalls should the chaplain avoid in approaching her? And what can the chaplain do to earn her trust?

CHAPTER TWELVE

Marketplace Chaplaincy

Marketplace chaplaincy is a specialized field within chaplaincy which provides pastoral care for businesses and their employees. These businesses include large corporations, trucking companies, athletic organizations, and even casinos. As health care continues to be a growing concern for both businesses and workers, companies have been forced to find alternative ways to deal with the mental health issues that can lead to costly absences, poor production, and growing health care costs. The editors of the "Winning Workplaces" website summarize this goal in the following way:

> In searching for a personalized yet affordable way to help employees deal with personal issues that can influence their performance, a growing number of business owners, leaders and HR managers are turning to chaplains who undergo specialized training beyond their seminary education to enter into workplaces.[1]

Church of God Industrial Chaplain David Manning,[2] explains that the essence of pastoral care is to provide care to "people at large." Marketplace chaplaincy or "industrialized chaplaincy," recognizes that all people have needs. Typically, when one thinks of chaplaincy it is in a military, hospital, or prison setting. Chaplain Manning notes that all people have needs, and the expansion of chaplaincy into the industrialized/marketplace setting is a necessary response to this awareness. He states: "The thought behind [marketplace chaplains] is that we minister many times in a cubicle instead of a foxhole. We minister to people who are in prisons of the mind and spirit not necessarily behind physical bars. And, we minister to those who are functionally depressed, but not to the point of clinical help."[3]

---

1 For full article, "Workplace-based Chaplaincy Eases HR Burden", see the Winning Workplaces web site at: www.winningworkplaces.org/library/features/workplace-based_chaplains.php. ©Winning Workplaces. Reprinted with permission.

2 Chaplain Manning serves on the Executive Committee of the CACPC board at Erlanger Hospital, which oversees the CPE program in Chattanooga. He is an Ordained Bishop and an endorsed chaplain.

3 Chaplain David Manning, Covenant Transports, interviewed by Brandelan S. Miller, Cleveland, TN, 9/23/09.

Chaplaincy ministry is having a profound effect on companies. It is a cost-effective benefit to both employer and employee. Employees at all levels have access to the care provided by chaplains, who maintain a neutral presence in the work context. This allows them to work through the many stresses that come with marriage, family, and career. As workers process life issues, it impacts their well-being. Healthy employees (holistic healthy) mean healthy productivity. Given the strong link between mental well-being and physical health, the potential exists for reduced health care costs for the company.

Education, Endorsement and Training

Since this field of chaplaincy is still fairly new to companies and organizations, a generalized educational background has yet to be established. As Chaplain Manning points out, this position often evolves out of a company's awareness that the need exists. Filling the position may simply be the result of looking inward to those employees who are licensed ministers. Other companies may look for something more extensive, such as CPE credits, etc. However, as this field grows, a more generalized and formalized criterion will surely emerge.

Paget and McCormack[4] offer the following list as a general prerequisite for chaplaincy in corporate America:

- General requirements: seminary training, ordination from an ecclesial body, endorsement by a legitimate endorsing agency, and at least 1-2 CPE credits

- Specialized training: marriage and family therapy, grief counseling, conflict resolution, and interpersonal relationship therapy

- Certification: critical incident management and suicide intervention

The authors also note that, due to the diverse needs of both administrators and employees, any additional specialized training would be beneficial for the chaplain.

Functions

The role of the industrial chaplain, while sharing many of the common functions of other chaplaincy fields, is very unique. These chaplains may carry out additional functions for the company, such as, new employee orientation or policy and procedure development. The specific job description may vary by employer. However, there are roles common to this type of position. For example, the chaplain is a spiritual leader/pastoral caregiver, counselor, and administrator.

4   Paget and McCormack, *The Work of the Chaplain*, ch. 6.

Spiritual Leader

As spiritual leaders, chaplains may hold scheduled Bible studies or interfaith services. They may organize memorial services in honor of significant historical dates, such as 9/11 or Martin Luther King, Jr. Day. Whatever the specific task, the goal is to pastor the company community. "Depending on the support level of the business, a chaplain may either have total access to help others or only limited access, such as offering to pray for them. At Covenant Transport we have, at times, during a local or national crisis, gathered as a group to pray over the event. I have held Good Friday events, 911 remembrances, and memorials for those who have died among us. I have actually done weddings on the campus. Again, it depends on the level of support given by a business as to what and how far a chaplain can go with support for the employees."[5] Chaplains may also be used in death notifications for immediate family members, co-workers, bosses/supervisors, etc.

The chaplain plays a vital role as encourager in an otherwise demanding and dehumanizing setting.[6] Therefore, chaplains must be a source of hope and encouragement to their community as they face the challenges of high turnover rates and demanding workloads. Of course, that hope must not be false or misleading; rather, it must be grounded in the belief that the community and individuals of the community can weather life's most difficult trials, even through lay-offs, terminations, and structural changes.

Counselor

As with all chaplaincy settings, counseling is a big part of the job description. Depending on the specific organization, the expectations may differ. Chaplains may be seen as nothing more than an onsite counselor with a theological degree, or as Chaplain Manning points out, "Counseling is a large part of the activity, but in many cases it is not the formal, office visit structure. It is more of, 'Hey, can I talk with you for a moment?'" Whatever the program looks like, marketplace chaplains must be skilled and trained in pastoral counseling.

Today, there are many models for pastoral care in the industrial setting. Some simply evolve out of a need; others are a form of traditional Employee Assistance Program emphasizing mental health. However, there are programs, such as the Valley Baptist Value Partners of Cameron County[7], Texas, which partners with local businesses as an alternative to

---

5 Chaplain David Manning, Covenant Transports, interviewed by B. Miller, Cleveland, TN, 9/23/09.

6 Paget and McCormack, *The Work of the Chaplain*, ch. 6.

7 http://www.valleybaptist.net/valuePartners/index.htm

an "Employee Assistance Program."[8] This program seeks to provide holistic care to employees, similar to what you might find in a hospital setting. Whichever model is used by a given business, chaplains must comply with the expectation of the employing agency. Chaplains who are unable to meet the criterion outlined by a company should rethink their employment with that organization.

Administrator

Industrial chaplains are administrators, also. They may be asked to consult on matters of policy or help with transitions in leadership. They may serve on an ethics committee, or they may serve as a mediator between supervisors and workers.[9] Whatever the role, chaplains must remember they are always a neutral party. Their hope is—as mentioned in volume one— to redeem these systems through moral and ethical standards that lead the company towards humane and ethical operations.

Chaplains also provide insight into the religious needs or concerns of individuals within the community. For example, the chaplain might suggest a party that celebrates both Christmas and Hanukkah if Jewish workers are present. Chaplains may also be called upon in matters of understanding cultural and religious values of a given faith system which may affect the working community.

Critical Issues[10]

"Industrial chaplains may find themselves involved in a local crisis at a plant, office or any other setting where people may be in stress or conflict due to their job. Most recently, I have been spending a lot of time encouraging folks due to massive layoffs." — Chaplain David Manning, 2009

The marketplace setting has its own unique issues, particularly when dealing with the stressors of daily career decisions and matters. Several

---

8 An EAP is a program offered by employers to help employees deal with personal or employment issues that may adversely affect their work performance. The idea is that a healthy psyche will lead to better productivity.

9 Paget and McCormack, *The Work of the Chaplain*, ch. 6.

10 Materials used for this section were written with the help of the Church of God Chaplains Commission. For more detailed reading on the issues addressed in this section, please see the COG Chaplains Commission's *Community Service Chaplain's Manual, 2008*. Used with permission from COG Chaplains Commission. ©2008.

closely related issues must be dealt with in this section: knowing and following the expectations of the employing agency and issues of stress.

Knowing and Following the Expectations of the Employing Agency

Any ministry outside the walls of the church has its challenges. While there are often similarities between the many fields of chaplaincy, each has its own unique issues to contend with. For marketplace chaplains, it is essential to understand the internal functioning of the organization (daily routines, policies, and procedures) as well as the flow of authority.[11] These two concepts are what make the organization's system work. If a chaplain cannot function within that system or has not taken the time to educate him/herself on the functioning of the system, then s/he will fail.

Chaplains, though they may not see the importance of company policy in the daily giving of their services, must not overlook the value and necessity of those policies or the value placed on them by employers. While they may not seem as important as providing excellent and professional care, they are the framework for the internal functions of the organization. Without it, the administrators have no way of managing an orderly work environment. They are the guide to company expectations, they identify what the working relationship will look like with care recipients, and they identify "who, what, when, where, why, and how" care happens. Suppose an employee is struggling with some kind of addictive behavior. The policies and procedural manual will identify exactly what the institution's responsibility is to the employee.

The policy and procedure manuals also give insight into another aspect of the workplace environment: chain of command. The chain of command determines the "who" and "what" of chaplaincy. The chaplain must understand who approves the care relationship and what that looks like in the work environment. For example, the supervisor may approve six sessions with the chaplain for a woman grieving the death of a spouse, but the supervisor may only approve them at the end of the day on Fridays. "Although chaplains will normally have free access to the administrators and the supervisors, if they attempt to assist employees while violating the chain of command, it can become problematic for both the employees and the chaplains. The responsibility to *learn, understand,* and *abide by* the departmental chain of command lies with the chaplains."[12]

Understanding Stress in the Workplace

It is certainly understood that the workplace can be very stressful. Employees and supervisors/administrators not only deal with the common

---

11 *CSC Basic Manual*, 2008.

12 *CSC Basic Manual*, 2008, pg. 89.

stressors of productivity, deadlines, customers, advancement opportunities, layoffs, etc., they also have stress from their daily lives. These two worlds collide in the work environment, creating an atmosphere that can be hostile or intimidating if the stress isn't managed and monitored in an effective and positive way. A well-informed chaplain can be a necessary player in creating a positive work environment. Trained chaplains not only understand stress, they can recognize indicators of extreme stress and offer assistance in managing and reducing the individual's experience of the stress.

Stress may be seen as a person's *internal response* to a troubling event or recurring situation. Everyone experiences stress to some degree every day: a backed up highway, a postponed meeting, a sick child. All of these things can cause a measure of anxiety in the lives of individuals. However, these experiences rarely become unmanageable. This is called *general stress*; it is stress that occurs in the daily rhythms of our lives.

General stress can be experienced in one of two ways: eustress and distress.[13] Eustress refers to the stress that comes from positive experiences, such as a promotion or an upcoming wedding. Even though the stressor is a desired event or change, it will cause some measure of tension in the life of the recipient. Distress is that stress which comes as a result of a negative experience, such as relational or financial problems. Distress is manageable and a natural part of life. The problem comes when distress becomes unmanageable or increasingly more intense as a result of a recurring or crisis situation.[14] According to the APA, prolonged stress can damage physical health. Chaplains should identify symptoms of stress that may lead to personal and professional difficulties. Symptoms that an employee or supervisor may be overstressed include: irritability, fatigue, problems concentrating, increased anxiety, or loss of sleep.

When stress is prolonged, intense, and/or untreated, it can lead to more serious conditions known as Critical Incident Stress (CIS) or Post Traumatic Stress Disorder (PTSD).[15] In short, CIS or traumatic stress occurs when people experience a severely traumatic situation or recurring traumatic events. In the case of a traumatic experience, chaplains should be alert for the following symptoms: "shock, withdrawal, nausea, sleep disturbances, sexual dysfunctions, hyperventilating, suicidal thoughts, cynicism, time distortion, and problems with authority figures."[16] Chaplains working in these settings must be prepared and trained in CIS

---

13 *CSC Basic Manual*, 2008.

14 American Psychological Association, "Stress," APA website. http://search.apa. org/search?query=stress.

15 *CSC Basic Manual*, 2008.

16 *CSC Basic Manual*, 2008, pg.103.

debriefing, a complicated and necessary follow-up to traumatic situations.

PTSD, likewise, is an emotional and physical response to a traumatic event, however, those who experience PTSD, "experience trauma along with intense fear, helplessness or horror and then develop intrusive symptoms (such as flashbacks or nightmares)."[17] Individuals who suffer from either of these conditions will experience difficulties in managing their daily life.

Facts about PTSD:[18]

- About seventy percent of U.S. adults have experienced a severe traumatic event at least once in their life, and one out of five go on to develop symptoms of PTSD.

- Approximately eight percent of all adults suffer from PTSD at any one time.

- Children and teens included, an estimated five percent of all Americans will develop PTSD during their lifetime. That's more than thirteen million people.

- About one in ten women will develop PTSD symptoms during their lifetime. That is double the amount of men who will develop PTSD because women are more likely to be victims of domestic violence, rape, or abuse.

- Almost seventeen percent of men and thirteen percent of women have experienced more than three traumatic events during their life.

While the nature of the stressor must be taken into account, the greatest factor in combating stress and stress management is to understand how individuals internalize stressors. For example, a wedding may cause different responses in different people; for one, it may be seen as an overwhelming expense or a major social event that needs to be perfect; for another, it may be the symbol of welcome change and a new beginning. Chaplains who help care recipients work through their perception of an event, life change, or crisis may do more than encourage a stressed worker; these chaplains equip the recipients to handle future stressors better.

---

17 American Psychological Association, "Stress"; The *CSC Basic Manual* (2008) provides a more extensive list of symptoms to be aware of on page 101. Physical: fatigue, chest pain, dizziness, elevated blood pressure, vomiting. Behavioral: withdrawn, inability to rest, alcohol consumption, suspiciousness, antisocial acts. Cognitive: confusion, loss of time, disturbed thinking, nightmares, intrusive images; emotional: anxiety, panic, fear, depression, feeling overwhelmed. Spiritual: anger at God, questioning of basic beliefs, loss of meaning and purpose, sense of isolation from God, and uncharacteristic religious involvement.

18 American Psychological Association, "Post Traumatic Stress Disorder", APA website, http://www.apa.org/helpcenter/traumatic-stress.aspx.

Chaplains who have taken the time to become educated in this area are an asset to employers. They help individuals cope more constructively with life and internalize stressors in a positive and empowering way. Their goal is to assist care recipients in developing lifelong coping strategies. This does not negate the necessity of being a caring and attentive presence in the midst of a recipient's traumatic moment. Chaplains still need to be available for individuals and families in crisis, however, proper training in stress detection and stress management will provide additional and necessary skill sets.

EXCURSUS

Campus Chaplaincy[19]

All of us would agree that college students represent some of the brightest young people the world has ever seen. They are gifted and talented. However, when it comes to their personal and spiritual lives, they need mentors, pastors, and guides. They need strong foundational support amid the turbulent transitions and temptations of campus life. Campus chaplains are the needed connection to provide ongoing personal support on campus. Many universities now admit that chaplains are one of the vital links to student success. They provide continuity between the care and support of home and the care and support of the college setting.

Training And Endorsement[20]

The requirements for employment as a campus chaplain are very similar to those of most full-time chaplains. Chaplains must complete at least a four-year degree, with many schools requiring a master's degree

---

19 Campus Chaplain John Unthank collaborated with our efforts to create an insert on this specific area of chaplaincy ministry. He is currently a full-time campus chaplain for the University of Tennessee in Knoxville, Tennessee. His efforts to assist us in the writing of this excursus are greatly appreciated.

20 Organizations which promote campus chaplains and may be a necessary resource for those pursuing this area of ministry include, but are not limited to: Church of God Campus Chaplaincy: Youth and Discipleship Department, http://www.cogyouthanddiscipleship.org/styled/page11/alphaomega.html; Intervarsity Ministries, http://www.intervarsity.org; and Baptist Collegiate ministry, http://www.bcmlife.net.

in theological studies. In addition, campus chaplains need training for this specialized ministry. Once chaplains have completed the necessary training, they are eligible to apply for endorsement from their denomination's chaplains commission or another recognized agency. This endorsement is a requirement of most major secular schools and is a prerequisite to productive university and chaplain relationships.

Campus Ministry Practices

Campus chaplains are pastors to the university at large and to the students of their denomination specifically. They begin immediately to fill the gap of the home church pastor or youth pastor. Personal student support can include personal meetings with students, emails and other electronic communication, and cards or letters through campus mail. More importantly, chaplains are a pastoral presence. They listen and they offer advice and guidance for students as they face challenges and difficult transitions. Keeping the student communication channel open is vitally important to the overall success of the students and the influence of the campus ministry.

Campus chaplains also provide personal support to the university administration, faculty, and staff through relational ministry and presence. The concept of a ministry of "presence" is one of the most important aspects of the overall campus ministry. While each campus ministry takes on its own unique niche of ministry in relationship to the campus, most have the following practices in common:

Bible Studies and Discipleship Training

Campus chaplains provide various opportunities for Bible studies, including large group studies and small, intimate group studies: these are usually held in student dorms. These Bible studies are extremely interactive and relevant to campus life issues. They are led mostly by campus chaplains, but can also be led by gifted and mature student leaders. Having a strong discipleship training module for students is a must for them to grow and practice their faith in the campus environment.

Campus Evangelism

Each campus is its own mission field. With that in mind, each effort at campus evangelism must be carefully designed to relate to the culture of the university and the students. Campus evangelism ranges from large campus worship events with all the elements of a worship service to smaller outreach events, personal encounters, and witnessing.

One of the highest priorities of college students today is making a difference in the lives of the needy. Community service outreach opportunities provide that outlet for both students and university staff. Examples of this type of collegiate outreach include: ministry to the homeless in the inner city, involvement in Habitat for Humanity building projects, ministry to senior adult homes and nursing facilities, and environmental projects.

Critical Issues

Campus chaplains have the opportunity to operate in a unique situation. Students are learning to function independently, managing their school work, developing new relationships, working, and giving time and energy to extra-curricular activities and sports. Some of those students are also trying to unite their faith and spiritual growth with the many other facets of college life. Chaplains who minister in this setting must not only be prepared for the complex issues of older adolescent life, but be aware of the critical issues inherent in college ministries. While campus chaplains wrestle with common chaplaincy issues, one that may be unique to this particular setting is the ministry's financial support.

Campus chaplaincy is a full-time ministry; however, many universities do not budget for chaplains. These chaplains operate under the umbrella of para-church organizations and must acquire their yearly income through fundraising. While many chaplains do this successfully, a portion of their ministry time must be spent fundraising. Chaplains who go into this area of ministry must have the ability to network and successfully raise money for their livelihood, or the financial stress may become too burdensome to bear.

Conclusion

The need for chaplaincy in all areas where men, women, and young people work, learn, and interact is evident. Everywhere people co-exist, there is need for ministry. Chaplaincy can provide much-needed assistance for individuals and families as they seek to navigate life's pains, pleasures, and disappointments. Chaplains must be a voice of guidance, love, and acceptance to all who seek them out. The industrial chaplain must be an unwavering image of faith and encouragement in times of economic hardship and uncertainty. In all the settings examined in this text, the chaplain must be a willing participant in the lives of individuals, families, and communities as they navigate through all of life's seasons.

CHAPTER TWELVE
Questions for Further Reflection

1. In your own words, write a paragraph describing at least two benefits of having a chaplain in the workplace. Give examples to support your answer. (5 points)

2. In a well-developed paragraph, describe how you might "sell" the concept of marketplace chaplaincy to a local organization. Remember, a secular organization may not share your views on the value of spirituality. What else might you include in your proposal that is both spiritually-focused and business-savvy? (5 points)

3. Define the following terms in your own words: general stress, eustress, distress, CIS, and PTSD. (5 points)

4. According to Unthank, why is campus chaplaincy a legitimate, professional ministry? Please respond in three to four complete sentences. (5 points)

Case Study: Case studies are provided for class discussion. The goal is to get you thinking about how you might approach ministry from the perspective of a chaplain. Reflect on the class materials and prepare/develop a response to the following case study:

> Anna lived in the college dorms. Her roommate was not a Christian. Anna had lived a very sheltered life and was from a very conservative home. Her roommate soon began to drink in the dorm room (not university policy) and also began to come in at all hours very drunk. Then she began to sneak her boyfriend into the dorm room and engaged in sexual behavior with him in the room. Anna kept this quiet for quite a while. She often just left her room while the roommate and her boyfriend were present and stayed out of the room in a student lounge all night. When she shared her dilemma she was at her breaking point. How did Anna feel inside? What were the internal conflicts? What could she have done about the problem? Why did she not do anything? What could the campus chaplain do to help her in this situation?

CHAPTER THIRTEEN
Volunteer Chaplaincy

C haplaincy ministry is somewhat different than traditional church ministry. In the past, the church has tended, for the most part, to remain within the four walls of the church building or at least on the church property. Chaplaincy is different in that it seeks to pastor the church *and* the community by caring for the hurting in all settings. These professionals provide skilled care in run-down apartment buildings and federal buildings, in homes through Hospice and in large community hospitals, and as full-time staff and volunteers. Volunteer chaplains in particular are an essential piece of the pastoral care model, making possible a level of individualized and personal care that is difficult for paid chaplains to provide with the many demands of full-time staff.

While much of the material in this book is geared toward those seeking full-time chaplaincy positions, each chapter is relevant for volunteer chaplains as well. Both are necessary for effective pastoral care programs. In this chapter, the focus will be narrowed to the unique and vital contributions of volunteer chaplaincy, including a look at two specific volunteer models of chaplaincy ministry: community service chaplaincy and local church chaplaincy. This chapter will also be important for those who plan to be full-time, paid chaplains; they will need to coordinate with the volunteers who will make up much of their team.

Legitimacy

The people of God believe they are divinely called to lovingly care for and serve others (in the church and beyond), and they believe the Holy Spirit can reach the heart of the hurting with the Gospel of Jesus Christ for salvation. This is the essence of the Gospel message and the motivation for thousands of volunteer Christian workers. The problem is that the need is vastly greater than the response. Volunteer chaplaincy is one way the church has responded to the immense needs of individuals and communities around the world. While this ministry has been gaining momentum, we must recognize that volunteers have been a part of ministry's story from antiquity. Today, volunteers—through chaplaincy— are much more organized and better trained to deal with the varied needs of care recipients.

As chaplaincy ministry continues to grow, institutions and organizations are unable to keep up with the demands of those seeking spiritual guidance at work, in prison, or in the hospital. The answer has been the enlistment of teams of volunteer chaplains worldwide. These teams of volunteers are vital, particularly for full-time chaplains who have the great task of overseeing hundreds—even thousands—of care recipients each year. Without volunteer chaplains, the demands of spiritual care would be impossible to meet. Furthermore, financial constraints on companies often do not allow for them to be staffed with full-time chaplains. In fact, in most countries, chaplaincy is approached primarily as a volunteer ministry.

In the United States, "volunteer" is often equated with a less-qualified worker; this is not necessarily true. Volunteer chaplains undergo extensive training, preparation, and accountability. They also have access to continued education and training in specialized areas, such as grief counseling or disaster relief. These volunteers often provide a depth and quality of care that full-time chaplains are unable to supply due to time constraints and administrative duties. Volunteers have the luxury of a singular purpose: care. Because of the contributions of both volunteer and employed chaplains, chaplaincy is one of the strongest specialized ministries in the world.

Theology of Care

We live in a world of conflict, pain, disappointment, disease, tragedies, hatred—you name it. Our world evokes the most provocative questions from its inhabitants. "If there is a God, why then is there so much suffering?" It is this kind of question that begs for the participation of the Church in a world that is thoroughly fragmented, wounded, and in many cases, hopeless. We can ill afford to let secular society be the first to give an answer to these provocative questions. By being there as Community Service Ministers, we can evoke in that person and/or family members the reality that through such pain, we may never have the final answer, but we know one thing for sure: God is never absent from the pain. As His Community Service Caregivers, we go beyond the gates of the city, ministering to those who are in need as if ministering to Christ Himself. As the Word of God says, 'Whatever you did for one of the least of these brothers of mine, you did for Me.'[1]

The mystery of God in this passage is that He is not only in the midst of the ministry experience, He is present in us as we minister, and present

---

1   Robert D. Crick, *Community Service Chaplains Manual*, 2008, pg. 38.

in those who receive our care. Where is God in the midst of crisis? Maybe the more appropriate question chaplaincy challenges us with is "where isn't God in the midst of crisis?" His sacred presence is a reminder that He is with us and with them, He is fully immersed in the ministry experience, and He is committed to being with the widow, the orphan, the immigrant, the sick, the wounded, and the least of these. His sacred presence points to the sacred nature of care ministry.

The second lesson this passage teaches is the value that God Himself places on the least of these. "Caring for, serving, and loving the *unlovely*, the *dissimilar*, and even the *despicable* in our communities is an act of obedience and worship in which God is actively present. Not only is God present in these loving acts, but Jesus Christ is present as Creator, Healer, Encourager, and Savior."[2] The passage connects eternal reward and blessing with compassionate care for the needy. His lesson is not a suggestion to remember those in need; it is an imperative for the obedient Christian life.

It is often easier to minister to the mentally stable, good workers with steady jobs, and those with good hygiene. It is not as easy to sit with a beggar who hasn't bathed in months. It is not easy to walk with the mentally ill or those struggling with addiction; yet the righteous serve in such a capacity. And they do so with humility, compassion, and love. Chaplaincy is a model that reflects this imperative ordained by Christ. In fact, it was so important to Him that He presents Himself not as the caregiver, but as the recipient (Matt. 25:40).

Care Precedes Evangelism

As Jesus ministered to many individuals as recorded in the Gospels, a model of care was revealed. Care must precede evangelism when the care recipient is in the midst of a crisis. The lame man lying on his mat and the woman caught in adultery are examples of individuals caught in the midst of personal crises when Jesus entered their lives. In these and many other instances, Jesus responded to their immediate needs before responding to their spiritual needs.

This does not discount or water down the Truth that convicts the heart of the unbeliever. It does not mean that evangelism is less significant in the model of care. It is simply more practical to deal with the immediate needs before offering them the Good News. The practicality of this model can be best understood through illustrations of those who suffer in a physical way. For instance, a man who is naked and exposed to the cold will be a more receptive listener if he is warm and clothed. The message of a compassionate Christ is given a more relevant context when the man's physical condition

---

2 *Community Service Chaplains Manual*, 2008, pg. 22.

is given the same care as his spiritual condition. And for those who have not experienced the love of Christ, His love makes more sense when realized through a compassionate caregiver. Luke 10:30-37 states:

> In reply Jesus said: "A man was going down from Jerusalem to Jericho, when he was attacked by robbers. They stripped him of his clothes, beat him and went away, leaving him half dead. A priest happened to be going down the same road, and when he saw the man, he passed by on the other side. So too, a Levite, when he came to the place and saw him, passed by on the other side. But a Samaritan, as he traveled, came where the man was; and when he saw him, he took pity on him. He went to him and bandaged his wounds, pouring on oil and wine. Then he put the man on his own donkey, brought him to an inn and took care of him. The next day he took out two *denarii* and gave them to the innkeeper. 'Look after him,' he said, 'and when I return, I will reimburse you for any extra expense you may have.'
>
> "Which of these three do you think was a neighbor to the man who fell into the hands of robbers?"
>
> The expert in the law replied, "The one who had mercy on him."
>
> Jesus told him, "Go and do likewise." (NIV)

Note that the Good Samaritan didn't see a Jew or a Roman, a rich or a poor man, "one of us" or "one of them;" rather, he saw a man in need of care. He didn't stop to ask if the man knew God; he simply carried the man to a place he could heal from his wounds.

"Chaplains of the twenty-first century must assume this attitude and mentality to be effective in ministry 'outside the gate' of the traditional church. [They] must be willing and intentional about providing care for the hurting in their community.... [They] must not walk by on the other side of the road refusing to see the needs of those around them. Chaplains of the twenty-first century must respond positively and purposefully to Jesus's challenge to '*Go and do likewise.*'"[3]

Chaplains must be cautious not to misuse this model. In the past, ministers with good motives have used the "Good Samaritan" model as a manipulative tool to bring people to Christ. The model was set up so that care recipients were made a captive audience to the Gospel message

---

3   Church of God Chaplains Commission, *Community Service Chaplains Manual*. (Cleveland, TN: Pathway Press, 2008) pg. 25. Permission granted by COG Chaplains Commission.

as payment for food, clothing, shelter, or other provisions. This kind of ministry response removes the power of the compassionate Christ to provide holistic and restorative healing in the life of the recipient, and diminishes the priceless value of grace extended to humanity through His work on the cross.

Theology of Volunteers

The concept of volunteers did not exist in the ancient world; helping one's neighbor was simply a part of their civic and religious duty. When the Israelites didn't help their neighbors, they were harshly judged by God (See Micah and Amos). The theme of care flowed into the teachings of Jesus, who instructed the people to care for those in need. Inherent in the ancient instruction was an understanding that care was freely given to those in need. For example, in the story of the Good Samaritan (Luke 10:25-37), the Samaritan assisted the man who had been brutalized and left on the side of the road to die. While they would not have used the term, this *is* an example of one who volunteered his resources, his safety, and his time in order to care for his "neighbor". Like the Samaritan, volunteers neither receive nor expect to receive any compensation for their ministry to individuals and families. They care because Christ did, and they do so because they love others and feel commissioned to ministry.

> "If the church is to carry on His ministry, it will be engaged in some form of ministry to the needy and the suffering."
>
> — Millard Erikson, Christian Theology

Jesus says in Matthew 25:31-46 that the sign of a true believer is one who does as Christ did: feeding, clothing, and giving a drink to those in need. They do so voluntarily, motivated by love of God and, consequently, love of others. In contrast, 1 John 3:17-19 states,

If someone has material possessions and sees a brother or sister in need but has no pity on them, how can the love of God be in that person? Dear children, let us not love with words or speech but with actions and in truth. This is how we know that we belong to the truth and how we set our hearts at rest in His presence....

And James 2:15-17 states,

Suppose a brother or a sister is without clothes and daily

food. If one of you says to them, "Go in peace; keep warm and well fed," but does nothing about their physical needs, what good is it?

These passages reiterate the truth that caring for our brothers and sisters (or neighbors, as illustrated by Jesus) was never intended for professionals, although it is a blessing that we have them. Care for the hurt, traumatized, hungry, or bereaved was a response to taking on the likeness of a compassionate and giving Christ. It is the act of loving with sincerity through humble giving of self and resources to those in need (Romans 12:9,13). Volunteer chaplains live this conviction through the sacrifice of time, personal resources, and immeasurable love. Volunteer chaplaincy is not and cannot be bound by the invisible lines between "us" and "them." It is the duty of these chaplains and all believers to provide care to a neighbor they don't understand and even to those they see as their enemies.

This is certainly not a "kill them with kindness" message. That unfortunate and too-common approach to care has its origins in Romans 12:20, which states: "If your enemy is hungry, feed him; if he is thirsty, give him something to drink. In doing this, you will heap burning coals on his head." Of course, "kill them with kindness" is certainly not the point of Paul's teaching. Some scholars believe the image of burning coals was tied to the value of fire (for heating, cooking, etc.) in the ancient world. If a family's fire went out they were in serious trouble, so they would carry containers on their heads as they went house to house seeking neighbors to give them a burning coal in hopes of relighting the fire which had gone out. Similarly, Paul called for the people to give basic sustenance to those in need in hopes of rekindling a spiritual fire that had gone out. What an image of volunteer chaplains who offer their ministry with the hope of lighting a spiritual fire in those they serve. This is why chaplains choose the model of care first (giving of their resources) and evangelism second (hoping that our coal will light a fire).

James sums up this theology of volunteerism in his letter (James 1:27, ESV): "Religion that is pure and undefiled before God, the Father, is this: to visit orphans and widows in their affliction, and to keep oneself unstained from the world." There is no better image of volunteer chaplaincy. It balances care of those in need with recognition of the stakes: this ministry is carried out amid a stained world, and we must minister without becoming stained ourselves. While there are certainly temptations in every venue of ministry, it is those not readily visible that often trip us up: cynicism, loss of faith in humanity, and disbelief that anything of significance can happen in extremely depraved areas. These are the temptations that can cause the greatest stains on chaplains. Volunteers must remember they are more than necessary; they are vital, and their work is making a difference every day in the lives of those they serve.

As Scripture identifies, volunteers are the essence of God's vision of care for hurting families, grieving widows, and victims of disaster. Volunteers make their mark all over the world as they feed, clothe, medicate, counsel, and help bury the dead of the victims of the world's circumstances. Without volunteers, this vast ministry couldn't possibly reach so many people every year.

Critical issues

Disconnection from the Local Body

All chaplains must be sent by the local church into the world to minister as representatives of that particular faith community. The danger is that too often the chaplain disconnects from the local body while serving outside its gates. According to Chaplain Jake Popejoy,[4] an FBI Chaplain of six years and the Coordinator of CSCs and International Training for the Church of God Chaplains Commission, the reason for this can be three-fold.

First, denominations often have a narrowed view of the ministry venue. They unknowingly place more value on the ministries which are visible within the church, ignoring the value of marketplace ministries which define the mission of chaplaincy. As a result, a major component of the Great Commission is missed or overlooked in ministry structure. Therefore, chaplains who are active volunteers in hospitals, nursing homes, fire departments, or businesses are not as readily recognized as ministers within the local body—in part because no one in the church sees the ministry of these community servants.

Second, the local church is not the only one at fault; lay ministers have discovered a new, brilliant, and beautiful opportunity to minister within the community. "The pastor/layperson who is serving in the capacity of a [volunteer chaplain] is now immersed in an environment of unchurched and often unconverted people; they begin to see conversions and changed lives on an unprecedented scale."[5] As a result, "The minister may begin to see this 'newness' as the result of employing nontraditional methods and models; consequently, alienating them from the local body, which is really

---

4 Chaplain Jake Popejoy, PhD, Church of God Chaplains Commission, interview by Brandelan S. Miller (email correspondence), Cleveland, TN. July 25, 2010.

5 Ibid.

the roots of chaplaincy."[6]

Third, volunteers may serve in settings that are considered "high-powered." such as law enforcement, corrections, fire departments, etc. With such settings, Popejoy warns that these adrenaline-producing situations can become addictive. The exhilaration which comes from a high-risk position cannot be reproduced in a traditional church setting. The disconnection occurs when the minister and/or layperson carries out their chaplaincy ministries with little or no accountability to a local church, pastor or regional ecclesiastical office.

Diversity and Sensitivity

Volunteer chaplains must remember that they will serve among people with diverse economic, educational, religious, ethnic, and family backgrounds. God is a creative God. Instead of another message of mere tolerance, we suggest that a Christian approach to diversity is love and compassion for, and inclusion and celebration of individuals and all they bring to the ministry experience. We do this with the intent of loving as Christ loved; however, we also do it with full awareness of the Great Commission's command to make disciples of *all* people. Without the extension of such love, we have no right to ask care recipients to trust us to lead them to the Christ we misrepresent.

Sensitivity in diverse settings is also a must. Volunteers must be sensitive to language that is degrading, judgmental, exclusive, or wounding to care recipients. For example, chaplains should be aware of language that is exclusive rather than inclusive (clergyman v. clergy, man power v. work force, and congressman v. member of congress). They must be sensitive to culture, gender, and economic differences; they must be sensitive to the unique needs of the recipient while being aware of the broader issues the recipient may struggle with given his/her personal history and background; and they must be sensitive to their own mistrusts, agendas, personal

Volunteer Opportunities:

1. NASCAR
2. Truck stops
3. Airports
4. Hospice or other clinical settings
5. Law enforcement
6. First responders
7. Public schools
8. Juvenile courts
9. Homeless centers
10. Prisons/jails
11. Athletic events
12. Casinos
13. Housing complexes
14. Disaster relief
15. Immediate responders
16. Campus
17. Any other venue you can conceive of or feel called to...

---

6 Ibid.

history, biases, or unhealed wounds that they bring into ministry. Personal awareness can remove barriers that will prevent the Spirit of God from manifesting healing, reconciliation, personal empowerment, and most of all, salvation.

Finding Professional Associations

Professional associations can be very beneficial to chaplains at every level. They provide the most current information about trends and issues, new developments in the field, professional growth through conferences or independent study programs, and networking.[7] Another benefit to professional associations is that many organizations look for chaplains who are affiliated with certain associations. Without membership, ministry opportunities with certain organizations might not be open to the chaplain.

A growing problem among volunteer chaplains is the issue of finding reputable associations to be affiliated with in addition to their ministerial credentials. These associations are not cheap; in some cases, chaplains pay a significant amount for memberships while receiving none of the benefits a good association provides, such as newsletters, journals, or conferences. Chaplains shopping for memberships should ask other chaplains or their chaplains commission for recommendations (see Appendix A for a list of professional associations).

Survey of Volunteer Chaplaincy

Volunteer chaplains are found in every venue of secular culture, from the United States government to small private organizations; from first responders (all over the world) to community outreach centers localized in some of the world's poorest and neediest areas. Chaplaincy is not an American invention; it is a worldwide accepted model of ministry to communities and individuals in crisis. Its greatest asset is the hundreds of thousands of volunteers who ensure that ministry reaches all people everywhere. Without the vast number of volunteers which undergird this ministry, it would be impossible to accomplish the great vision and mission of chaplaincy in all places, everywhere. Here is a list of some of the places volunteer chaplains are found.

Hospice Chaplaincy

Hospice chaplains offer care to individuals who are in the final stages of dying. This particular field is one of the fastest-growing areas within

---

7 The GradSchools.com Team, "The Benefits of Joining a Professional Association," GradSchools.com, August 2010, www.gradschools.com.

chaplaincy.[8] One reason for this is that fewer individuals have a member of the clergy or a church to which they can turn when dying. Another reason chaplains may be gaining popularity is that they provide a non-anxious, spiritual presence in the midst of unanswerable questions about life, death, and suffering. Chaplains offer guidance to the dying as they seek peace about unreconciled family relationships, unforgiveness, guilt, etc. Often this care is done in the homes of the dying, and many times it is done in the midnight hours when care recipients are taking their last breaths.

The job of the hospice chaplain is so important. "In the hospice idiom, [they] make dying easier.... Some chaplains refer to what they do as fostering a more "successful" experience—by whatever definition of success can be negotiated in the final hours between a dying person and a compassionate stranger."[9] This may be a sacred religious moment between two sojourners, or it may be a conversation between two people about life and all its complexities. The conversation may be one-sided and full of rage, or it may be a gentle movement toward acceptance of death. Chaplains don't manage the dialogue or the processing of death; they simply walk alongside the care recipient as a compassionate presence during their journey.

NASCAR Chaplains

The ministry of the NASCAR chaplain is immense. Chaplains have been serving in the NASCAR community for more than twenty years through organizations like the MRO (Motor Racing Outreach).[10] They provide pastoral care at all Sprint Cup, Nationwide, and Craftsman Truck Series events. Their target community is more than the famous faces who race around the tracks; they minister to the spouses and children of competitors, offering childcare and other service programs. They are present for the near-death and fatal accidents that are an unfortunate part of the sport. They marry couples, rejoice in births, help process defeat, and celebrate victory. In addition, they provide ministry to crews, the media, and fans. Anyone who shows up at a race is a part of the community to which these chaplains offer care. NASCAR chaplains pray for those who need prayer and offer chapel services and Bible studies on a regular basis. They are a reminder that life is bigger than the racetrack.

---

8   Paul Vitello, "Hospice Chaplains Take up Bedside Counseling," *The New York Times*, October 28, 2008, http://www.nytimes.com/2008/10/29/nyregion/29hospice.html?_r=1&pagewanted=2.

9   Paul Vitello, 2008, pg. 1.

10 Dave Rodman, "Former MRO Chaplain Gives Life Lessons In New Book", NASCAR.com, August 21, 2008, http://www.nascar.com/2008/news/features/08/20/dbeaver.book.devotions.nascar/index.html.

Two general ways volunteer chaplaincy is carried out is through Community Service Chaplains and Local Church Chaplains. Community Service Chaplains (CSCs) are individuals (predominantly licensed ministers) who minister in the community on behalf of an agency. Local Church Chaplains (LCCs) are teams of laypersons who are sent by the local church to provide ministry within the community on behalf of the church. There are benefits and complexities to both of these models, which we will explore.

MODEL I

Community Service Chaplaincy

The Community Service Chaplains (CSCs) understand their role to be that of service and contribution. The service is to the men and women of the organization being served, to [the] church which recognizes the need to minister in the marketplace, and to our Lord and Savior Jesus Christ. The contribution of each chaplain is of his/her time, talents, care, professional expertise, and often personal resources. This is done with a genuine love for those who serve our communities and citizens.[11]

Like full-time chaplains, CSCs are trained for this specialized ministry. While they are considered volunteers, this does not lessen their value or their professional qualifications. CSCs are often professional clergy or credentialed clergy who feel a call to minister to the local community. They are provided general and initial training in subjects like human behavior, pastoral care, and "spiritual guidance." (Pastoral care providers are leaning away from words like "counseling" due the legal issues that surround this specialized field of training. It is suggested that phrases such as "pastoral care" or "spiritual guidance" be used when referring to any type of "counseling" that may take place, leaving that particular term for professionals in the field. By differentiating between the two, chaplains can lessen the likelihood of legal ramifications that professionals are insured against.) CSCs are provided with many opportunities for continued education and practical, professional experiences. In addition, they are actively committed to enriching the lives of the people they serve by

---

11 Church of God Chaplains Commission, *Community Service Chaplains Manual*. (Cleveland, TN: Pathway Press, 2008).

providing the emotional and spiritual guidance necessary for daily living and effective work.

Training and Endorsement

Community Service Chaplains, as volunteer chaplains, work as professional pastoral caregivers within various community settings. CSCs often work under or with a staff chaplain who oversees the spiritual care department of an organization. Since the majority of CSCs are professionally-trained clergy, it is expected that these volunteer workers work at the same level of professionalism and skill as full-time chaplains. Credentials are an important piece of the puzzle because public organizations will note the difference between credentialed pastors/chaplains and laypersons. In addition to a ministerial license, CSCs must complete a similar (but less extensive) certification process in order to be a volunteer chaplain in many settings.

Training

CSCs in most denominations are required to take a basic chaplaincy training course. This is often through their chaplains commission, if the denomination has one. The basic chaplaincy course will typically cover three areas: law and practice, core skills, and specialized ministry.

Studying law and practice, chaplains become familiarized with common ethical issues, how to offer spiritual care in a pluralistic society, confidentiality and privilege, and the Lemon Test.[12] The goal is to provide volunteers with a basic understanding of their limitations and the opportunities available in spite of the separation of church and state.

A second area of study is core skills. These include stress education, Critical Incident Stress management, disaster response, suicide and death notifications, domestic violence, and grief. (We touched on some of these in chapter twelve.) Stress, trauma, and grief are among the top issues that chaplains will confront. Families making end-of-life decisions, officers in the line of duty, and employees facing downsizing or personal life issues may experience any of these issues any given day. And these are just the basic or core skills that entry-level chaplains must master.

A third area is an introduction to the various specialized fields that chaplains may choose. Each context requires some kind of specialized training. Law-enforcement chaplains will need to undergo specific training to understand the mindset, risks, and community of the agency.

---

12 The Lemon Test helps determine separation between church and state. We will discuss it in more detail in the chapter on ethics.

Clinical chaplains will need to become familiar with the way hospitals expect chaplains to approach care, particularly as they understand their limitations as a healer, comforter, and evangelist.

These classes are merely introductions to more comprehensive and advanced courses on these subjects. Chaplains are encouraged to take additional training courses that are specific to the area they serve. For example, if a CSC is called to work at a county jail, s/he will need to receive training specific for that specialized context. The same is true of industry, military, corrections, hospitals, and schools. CSCs will also want advanced skill training as they become more and more acquainted with the particular issues present in their context. For example, CSCs will certainly want advanced training in the areas of suicide and suicide prevention when working among law enforcement officers or inmates.

In addition to formal training, experience as a pastor or lay minister provides necessary practical knowledge for developing chaplains. A chaplain should have at least two years of experience in some ministerial capacity. This lays a foundation for serving individuals and families in a variety of capacities.

Endorsement

Not all institutions will require volunteer ministers to be certified chaplains; however, most will request some kind of certification indicating that a religious entity is responsible for the volunteer. An endorsement for a community service chaplain indicates that the chaplain has taken the necessary steps to prepare and train for ministry in a pluralistic setting. Each denomination will have its own process that takes place through its endorsing agency, such as a chaplains commission. Many may require a police background check. In the CSC model, chaplains are recognized by the church, but held accountable by outside agencies, such as a state or general office. Volunteers seeking to be endorsed by their denomination should contact their denominational headquarters or chaplains commission for an outline of the specific endorsement process.

Responsibilities

The responsibilities of Community Service Chaplains are very different from those of full-time, professional chaplains. As volunteers, they normally do not participate in ethics committees; they don't balance the spiritual care budget; and they don't perform any of the administrative duties that come with a paid staff position. The particular responsibilities of a Community Service Chaplain are outlined by the organization they serve. This may include state legal codes and agency rules that hold the

CSC to a standard similar to that of an employee, lest they place the agency in a compromising position regarding security, confidentiality, and liability.[13] Generally, law enforcement chaplains, hospital chaplains, and institutional chaplains are responsible for death notifications, stress debriefings, and pastoral care (baptism, prayer, spiritual guidance/pastoral counseling, or preaching). CSCs are attached to the institution; they are responsible for understanding their duties and fulfilling them with excellence and integrity as professional clergy in a secular work environment.

Another aspect of a CSC's role is legal responsibility. Legally, chaplains are considered professionals, bound to the same legal responsibilities as those employed by the institution and as those assumed by a licensed minister (such as confidentiality and privilege). CSCs must also be responsible to the endorsing agency for accountability and continuing education opportunities.

For senior pastors who are also CSCs, chaplaincy duties fulfill their responsibility to the community. They serve as a bridge between the gated community of the church and the community outside its gates. As a benefit, CSC ministry keeps the pastor—and therefore, the church—in touch with the cares and concerns of those in the marketplace. Chaplaincy creates an opportunity for the church to broaden its influence and fulfill its responsibility to be a light to the world. For CSCs who are called and credentialed ministers but not pastors of a church, this ministry is the only way they fulfill their calling. In many instances, they will do more ministry per hour and per person than the average local pastor.

Summary

The opportunities of volunteer chaplaincy are expanding exponentially. Chaplaincy began with more traditional settings, such as the military and prisons, and has grown into a vast ministry. This is due in part to the success of volunteer chaplaincy which has expanded into other venues and associations. Volunteers are present at almost every major event, such as NASCAR or the Biker's Association. Volunteers offer comfort and care to families in low-income housing complexes, casinos, truck stops, airports, and sporting events; volunteers are present in disaster relief through organizations like the Red Cross and FEMA; and volunteers minister on a regular basis in benevolence/care centers and Gospel rescue missions around the world.

The rapid growth of chaplaincy is occurring for many reasons, one of

---

13 Chaplain Jake Popejoy, PhD, interview.

which is that full-time chaplains can no longer personally reach all who have been entrusted to their care. In fact, chaplaincy ministry is dependent on and sustained because of individuals who volunteer their time and resources to make a difference in communities all over the world. Full-time chaplains have growing administrative responsibilities which limit their opportunity to meet regularly with care recipients. Volunteers do not have those responsibilities, which frees them to have more one-on-one contact with care recipients. Because of this, they are treated—ecclesiastically, legally, and professionally—as full-time chaplains.

MODEL II
Local Church Chaplaincy

In this postmodern era, the church needs more than the traditional paradigms of ministry if it is to remain relevant and accomplish its mission of fulfilling the Great Commission (Matthew 28:19-20). No longer can the church expect people to come just because the church is there; rather, it is necessary for the church to go to the people of the community simply because they are there. It is in the community that the church should shine. It is there the church is able to minister to people and demonstrate the love of Christ through caring and compassionate outreach. This loving care results in relationships with people from the community which provides the platform for sharing the gospel and leading people to salvation.

Local Church Chaplaincy[14] is a ministry paradigm which can enhance and complement the care ministry or outreach ministry for any church of any size. How this model differs from traditional chaplaincy models is that a church is trained and equipped to provide chaplaincy ministry, instead of an individual sent by the church. It can be used to whatever extent that the church pastor and leadership determine. And it will succeed to the extent that the senior pastor is committed to it. Some churches have embraced this paradigm in all of the care, benevolence, and outreach ministries of the church. Other churches have implemented this chaplaincy model in more traditional settings, such as police, fire, jail, hospice, hospital, and nursing homes. Regardless of how this paradigm is utilized within a believing

---

14 The material in this section was written with the help of the Church of God Chaplains Commission who contributed material through interviews and through their published manual, *Local Church Chaplaincy Manual*, ©2009 COG Chaplains Commission. Used with permission.

community, the church must recognize that chaplaincy ministry is a rapidly growing and rapidly expanding interdisciplinary field, particularly in unconventional community settings.

What are LCCs?

Local Church Chaplains (LCC) are chaplains who care for and serve the church and the local community.[15] The senior pastor is the key player in this model. S/he sanctions the LCC model of chaplaincy ministry; s/he develops and adapts the LCC model to fit within the vision and mission of the church. The team is comprised of laypersons, pastoral staff, and others within the church who share a call to bring ministry to the community. The church, not the chaplains commission, is responsible for training and certifying these chaplains. And the senior pastor, not the chaplains commission, holds the church's chaplains accountable for their ministry. In summary, all administrative aspects and execution of ministries comes from within the local church body. While it is self-sufficient, the church is no longer self-contained or segregated from the community it is purposed to serve.

Finding a place to serve and care for individuals and families in need is not difficult; wherever there are people, there are needs—financial, relational, emotional, physical, provisional, and spiritual. Churches that implement this model have chaplains serving in many contexts of ministry, both in the church and in the greater community. The distinctive characteristic of this model is that it assumes everyone is able to offer some level of care to their neighbor. Not everyone can give financial assistance, but anyone can bag groceries from the food bank. Not everyone can give a lengthy theological response to suffering, but, with a little training, anyone can sit with a terminally ill patient and listen to their fears, their hopes, and their faith struggles. The benefit of this model is that it opens the church to the community, and, when that is done well, the community opens itself to the church.

The Function of the LCC

The LCC is unique in that it is not simply a call to an individual; it is a call to a body of believers who truly believe in the mission of Jesus Christ, although many individual members discover their specific call to minister

---

15 This model is more fully outlined in the *Local Church Chaplaincy Manual*. It is a concept/model designed by the Church of God Chaplains Commission. For more information, request materials from the COG Chaplains Commission. *Local Church Chaplaincy Manual* (Cleveland, TN: Pathway Press, 2009).

as a result. CSCs are often pastors who have a call to reach the community. It is very difficult to accomplish that task individually; however, if a pastor commissions the body to share in that call, they more capably reach out to the community. (This must come from the pulpit.) In doing so, the local church can become a light of caring concern for the people that exist beyond the iron gates of our Christian community. The church is not accidental; its construction was an intentional part of God's plan to minister to a specific area.

The LCC is an intentional attempt at breaking down the "iron gates" that have separated the church from the hurting people of society. Its purpose is two-fold: providing care ministry and discipleship.[16] LCC is a care ministry because it calls the church to minister to all people everywhere. It is discipleship because theological reflection and evangelism are actualized through compassionate care and intentional equipping of the saints through continuing education and skills development training. Ideally, this model seeks a balanced approach to chaplaincy in which the chaplains serve equally in the church and in the community.[17]

Opportunities within the Church: (please note: this is not an all-inclusive list)

Lay counseling (spiritual guidance): bereavement, marriage and family, etc. (Please note that issues which are outside of the expertise of the LCC should be referred to a professional)

Benevolence: caring for families in need of food, shelter, or other basic needs.

Clinical ministry: caring for members who are hospitalized (long- or short-term, such as nursing homes, mental institutions, in-home care, and short-term hospital stays).

Ministry to widows: caring for members of the body who are having difficulties transitioning into life after the loss of a spouse. For example, if the deceased spouse took care of all the financial matters, the widow(er) may need someone to teach teach him/her how to balance a checkbook, where to go to pay the light bill, etc.

Ministry to seniors: caring for members of the older adult community who express concerns for their ability to provide various kinds of self-care; this may include anything from lawn care to issues of personal hygiene to meal deliveries.

Jail ministry: caring for members and/or families who are incarcerated or

---

16 Chaplain Tom Offut, D.Min., The Church of God Chaplains Commission, interviewed by Brandelan S. Miller, phone conversation, Cleveland, TN, August 31, 2010.

17 Ibid.

who have loved ones that are incarcerated.

Opportunities within the Community: (please note: this is not an all-inclusive list)

Clinical settings: hospitals, nursing homes, shut-ins, hospice, etc.

Corrections: inmates, officers, correctional officers, etc.

Benevolence: care of low-income families, families in temporary crisis, etc.

Crisis Centers: domestic violence, rape and suicide hotlines, etc.

Lay Counseling/support groups: crisis hotline, Celebrate Recovery groups, AA, etc.

Disaster Relief: FEMA and Red Cross trained/certified, disaster relief center, etc.

Training and Qualifications

Since preparations for becoming an LCC are primarily done at the local church level, the chaplains commission meets with the pastor and the prospective LCCs for an initial training and introduction into the practice of chaplaincy. This training is not as extensive as that of full-time, professional chaplains or Community Service Chaplains. However, the senior pastor, as a trained and licensed member of the clergy, will implement continued education opportunities for his team of lay ministers. (Some areas that are worthy of consideration in training LCCs include death and dying, suicide, addiction, inclusivity, and healthy boundary setting.) This is to reinforce the idea that the LCCs are commissioned and sent out by the pastor and the local church. The pastor is responsible for endorsing and certifying the members of his/her team.

Responsibility of LCCs

Local Church Chaplaincy invites a team to share in the responsibilities of the chaplain. Depending on the size of the church, these responsibilities may differ. However, having a clear description of the expectations and roles of those involved will allow leaders to serve with much more confidence and clear parameters. The following list is an example of possible roles and responsibilities.[18]

The **Care Pastor** is responsible for all of the care, benevolence, and outreach ministries of the church, including the "HELPS"

18 Church of God Chaplains Commission, *Local Church Chaplaincy Manual*, 10-12.

ministry. The Care Pastor is also responsible for overseeing both the Disaster Response and Care/Chaplaincy Training programs.

The **Director of Disaster Response**, possibly the Care Pastor or the Senior Pastor, requires someone with both leadership ability and administrative skills. The Director of Disaster Response will be the authoritative person to activate and deploy Disaster Response teams in the event of a disaster. If a person other than the Care Pastor or Senior Pastor is appointed as the Director of Disaster Response ministry, it should be made clear to all members of the Care/Chaplaincy team and the entire church body.

The **Care/Chaplaincy Training Coordinator** is responsible for training the ministers and chaplains for their given outreach program(s). Chaplaincy training brings a new dimension to the outreach programs of the church by enhancing the saints' skills in ministering to people outside the church. Additionally, this training will strengthen their skills for ministry within the church.

Lay Leaders, working directly under the Care Pastor, are used to fill the following positions: Evangelism Director, Chaplains of the various ministry emphases, Director of HELPS Ministry, Local Benevolence, and Outreach Director.[19]

An Example of the LCC in Action

The East Flatbush Church of God, located in Brooklyn, NY, is pastored by Dr. RC Hugh Nelson. Pastor Nelson caught a vision to "take his city for Jesus Christ" by training and deploying chaplains throughout the greater Brooklyn area. He found the LCC model as the most effective model possible for fulfilling his lofty vision. Dr. Nelson, with the help of the Chaplains' Commission, has trained more than 100 of his credentialed ministers and key lay workers for chaplaincy ministries. Chaplain Gloria Edwards, his Local Church Chaplaincy Director, has received specialized training, and

---

19 The Outreach Director has the responsibility for all outreach, evangelism, and mission projects. Some outreach programs will be ongoing, and some will be one-time events. The director will organize evangelistic projects for the community, such as Adopt-a-Block, passing out tracts, and random acts of care, and will seek opportunities to minister to the community during events such as fairs, sporting events, or wherever it might be possible to reach people for Jesus.

now leads a team of chaplains each week in reaching out to their streets, feeding centers, jails, and even street gangs.

This ministry has developed a caring ministry to the needy families of the Brooklyn area. Chaplains make themselves available to give clothes and food to the needy right in front of their church building. They have also partnered with the public school in their area to care for and serve needy families. Each Saturday at the school campus there is a carnival atmosphere as chaplains minister to families and children. They provide a meal, games, Christian instruction classes, Christian music, and much more to the people who attend these events.

Each week, the East Flatbush Church has core lay chaplains who stand ready to care for and serve hurting people. This church's chaplaincy witness gives testimony of their exciting ministries beyond the gates of the church building. Pastor Nelson also feels that a church must have a solid ministry "within the gates" with worship services, grief support groups, nursing home and medical facility ministries, discipleship classes, specific training for ministry, and many other ministries. These chaplaincy ministries are what make a local church strong and obedient to their Lord in fulfilling the mandate of Christ to care for and serve others. The LCC meets the need for a sound biblical ministry model in the East Flatbush Church of God.

— COG Chaplains Commisson, Weekly Update, 2009

Critical Issues

Selection Process

There are many critical issues that may arise among LCCs; the first is selecting a team of qualified individuals to take on the great task of chaplaincy ministry. The responsibility for this selection process rests with the pastor and those he leans on for guidance and wisdom. Because of their presence within the community, it will be necessary that only those laypersons that are responsible, trustworthy, dependable, and mature should be given the privilege and responsibility of this ministry. Furthermore, pastors must be certain that the LCCs have been called, confirmed, and sent by the church into the community. In addition, pastors should look for those individuals/laypersons who are teachable leaders, growing and maturing disciples, steadfast in their witness and membership, and submissive to those the Lord has placed over them.

A program that is largely focused on the care of the poor in a largely wealthy community may miss the opportunity to serve the broader needs of the area. While the concerns of the poor must be addressed, there may be other, more pressing issues worth noting. Maybe the community, though wealthy, has a large number of individuals struggling with addiction. In that case, the LCCs may want to focus their attention on addiction recovery through programs such as Alcoholics/Narcotics Anonymous or Celebrate Recovery.

A church that seeks to build an effective team of Local Church Chaplains must know the issues and concerns that pertain to the community it serves. This is not only important for those who could potentially benefit from the ministry offered through chaplaincy, it is important for the team, whose resources and time are being pulled together to offer a viable and necessary ministry. In other words, it is extremely important and prudent to assess the needs of the community so that specific needs can be addressed and are not overlooked. One place to start is to ask city officials for their input on what the major concerns in the area are and what the church can do to be of service.

Summary

God seeks to get the church's attention in these last days. Our Lord desires to re-commission His church for community ministry. Local Church Chaplaincy is a response to that call and commission. Chaplaincy is not a place of ease or comfort; it requires the church to be present in the soiled grittiness of human existence. Those who answer this *corporate* call will find chaplaincy ministry beyond the walls of the local church as a necessary response; they must go where the people are.

Chapter Conclusion

Chaplaincy ministry is a growing enterprise of skilled professionals and equipped volunteers. As it expands, finding more and more places to permeate secular society, it continues to change how the secular world views the role of spirituality in the workplace, in recreation, in health systems and in all other places chaplains are found. The reality is that society is becoming more aware and interested in personal spirituality— whatever that may look like individually. However, they are not looking to Christian churches to find the answers to their spiritual longings. Chaplaincy, as designed by God, positions individuals and entire church bodies (as LCCs) in places where the church has historically refused to go. There, they are finding men, women, and young people who long for the hope and presence that chaplains offer. As our world continues to become less trusting of the church, chaplaincy may be the necessary response to the world's thirst for a spiritual awakening beyond the borders of the church community.

CHAPTER THIRTEEN
Questions for Further Reflection

1. How is chaplaincy different from traditional church ministry? Please be specific in your answer and remember to use complete sentences. (5 points)

2. In your own words, explain what a CSC is. Your definition should summarize the various attributes of the CSC identified in the chapter. (5 points)

   For the next two questions, refer again to the story of the East Flatbush Church of God in New York. Then answer the following questions with complete sentences:

3. Who gave authority for this local church chaplaincy program and empowerment to its chaplains? How important is training for this specialized area of ministry outside the gates of the local church (see Eph. 4:11-16)? (5 points)

4. Discuss how God can use crises as opportunities for witnessing if a church is ready to care and serve others. What are some hindrances when ministering to underprivileged families? In jails and prisons? In medical facilities? To the homeless? Others? (5 points)

CASE STUDY: Case studies are provided for class discussion. The goal is to get you thinking about how you might approach ministry from the perspective of a chaplain. Reflect on the class materials and prepare/develop a response to the following case study:

Six months ago a young girl and her family were returning from church. With the roads slick and wet, the girl (age seventeen) lost control of the car, ran a red light, and impacted another vehicle. As a result of the accident, a small child (her five-year-old brother), and her mother and father were instantly killed. The accident left the young girl permanently scarred (with the possibility of extensive plastic surgery). The family is devastated by this horrible accident. There are two older brothers and one married sister left.

As a result of this family crisis, how will the local church chaplain respond to the following?

1. How will your previous experiences with grief help/hinder your work with this grieving family?

2. Will this family's concept of God, judgment, grace, the church, and other theological issues be changed?

3. How will you help the young girl who was driving the car deal with her guilt? The anger of her family? Other issues?

4. What resources and persons will you need to work with this family?

CHAPTER FOURTEEN

Ethics, Morality, and the Law in Chaplaincy:
"Doing the right things for the right reasons"

E thics is a vast field of study. Its impact can be found in every system, government (religious and secular), and workplace, because ethics provides a frame from which groups decide what behaviors and attitudes are acceptable. In the field of chaplaincy, it is imperative that chaplains have processed through their beliefs and established a specific ethical framework. Furthermore, they must have a clear understanding of the ethics and laws that undergird the workplace and a clear understanding of how their moral convictions and ethical foundations are lived out in the public setting and within the constraints of governing laws.

First, ethics and morality are often used interchangeably; they are distinct concepts that are dependent on one another. For our purposes, we will define ethics as the "*process* of determining right and wrong," and morality as "the actual *content* of right and wrong."[1] In other words, morality is the behavior or system that results from deciding what is right and wrong. Second, every program or institution that a chaplain works within will have its own set of ethical codes based on laws pertinent to that setting. It is imperative that chaplains are aware of those laws, as well as standards put forth by the employing organization. Third, chaplains must define for themselves that specific code from which their faith is derived and practiced in the professional arena. For example, integrity and trustworthiness are a must for all chaplains in all settings. This personal code has a practical application scripturally and professionally. In this section, we will attempt to briefly understand the evolution of such personal ethics; interpret them legally as related to chaplaincy ministry; formulate a practical, ethical approach; and apply them to personal practice.

Examining Popular Approaches to Ethics

Where Do Our Current Ethical Practices Come From?

It is very important to note that Scripture is a Christian's primary source for ethics; however, there are many layers which affect how we approach

---

1   Scott B. Rae, *Moral Choices: An Introduction to Ethics* (Grand Rapids, MI: Zondervan, 1995), 15. Emphasis added.

the topic of ethics. Let's clarify; we are ultimately affected by many outside factors in processing right and wrong, but we must always come back to our foundations in Scripture. Many differentiate this as Truth (Bible) and Values (tradition/culture). Among those factors are Scripture/religion, culture/family, society, education, and experience. In the secular setting, it is very important for chaplains to hold to their ethical Truths while embracing the ethics of professionalism and law.

Scripture/religion:

As Christians our primary standard of measure comes from Scripture.[2] However, even this is a limited approach since our personal background and experiences act as a filter in how we read and interpret Scripture. In addition, we are influenced by the traditions and bylaws of our ecclesiastical affiliations.[3] Just as the political spectrum is diverse, so is the church. Denominations, while maintaining certain core beliefs of right/wrong, have been diversified by political topics and social issues. For example, female preachers are still an issue the church is working out. In some denominations, women cannot preach or be deemed ministers; in other denominations, women have just as much opportunity as men; and many other denominations find themselves somewhere in between, giving to women limited pastoral authority. Whether we want to admit it or not, the political and social landscape will shape how we interpret right from wrong.

Cultural Relativism:

Cultural relativism refers to those ethics which are determined to be relative to a specific cultural group and/or family of origin.[4] As Christians, we subscribe to specific norms of right and wrong. Other cultural groups may not share in that same standard of measure. For example, pre-marital sex, in Christian circles, is still considered a sin. However, other cultural groups may not share in that conviction. In conservative Muslim circles, women who uncover their heads in public can be put to death. In western cultures, women are not held to such rigid modesty.

Society:

Our use of social relativism refers to the legal system of a given society that defines for the people certain rights and wrongs in behavior. Not all moral issues are legal issues. The example cited above on consensual,

---

2   Kyle Fedler, *Exploring Christian Ethics: Biblical Foundations for Morality* (Louisville, KY: Westminster John Knox Press, 2006); Steve Wilkens, *Beyond Bumper Sticker Ethics* (Downers Grove, Il: InterVarsity Press, 1995).

3   Fedler, *Exploring Christian Ethics: Biblical Foundations for Morality*; Steve Wilkens, *Beyond Bumper Sticker Ethics*, (Downers Grove, Il: InterVarsity Press, 1995).

4   Steve Wilkens, *Beyond Bumper Sticker Ethics*.

adult, pre-marital sex is a moral issue not bound by law. For example, while homosexuality is not forbidden by the law, gay marriage in many states is not legal – and this is rapidly changing. In this sense, homosexual partnerships have been a moral issue for many that have also had legal limitations.

Education:

The amount of schooling or the quality of the education can contribute to the ethical approach taken. Generally, education broadens our understanding of the human mind, behaviors, and motives, as well as our understanding of the Holy Scriptures (for Christians). An education can equip us with the tools to critically assess a given dilemma which would require us to decide what is right or wrong based on our understanding of Scripture, policies, and law.

Experiences:

According to Kyle Fedler,[5] experience shapes how we process right and wrong, affecting it on two levels. "First, our experiences shape our reading of Scripture. Second, experience might function as an independent source of knowledge. Again, no one comes to Scripture as a totally blank page; we come with a world of experience"[6] which filters the way we understand the Bible. The example that Fedler gives is that of receiving God as Father.[7] He suggests that our own relationships with our father or father-figures will inform our perception of our Heavenly Father. Those who had fathers who were abusive or who abandoned the family may perceive God the Father as frightening or rejecting. The believer may never feel worthy enough to receive the Father's unconditional love. Furthermore, those who have experienced powerlessness and oppression may find it difficult to relate to passages that call for them to submit to all authorities.[8]

In addition to our own experiences, we can gain useful insight from the experiences of those around us. Chaplains are surrounded by personal narratives: those they minister to, their families, their church friends, and their peers. These resources provide another source of guidance in the evaluation of our decision-making processes and belief systems.[9] Those experiences can enhance that process, especially since our own experiences are so limited. Just as personal experiences can bring Scripture into our own lives, the experiences of others can bring a shared and more broadened reading of Scripture.

5 Fedler, *Exploring Christian Ethics: Biblical Foundations for Morality*.

6 Ibid.

7 Ibid.

8 Ibid.

9 Ibid.

Precedent Setting for the Constitutionality
of Religious Programs

Ethics and Law:

When discussing ethics and law three terms are essential to know and define: confidentiality, mandated reporting, and privilege. **Confidentiality** refers to the duty of clergy (or other specific vocations) to hold in confidence information disclosed to them.[10] However, there are times when that privileged communication must be violated according to the law: *reasonable belief the recipient is a threat to self, others, or country*. This is different than chaplain-client privilege. **Privilege**[11] is the legal dimension that protects client confidentiality in court matters unless given consent by the client. One is a matter of moral obligation upheld by the given faith tradition; the other is a legal matter upheld by the government.[12] There are times when the chaplain will have to decide whether or not to break confidentiality. Beyond being a threat to self, if a client has disclosed information concerning abuse, chaplains have an obligation to report this to the authorities. This is called mandated reporting. **Mandated reporting** refers to certain individuals, such as clergy, who are mandated by law to report any suspicions of child abuse.[13] Many states have also added elder abuse (ages 60+) to mandated reporting. This must be done in a timely manner, usually about 36 hours after suspecting the abuse. A recent example of this is the school district being investigated in the suicidal death of a girl who had been repeatedly and overtly bullied at school. The faculty, administration, and students were aware of the behaviors, yet did not report the bullying. One incident in particular occurred in the school library the day of her death. The librarian reported the incident to the administration the day after the young girl's suicide. The result of this is a new law in the state of Massachusetts mandating teachers to report such activities within a specified time frame.

Supreme Court Rulings:

In 1971, three similar cases were being heard by the United States court system: Lemon v. Kurtzman, Earley v. DiCenso, and Robinson v. DiCenso. All three of these cases were tied to the issue of state money being distributed to parochial schools.[14] The issue focused on the separation

---

10 Ibid.

11 Paget and McCormack, *The Work of the Chaplain*.

12 Ibid.

13 Ibid.

14 The Oyez Project, *Lemon v. Kurtzman, 403 U.S. 602 (1971), Oyez: U.S. Supreme*

between church and state. For example, under Pennsylvania educational policies, the state gave money to non-public schools for materials and teacher salaries for secular subjects, such as history or math.[15] Essentially, policies like these in this and other states "made aide available to 'church-related educational institutions.'"[16] The most famous was Lemon v. Kurtzman, a Supreme Court case, which addressed the issue of "the constitutionality of ministries—or church related services—which may conflict with the position of church and state relationships."[17]

In the case of Lemon v. Kurtzman, "The Court found that the subsidization of parochial schools furthered a process of religious inculcation, and that the 'continuing state surveillance' necessary to enforce the specific provisions of the laws would inevitably entangle the state in religious affairs. The Court also noted the presence of an unhealthy 'divisive political potential' concerning legislation which appropriates support to religious schools."[18] This conclusion was made based on a three-prong decision which has since become a checkpoint for deciding separation between church and state: 1) it must have a secular legislative purpose; 2) its primary effect must not advance or inhibit religion; and 3) statute must not foster an excessive government entanglement with religion.[19] This test is known as the **Lemon Test**.

An Examination of the Lemon Test

1. The statute must have a secular legislative purpose.[20] However, the court clarifies that the presence of a religious purpose does not automatically doom a law or practice as long as a secular purpose also exists. For example, Carter v. Broadlawn Medical Center[21] challenged a hospital chaplaincy program. Courts ruled that, while religious purpose was present, it must also have the secular purpose of holistic healing. As long as there is a valid secular purpose, religious benefits could be present without violating the first prong of the Lemon Test.

Court Media (http://oyez.org/cases/1970-1979/1970/1970_89).

15 Ibid.

16 Ibid.

17 Robert D. Crick, et. al., *Community Service Chaplaincy Manual,* (Cleveland, TN: Prepared and copyrighted by the COG Chaplains Commission, 2005).

18 The Oyez Project, *Lemon v. Kurtzman.*

19 Ibid.; Robert D. Crick, et. al., *Community Service Chaplaincy Manual,*; Robert W. Proctor. "Community Service Chaplaincy", dissertation. Haggard Graduate School of Theology, 2007. (Lemon test section by Proctor.)

20 Proctor. "Community Service Chaplaincy", dissertation.

21 Ibid.

2. The primary effect must not advance or inhibit religion.[22] The second prong prevents a statute from being deemed unconstitutional simply because it "harmonizes" with the basic tenet of a given religion. For example, the Carter V. Broadlawn Medical Center suit challenged the hospital on grounds that it violated the Lemon Test by paying chaplains to practice religion. The courts held that monetary benefits *can* be tolerated in applying the Lemon Test. "It distinguished the neutrality of employing a counselor with the versatility and training to help persons all along the continuum of religious dispositions from cases where the effect was more direct and selective."[23]

3. The statute must not foster an excessive government entanglement with religion.[24] According to Proctor, the third prong indicates that any governmental oversight is likely to violate the undue entanglement prong of the test. By oversight, this is referring to the determination of what is religious and what is not—inquiries into religious doctrine and detailed monetary or close administrative contact. Based on this finding, it is more constitutional to open something up to both religious and secular practices than to inhibit all religious practices.

The relevance of this part of the finding for chaplaincy is that it allows chaplains ample room and independence to fulfill their duties. However, if there are questions about constitutionality, chaplains may measure it based on the following summary:[25]

1. The program has a secular purpose also (i.e., holistic healing or morale).

2. It is religiously neutral. (pluralistic)

3. It avoids excessive religious entanglement.

4. It is a long-standing program (has a history).

The Chaplain as Moral Conscience:

Developing a Professional Ethic

Chaplains are surrounded by diverse cultural, religious, and experiential backgrounds. In that highly pluralistic and secular setting, chaplains must have a firm grasp on the ethical and moral standards by which they will operate. They must be fully educated on legal and corporate interpretations

---

22 Ibid.

23 Ibid.

24 Ibid.

25 Ibid.

of right and wrong as an employee and as an advocate for care recipients. However, they are also the moral conscience of the employing institution. They are a reminder that budgets and financial growth are not the only important factors when running a business. While law and company policy help police some of the unethical behaviors within organizations, a moral presence is a constant reminder that even legal behaviors can have negative effects on the company. In this sense, morality is different than ethics in that it is centered on biblical principles, not law. The question, then, becomes "how do chaplains—moral representatives—formulate a balanced ethical practice?"

A balanced ethical policy for chaplains should be formulated on three components: company policy, law, and Scripture. Every company holds their own ethical standards. Much of that is governed by the state and federal government. It is important for chaplains to at least be familiar with that policy or aware of where to get the information. If the company is large enough, it will have an HR person who is likely to have access to that information. Chaplains should request a copy for their office. It is equally important for chaplains to be aware of laws that impact that particular business. For example, if Chaplain Thomas works for a large, financial investment company, he needs to be somewhat familiar with the laws pertinent to those practices because he may be asked to advise the company on ethical policies.

The other part of this formula is biblical understanding. Chaplains must have a well formulated idea as to the difference between right and wrong. As religious representatives, the company, hospital, or unit will look to them to navigate through a multitude of situations that will require someone to keep the employing institution on course. The question becomes, then, how does one develop that moral voice? Consider the following case study:

> As a military chaplain, a strange request came from our Sergeant to me; it was a request from one of our commanders, which required that I show up at his hooch/tent to give him private communion. The only problem was I knew this Commander quite well, and I knew he had brought in a nurse and was having an affair with her. When I got to his quarters, per his request, I gave my response, "Sir, I can't give you private communion for two good reasons: one, it would discredit the communion service with me and the whole unit knowing your immoral behavior; and secondly, it would discredit me and my influence with the men and women of 'your unit.'" Needless to say, I was dismissed; and, not to my amazement, my immediate supervisor intervened on my behalf.

— Chaplain Robert Crick, D.Min

As a starting point, it is very important to develop a sense of right and wrong based on Scripture. This is why it is so important for chaplains to have solid training in theology or religious studies. In addition, it is important to routinely study Scripture as a way to stay grounded in what they believe and to grow in their understanding of the complexities of moral decision-making. Above all, that decision-making process must be governed and motivated out of love for God and neighbor. In the above example, the course of action was motivated out of commitment to the integrity of Scripture, love of the unit, and love for the Commander. It will be important for chaplains to remember that "right" rarely means easy or immediate gratification and will often come with a cost. In other words, chaplains must always do the right thing for the right reason.

Common Ethical Issues[26]

Sexual Harassment

Sexual harassment is a serious legal issue monitored by the Equal Employment Opportunity Commission under Title VII of the Civil Rights Act of 1964.[27] Because of the severity of this issue and its harmful effects on the working environment (including employee morale and productivity), chaplains need to make themselves aware of the laws and policies regarding sexual harassment in the workplace. Guides to these policies can often be found in the Human Resource Department. Both the employing agency and the federal government have guidelines and policies that can help chaplains understand and identify when sexual harassment is present. It is also important for chaplains to be aware of their own gender biases that may affect their working environment or relationships with fellow employees.

Should a chaplain be confronted with sexual harassment issues, s/he must follow appropriate procedures and protocol for reporting violations to the authorities. Not doing so could result in irreparable damages for the victim and the employer. While the hope is that a chaplain never has to

---

26 The ethical issues listed in this section are not comprehensive. There are many ethical issues that chaplains must be aware of. To learn more about these see the COG *Community Service Chaplaincy Manual*, 2008, created by the Church of God Chaplains Commission.

27 The EEOC defines sexual harassment as "practices ranging from direct requests for sexual favors to workplace conditions that create a hostile environment for persons of either gender, including same sex harassment. (The "hostile environment" standard also applies to harassment on the basis of race, color, national origin, religion, age, and disability.)" For more information concerning sexual harassment, please go to http://www.eeoc.gov/facts/qanda.html.

make such a report, it is extremely important to be aware of what classifies sexual harassment and how to properly report it.

Confidentiality

Most chaplains are licensed clergy and are held to the same professional standards as pastors. Confession and self-disclosure are sacred acts that occur in the presence of ministers or chaplains. Care recipients seek professional counseling or guidance from a chaplain as a person of the clergy, with an understanding that s/he will keep in confidence the personal information disclosed. It is a privilege to be entrusted with the laments of those in crisis; chaplains must protect that confidence by safeguarding all written matter from or recorded sessions with care recipients. Recipients' confessions should be treated professionally, like a verbatim; just the facts, with clarifying details included. The chaplain must also be sure that all records are safely stored; no one but the chaplain should have access to them. If a chaplain breaks confidentiality, s/he should expect to be terminated from the position and to have his/her license suspended or permanently revoked. The only reason to break confidentiality would be if the recipient threatened to (or the chaplain believes him/her to) endanger his or herself, another person, or the country.

Kindness through Equality and Fair Treatment

Central to the Christ-like heart is the belief and life practice that all people deserve to be treated fairly and kindly. If they are not careful, chaplains can find themselves—intentionally or unintentionally—engaged in activities or conversations that are condescending or degrading to specific groups. One group particularly worth mentioning is those with physical or mental disabilities.

Medical advances and a greater understanding of the capabilities of people with disabilities have opened the door for many to be integrated into the workplace. The challenge is to create an environment where all people can succeed. This may be as simple as having wheelchair-accessible doors or offering courses to help peers better understand both the limitations and the vast capabilities of people with various physical/mental challenges. (Disabilities are not limited to physical restrictions; learning, medical, physical, psychiatric, and speech/language disabilities are all included.) The Americans with Disabilities Act (ADA) website can be a great resource for chaplains in case any concerns arise in the workplace. [28]

Biases concerning religious, racial, ethnic, sexual, or economic backgrounds are another ethical issue confronted in the workplace. Chaplains must be aware that unfair perceptions and treatments of certain

---

28 The American Disabilities Act can be found online at: http://www.ada.gov/

groups still exist. For example, the Muslim community has recently come under attack. No kind of prejudice may be tolerated. Chaplains who are prejudiced lack the heart of Christ and misrepresent the mission and purpose of chaplaincy ministry.

A seemingly acceptable form of prejudice manifests itself in humor that targets certain groups. For example, the homosexual community is often the punch line for inappropriate jokes. Chaplains must *never* engage in such activities; they are not only unethical, they are also illegal!

The best solution to prejudice is to treat every person with compassion; to consider every person a human being, beloved and valued by God; and to extend kindness to all people equally.

Conclusion

Because chaplaincy is a ministry that exists beyond the gates of the Christian community, it is a very visible ministry. People look to a chaplain as a moral guide; if a chaplain behaves unethically, many will see and many will judge. That is why it is so important to use care and discernment when ministering in secular settings: chaplains not only represent their employing organization, they represent God and the Christian church. Chaplains interact daily with hurting people in the midst of great crises; these people are vastly diverse in ethnicity, race, economics, education, and religion. Developing and holding firmly to a Scripture-based ethical and moral foundation will help chaplains value the life and integrity of their care recipients and will also help them not to lose their moral compass.

The chaplain's foundation must be balanced between Scripture, law, and company policy. Leaning too heavily on one or too little on the other may lead to negative perception of the chaplain. Furthermore, given the legal climate of today, chaplains who are unaware of laws or misguided in their approach may lose more than a job; s/he may also be prosecuted. For this reason, it is imperative that chaplains be fully informed about the law, company policy, and Scripture.

CHAPTER FOURTEEN

Questions for Further Reflection

1. Explain the difference between ethics and morality in your own words. Provide an example to illustrate your point in three to five complete sentences.

2. If you were to create a bumper sticker for your vehicle, what would it say, and how would it reflect your core ethical beliefs? (Write three to five sentences.)

3. List the three levels of experience identified by Fedler that influence how we read and interpret Scripture as our guiding source. (Write three to five sentences.)

4. What is the Lemon Test and what are its three prongs?

CASE STUDY: Case studies are provided for class discussion. The goal is to get you thinking about how you might approach ministry from the perspective of a chaplain. Reflect on the class materials and prepare/develop a response to the following case study:

> The parents of a sixteen-year-old girl slowly begin to realize their daughter has a substance abuse problem. At age thirteen, their daughter had a serious accident in which she broke her leg in several places. During her recovery over two years, she used a painkiller excessively. Now she obtains the painkiller illegally and uses the drug for non-medical reasons. Her schoolwork has suffered and she forgets things. Her room is never clean and her personal hygiene is poor. She lies around the house a lot and is very depressed. The parents call you to discuss the matter. Reflect on of the following questions:
>
> 1. What can these parents do to help their daughter?
>
> 2. What professional(s) should the parents contact?
>
> 3. What biblical/theological or legal/ethical issues are involved here?

CONCLUSION

A Commitment to the Marketplace and the Temple

CHAPLAINCY

A Commitment to the Marketplace and the Temple

In our examination of the history and theology of chaplaincy from the earliest Old Testament times to the present day, we have concluded that it is important to understand the theology which undergirds chaplaincy, the history which has shaped it, and the professional practice which defines it in its various functions. This multi-disciplinary approach has led us to discover that chaplaincy, its principles, and its ministry possibilities existed in the very heart of God since the beginning of time. Furthermore, chaplaincy's principles and practices have serious implications for every aspect of Christian ministry. Chaplaincy is not just an avenue of care, but a theology and practice that should be evident at every level of ministry: locally, regionally, nationally, and globally.

We began our examination of chaplaincy with the assumption that God is the creator of all things, even the secular. The church must think of itself as having two dynamic responsibilities: first, to establish good, faithful, and responsible ministries within the proverbial gates of the Temple, i.e., the local church; and second, to lay claim equally to ministry outside the gates of the Temple, i.e. in the marketplace. We boldly lay claim to our place within the Temple and enjoy the benefits of the traditional ministries it provides (worship, Sunday school, youth ministries, and the list goes on), while equally claiming those blessed ministries which extend into the community. The bold reality is that a Christian is dynamically and deeply attached to both the church and the world. Both places are dwellings of Almighty God, and while those within the gates may have experienced Him personally, it goes without saying that God still claims every creature both inside and outside the gates as His own. Remembering this keeps the church from being overly invested in either context. To be attached only to the local church or denomination could cause us to view our wounded world from within our own protected "gated community." Such an attitude would assume that our responsibilities to God end at the altar. In reality, our responsibility as a Christian only begins at the altar; it is there we begin to deepen our relationships within the Temple and to claim our ministerial call beyond it. The ideal Christian is one who is rooted in the traditions and the ministries within the gates, while at the same time recognizing the call and making the commitment to minister outside the gates.

History has shown us that this has always been a part of God's plan. For the modern-day Christian, it is having one foot in the Temple and one foot in "secular" society. Both places belong equally to God, and it was His design that Jesus Christ, who illustrates best the principles of the Old and New Testaments, became the bridge between the Temple and the marketplace. He expects us to be faithful and use that bridge consistently, in order to keep ourselves deeply connected to both the ministries of the Temple and to the hurting humanity beyond its doors.

God never segregated the Temple from the marketplace as humanity often does. That is why we have shown, historically, that even the most rigid believer of the traditional Temple ministries had a passionate plea to consider—as God considers—that the marketplace is also His. So, even as we considered the traditions of the Old Testament, we found room in the strictest passages for the foreigner, the leper, and the non-Jew. However, there may have been times when the Temple, with its ritualistic adherences, appeared as a "gated community," detached from God's greater mission for the world. Again and again as the biblical story unfolded (from Noah's plea for the community's repentance to Jesus's death on the cross), the goodness and grace of God was never interpreted as just for those within the Temple, but for the entire world.

Jesus illustrated this global mission. He didn't just purposely violate the boundaries of those that were permanently attached to the Temple; He came to free them, so that, without losing the deep Temple heritage and practices, these Temple dwellers would take the very best of what they have learned at the altar of God and share it freely with a broken world.

Jesus, as the prototype chaplain/minister, was genuinely committed to the Temple, while equally committed to reaching and living among the disenfranchised within the community. God's vision for ministry beyond the gates did not die with the first-century church, though. It survived and grew in the life and mission of the early church and beyond. As history continued to unfold and the challenges of the church changed, God raised up men and women who kept alive this principle of a global God existing in relationship to both places; and, from this concept, chaplaincy was born. Although its beginning was lived out in the life of the laypersons and local pastors who saw fit need for care ministries in the local and global community, these precursors to chaplaincy represented the very best of the church for the cause of society's "least." As chaplaincy began to take shape under the guise of specialized ministries, these care providers sought training in Bible colleges and seminaries, and they sought the confirmation of the church for the call to carry out, on behalf of the temple, the ministry of the Lord Jesus Christ outside the gates. They were those selected to represent the church as specialized ministers, later called chaplains.

Ideally, every Christian should be trained for such a dual ministry. We should be as comfortable in the marketplace with our deep, biblically-based faith as we are in the Temple. If we find someone who wants to either dwell permanently in the Temple or the marketplace, we must challenge them towards this balanced ministry that we claim, not only as the core of chaplaincy practice, but as God's intention for every believer since the beginning of time. He did not save us from our sins to allow us to forget from whence we came. He delivered us from the pain and agony of our life outside the gates (salvation) so that we, now as mature Christians, can go "beyond the gates" with the good news for those who are trapped in a sinful life.

Of course, in recognizing the need for and value of bringing ministry to the people, we must likewise recognize and validate the significance of those things the community has contributed to the church. We cannot honestly evaluate the life and progress of pastoral care practices without acknowledging the contributions of secular society. For example, most of our standard, modern practices of pastoral care and counseling came from individuals that we would label as "secular," such as Freud. And yet, because God lays claim to both the church community and the secular community, we can say that He extracts from all of His creation principles and practices that provide deep emotional, physical, and spiritual care to hurting humanity.

By looking at all of the significant players who helped shape chaplaincy and the principles that it upholds, we come to discover that God is not limited by man-made boundaries. The reality is that God is a global God; He will lay claim to every person who is both within the church and within the community until the end of this present age. So it would be only natural to believe the resources that He finds in these two important entities would be used and shaped by Him, ultimately, for humanity's physical, social, emotional, and spiritual welfare.

While the integration of both the Temple and marketplace did not happen immediately, it did eventually unfold into a shape of ministry known today as chaplaincy care. The impact of those influences on the practice of chaplaincy is evident in how these global, creational principles function in the various ministries of chaplaincy care. For example, whether in the Temple or the marketplace, when we begin to feel ourselves as having ultimate authority, we miss that humble, deep experience that centers in the reality that we, like the rest of humanity, are at the mercy of Almighty God. Neither the marketplace nor the Temple belongs to us; it belongs to God Almighty. Chaplaincy—with its high demand that an individual be ecclesiastically trained and spiritually mature, while at the same time clinically trained and socially adept—humbly recognizes the limitations and boundaries present within all contexts while maintaining a submissive heart to God's ultimate authority and vision for humanity. When, finally, the last chapter is written, neither the earthly Temple nor the marketplace will be standing; they, like every knee that will bow and every tongue that will confess, will present themselves before Almighty God and dwell through eternity in a kingdom representing the very best of the Temple and the very best of the marketplace. When He comes to establish His Kingdom for all eternity, we would hope that He would find us actively involved, personally and spiritually, with both the Temple and the marketplace.

Ideally, when we are in the marketplace, the deep tenets of the temple (traditional faith) should be evident in our personal and professional approaches to life and ministry; and, when in the Temple, our language; our passion; our style of ministry; the things that we are most passionate about would reveal the great opportunities, responsibilities, and blessings of the marketplace upon our lives and our church. Chaplaincy, better than most ministries, illustrates the importance of being a genuine citizen of both the Temple and the marketplace.

It is often said of local pastors that they are at their best when they don't simply pastor a local church, but an entire community (the marketplace). This phrase is in no way intended to water down all of the traditional practices and ministries within the local church; rather, it emphasizes the fact that we are at our best when those practices and principles of the local church are shared, reviewed, and sometimes revised within the larger community. Chaplaincy leads the way in this regard.

For chaplains, there is no such thing as being "non-denominational." They are Baptists, Methodists, Presbyterians, etc. They are Fundamentalists, Evangelicals, Universalists, and all the other titles that fashion our identity and journey to a particular altar of prayer from which we come to understand that Scripturally, to fulfill our calling, we must, in addition to being faithful to the practice and ministries of our prescribed Temple, embrace the larger world which we call the marketplace. That doesn't mean that we restrict our ministry to people of our own faith group; rather, in ministering to this pluralistic society, we communicate to care recipients that the source of our care and compassion is found in the deep tenets of our particular Temple modality. And it is out of that deep faith and confidence that we reach out to people of all different persuasions and to those that claim no persuasion. We are *most effective* in the marketplace when we know and are confident in "who we are," and "whose we are." Likewise, we are *least effective* when we water down our identity. Therefore, the church, in the wake of internal and external changes, must identify and shape its ministry identity accordingly. However, the church must avoid thinking that it can become part of the marketplace by simply handing out goods through the gates of our exclusive, gated communities.

We, as a unified citizenship, must go to where the pain is the greatest; for it is only in that manner we will be able to literally minister to Christ. That is, the passage, "As you do it unto the least of these, you do it unto me," is to be interpreted literally, not figuratively. Therefore, in ministering to the pains of this world, we are allowed the holy privilege of ministering to Christ Himself.

Of course, the greatest challenge must be turned inward. This study is merely an introduction to the call that has led you to inquire about this specialized area of pastoral ministry. The question you must now ask is "Where do I go from here?" Although a difficult question to consider, it is one that must be answered in order to be compelled forward into a ministry arena that is challenging, mobile, non-traditional, and vastly diverse in context and demographic.

Appendix A
Professional Associations

Field	Association Name	Website
Correctional	American Correctional Chaplains Association	www.correctionalchaplains.org
Law Enforcement	International Conference of Police Chaplains	www.icpc4cops.org
Military	Military Chaplains Association of the United States of America	www.mca-usa.org
Industry/ marketplace	Marketplace Chaplains USA	www.mchapusa.com
Clinical	Association for Clinical Pastoral Education, Inc.	www.acpe.edu
	Association of Professional Chaplains	www.professionalchaplains.org
	Healthcare Chaplains Ministry Association	www.hcmachaplains.org
Campus	National Association of College and University Chaplains	www.nacuc.net
Race Track	Race Track Chaplaincy of America	www.rtcanational.org

Note: every denomination which endorses chaplains has their own chaplains commission.

Bibliography

Asquith, Jr., Glenn H, ed. *A Vision from a Little Known Country: A Boisen Reader.* Journal of Pastoral Care Publications, Inc., 1992.

Baxter, Richard. *The Reformed Pastor.* Edited by Hugh Martin. Richmond, VA: John Knox Press, 1956.

Bridges Johns, Sheryl. *Pentecostal Formation: A Pedagogy Among the Oppressed.* Sheffield, England: Sheffield Academic Press, 1993.

Bruchhausen, Walter. "Health Care between Medicine and Religion: The Case of Catholic Western Germany around 1800." *Hygiea Internationalis* 6(2): 197–194, 2007. http://dx.doi.org/10.3384/hygiea.1403-8668.0771177. (Accessed via CEST)

Church of God Chaplains Commission. *Community Service Chaplaincy Manual*, tenth edition. Cleveland, TN: Pathway Press, 2008.

Church of God Chaplains Commission. *Community Service Chaplaincy Manual.* Cleveland, TN: Pathway Press, 2005.

Church of God Chaplains Commission. *Local Church Chaplaincy Manual.* Cleveland, TN: Pathway Press, 2009.

Chrysostom, St. John. *St. John Chrysostom: Six Books on the Priesthood,* translated by Graham Neville. Crestwood, NY: St. Vladimir's Seminary Press, 1964.

Clebsch, William and Charles Jaekle. *Pastoral Care in Historical Perspective.* Englewood Cliffs, New Jersey: Prentice-Hall, Inc., 1964.

Coleman, Judith. "Prison Chaplaincy at Work." *Corrections Today*, August 2003.

Crick, Robert D. "A Covenant of Pentecostal Supervision." DMin diss. The Candler School of Theology, 1987.

"Drinking From Our Own Wells: Search for a Pentecostal Care and Counseling Paradigm in the Development of Contemporary Caregivers." Paper presented, Pentecostal Caregivers' Conference, Cleveland, TN. Reprinted with permission of Dr. Robert Crick, Director of the Church of God Chaplains Commission.

Dicks, Russell L. *Principles and Practices of Pastoral Care.* Englewood Cliffs, NJ: Prentice-Hall, Inc., 1963.

Fedler, Kyle. *Exploring Christian Ethics: Biblical Foundations for Morality.* Louisville, KY: Westminster John Knox Press, 2006.

Firet, Jacob. *Dynamics in Pastoring*. Grand Rapids: William B. Eerdmans Publishing, 1986.

Gerkin, Charles. *An Introduction to Pastoral Care*. Nashville: Abingdon Press, 1997.

Goll, James W & Michal Ann Goll. *Compassion: A Call to Take Action*. Women on the Front Lines Series. Shippensburg, PA: Destiny Image Publishers, Inc., 2006.

Holifield, Brooks E. *A History of Pastoral Care in America: From Salvation to Self-Realization*. Nashville: Abingdon Press, 1983.

Jett, Mickey. "Community Service Chaplaincy." Prospectus, Pentecostal School of Theology, 2009.

Johnson, John. "Seeking Pastoral Identity." *The Spurgeon Fellowship Journal*, (Fall 2007): 4. www.thespurgeonfellowship.org.

Kemp, Charles F. *Physicians of the Soul: A History of Pastoral Counseling*. New York, NY: The Macmillan Company, 1947.

Kubler-Ross, Elisabeth. *On Death and Dying*. New York, NY: Scribner, 1969.

McNeil, John T. *A History of the Cure of Souls*. New York, NY: Harper & Row Publishers, Inc., 1951.

Nouwen, Henri J.M. *The Wounded Healer: Ministry in Contemporary Society*. Garden City, NY: Image Books, 1979.

Oden, Thomas. *Becoming a Minister*. Classical Pastoral Care 1. Rev. ed. HarperCollins Publishers, 1992.

The Oyez Project. "Lemon v. Kurtzman, 403 U.S. 602 (1971)." *U.S. Supreme Court Media, Oyez*. http://oyez.org/cases/1970-1979/1970/1970_89.

Paget, Naomi K. and Janet R. McCormack. *The Work of the Chaplain*. Valley Forge, PA: Judson Press, 2006.

Proctor, Robert W. "Community Service Chaplaincy." Dissertation, Haggard Graduate School of Theology, 2007.

Purves, Andrew. *Pastoral Theology in the Classical Tradition*. Louisville, KY: Westminster John Knox Press, 2001.

Rae, Scott B. *Moral Choices: An Introduction to Ethics*. Grand Rapids, MI: Zondervan, 1995.

Rauschenbusch, Walter. *Walter Rauschenbusch: Selected Writings*, edited by Winthrop, S. Hudson. New York, NY: Paulist Press, 1984.

Rogers, Paul. "Correctional Chaplains Calming the Storms of Life for Staff and Inmates." *Corrections Today*, February 2003.

St. Francis of Assisi. *Francis and Mare, the Complete Works*, translated by Regis J. Armstrong and Ignatius Brady, 33. New York, NY: Paulist Press, 1983.

St. Gregory the Great. *Pastoral Care*. Edited by Johannes Quasten and Joseph C. Plumpe, translated by Henry Davis, "Ancient Christian Writers: The Works of the Fathers in Translation," no. 11. New York, NY: Newman Press, 1950.

St. Jerome. *To Paula*. "Jerome: The Principal Works of St. Jerome," Letter XXXIX. Christian Classics Ethereal Library website, http://www.ccel.org (accessed November 11, 2010), 2.

Westerhoff, John H. "The Church and Family." *Religious Education* 2, 78 no. (1983): 249-274. ATLA religion Database with ATLA Serials.

Wilkens, Steve. *Beyond Bumper Sticker Ethics*. Downers Grove, Il: InterVarsity Press, 1995.

Yancey, Dean. *Prison Ministry: the responsibility of all Christians is to minister to inmates and their families*. Publishing information not available.

IF YOU'RE A FAN OF THIS BOOK, PLEASE TELL OTHERS...

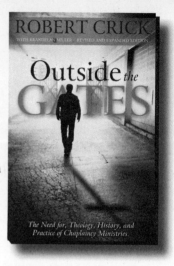

- Write about Outside the Gates on your blog, Twitter, MySpace, and Facebook page.

- Suggest Outside the Gates to friends.

- When you're in a bookstore, ask them if they carry the book. The book is available through all major distributors, so any bookstore that does not have Outside the Gates in stock can easily order it.

- Write a positive review of Outside the Gates on www.amazon.com.

- • Send my publisher, HigherLife Publishing, suggestions on Web sites, conferences, and events you know of where this book could be offered at media@ahigherlife.com.

- Purchase additional copies to give away as gifts.

CONNECT WITH ME...

To learn more about Outside the Gates, please contact me at:

Dr. Robert Crick

www.outsidethegates.org

rcrick@outsidethegates.org

You may also contact my publisher directly:

HigherLife Publishing

400 Fontana Circle

Building 1 – Suite 105

Oviedo, Florida 32765

Phone: (407) 563-4806

Email: media@ahigherlife.com